THE WORLD'S GREATEST
SERIAL KILLERS

ACKNOWLEDGEMENTS

Corbis UK Ltd/Bettmann 19, 23, 36, 118
Hulton Getty Picture Collection 40, 62, 63
Rex Features 47, 75, 78, 83, 93, 126, 129, 152, 168, 169, 179, 180

THE WORLD'S GREATEST
SERIAL KILLERS

Nigel Cawthorne

CHANCELLOR
PRESS

This 1999 edition published by Chancellor Press,
an imprint of Bounty Books, a division of
Octopus Publishing Group Ltd.,
2-4 Heron Quays, London E14 4JP
An Hachette Livre UK company

Reprinted 2000, 2001, 2002, 2003, 2005, 2006, 2007, 2008

Copyright © Octopus Publishing Group Ltd

ISBN: 978-0-753700-89-1

A CIP catalogue record for this book is available from
the British Library.

Printed and bound in the UK by CPI Mackays, Chatham ME5 8TD

Contents

Introduction

According to the FBI Handbook, a serial killer is someone who has murdered more than four people. This must have been done over a period of time, however – going down the local McDonald's and taking everybody out in one go does not count, because although the body count may be high, the perpetrator would be a spree killer, not a serial killer. In order to qualify as serial killer, the killings therefore have to take place one after another, like an old-fashioned newspaper serial (which is how the term came to be coined).

Indeed, the serial killer is a modern, mass-media phenomenon: although there were multiple murderers throughout history, such felons only became known as serial killers when the police discovered the bodies of their victims consecutively, the resultant press reports chilling the blood of the reading public and giving the impression that no one was safe.

Serial killers' motivations are often sexual. Some like to mutilate the bodies of their victims and sometimes resort to cannibalism. They seem to like to see how far they can travel beyond the usual bounds of morality. They frequently exhaust the possibilities and seem relieved when they are caught, quickly admitting their many crimes. In other cases they become so high on the thrill of living in a moral vacuum, in which every whim can be instantly acted out, that they become careless or unlucky.

Thankfully, most of the world's greatest serial killers described in this book have been caught. But beware: some of them are still out there.

1 ❖ Jack the Ripper

Jack the Ripper was the first serial killer to come to public attention. Although he killed only five women for certain – a pitifully low body count compared to those who came after him – he must count as one of the world's greatest serial killers because today, over a century since his savage murder spree ended, his name still chills the blood. In the East End of London, where he went about his gruesome business, tours of his murder sites are conducted. Experts still speculate about his identity. Each new serial killer that hits the headlines is compared to him. This is fame – or notoriety - indeed.

Jack the Ripper qualifies as the first true serial killer because his ten-week campaign of murder was a media event. Indeed, he courted the press, writing to the newspapers and giving them his sobriquet. He even sent them body parts of his victims that had been excised during his bizarre mutilation of their corpses. The Ripper's murderous activities gripped the public's imagination like no single individual's crimes before them and London was paralysed by fear. Again thanks to the mass media, Jack the Ripper was soon as famous in New York, San Francisco, Paris, Sydney and Berlin as he was in London. In Arles, the painter Vincent Van Gogh had been avidly following the accounts of his deeds in the French newspapers before he sliced off part of his ear (some biographers have concluded that he was influenced by the Ripper's method of dissection).

Whitechapel was the Ripper's stamping ground. In 1888, when the killings started, there were 62 brothels in the London district, along with 233 boarding houses that catered for prostitutes and their clients. On top of that there was also an army of older, pox-ridden, middle-aged alcoholics who offered their sexual favours in alleys and doorways for the price of a slug of gin.

On the night of 3 April 1888 the 45-year-old Emma Elizabeth Smith solicited a well-dressed gentleman. Later that night she collapsed in the arms of a police constable, saying that she had been attacked by four men. A foreign object had been shoved up her vagina and she died a few hours later. What connected her death to the Ripper's subsequent murders was the fact that her ear had been cut off. Then, on the night of 7 August 1888, Martha Tabram was stabbed to death. There were 39 wounds on her corpse, mainly around her breasts and vagina – the areas of the body that the Ripper liked to mutilate when he had the time. Both Martha Tabram and Emma Elizabeth Smith had been attacked from behind. The police assumed that (like the Ripper's later victims) the women had turned their backs on their client and had hoisted up their skirts for rear-entry sex when they were attacked. It is not known for certain that these two women were killed by Jack the Ripper, but their killer was never caught and their murders shared many similarities with the Ripper's slayings.

The first woman definitely to have been killed by Jack the Ripper was the 42-year-old Polly Nichols, whose body was found in Buck's Row, Whitechapel, at 3.15am on 31 August 1888. Although she had fought her attacker she had not cried out, for her murder had taken place under the window of a sleeping woman who had not been woken by the struggle. She also appeared to have turned her back on her attacker, who slashed her throat twice, so savagely that he almost decapitated her. There were deep wounds around her sexual organs, too, although no body parts had been removed. The doctors who examined the corpse speculated that the attacker had some medical knowledge and was possibly a doctor himself.

The police concluded that Polly had turned away from her killer during the assignation (a common practice among London street prostitutes of the time). She had therefore had her back to her killer when he pulled his knife, which was why she had not cried out. He had then put the knife to her throat and had pushed her forward on to it, which explained the depth of the wound. It also meant that the blood from the arteries and veins in her neck would have spurted forward, away from the killer, enabling him to escape from the scene unsullied.

With the murder of Polly Nichols the police realised that they had a maniac on their hands who seemed to be motivated by a hatred of prostitutes. Detectives were accordingly sent into the East End to search for men who mistreated prostitutes. The name 'Leather Apron' came up several times during the investigation and a shoemaker called Pizer was arrested. Although he used a leather apron and sharp knives in his trade, his family swore that he had been at home on the three occasions on which women had been attacked in this manner.

On 8 September 1888, in various pubs in Whitechapel, the 47-year-old Annie Chapman bragged that the killer would meet his match if he ever came near her. She was wrong, however. She was subsequently seen talking to a 'gentleman' in the street; having apparently struck a bargain they went off arm in arm. Half an hour later she was found lying dead in an alleyway. Her head was connected to her body by only a strand of flesh. Her intestines had been thrown over her right shoulder and the flesh from her lower abdomen over her left. Her kidneys and ovaries had been removed.

The killer had left a blood-soaked envelope bearing the crest of the Sussex Regiment. It had been reported that Martha Tabram had been seen in the company of a soldier shortly before her death and the newspapers now speculated that her wounds could have been caused by a bayonet or army knife.

Three weeks after the death of Annie Chapman the Central News Agency received a letter that gloated about both the murder and the tantalising clues that had been left. The author expressed his regret that the letter had not been written in the victim's blood, which had gone 'thick like glue', and promised to send the ear of his next victim. The letter was signed 'Jack the Ripper'. At last the murderer had a name. On 30 September 1888 the Central News Agency received another letter from the Ripper, apologising for not having enclosed an ear, as promised. But he nevertheless had exciting news for the papers, he wrote: he was going to commit a 'double' – two murders in one night.

At 1am on the night on which the letter had been received the 45-year-old 'Long Liz' Stride, a Swedish prostitute whose real name was Elizabeth Gustaafsdotter, was found lying in a pool of blood; her throat had been slashed. The delivery man who discovered her body heard her attacker escaping over the cobblestones. At around the same time the 43-year-old prostitute Catherine Eddowes was being thrown out of Bishopsgate Police Station, where she had been held for being drunk and disorderly. As she walked towards Houndsditch she met Jack the Ripper, who cut her throat, slashed her face and cut her ear, though not severing it completely. He also opened up her stomach, pulled out her intestines and threw them over her shoulder. Her left kidney was found to be missing altogether.

The murder of two women in one night – so soon after a letter from the Ripper promising just that – sent London into a panic. Queen Victoria demanded action, but the police had no idea where to begin. (The public did not even have that great fictional detective Sherlock Holmes to turn to, for he did not make his debut in *Strand* magazine for another three years.)

In a blaze of publicity, East End resident George Lusk set up the Whitechapel Vigilance Committee with which to patrol the streets. For his pains, two weeks later Mr Lusk received a small package through the post. It was from Jack the Ripper and contained half of Catherine Eddowes' kidney; the other half, an accompanying note explained, had been fried and eaten. On hearing this Queen Victoria concluded that the Ripper must be a foreigner: no Englishman would behave in such a beastly way, she asserted. A Cabinet meeting was called to discuss the matter and the government consequently ordered checks on all of the ships that were tied up in London docks. This action proved merely to be a huge waste of police manpower and in the meantime the Ripper continued on his grisly business.

On the night of 9 November 1888 Mary Kelly was seen soliciting a 'well-dressed gentleman' on the streets. Mary was unlike the Ripper's previous victims, being attractive and young – just 24. She was not a full-time prostitute, only going on to the streets occasionally, when she needed to pay the rent. She was furthermore killed indoors and was also the only one of the Ripper's victims to cry out. Despite her screams, the Ripper was not disturbed and spent more than an hour going about his dreadful task.

Mary Kelly's clothes were found folded neatly on a chair, from which it was assumed that she had brought her 'gentleman' back to her room and had taken off her clothes in readiness for sex. The theory was that it was then that he had pulled a knife. Unlike the Ripper's other victims, Mary had been facing her killer and had cried out on seeing the knife. Some time between 3.30 and 4am a woman who had been sleeping in the room above had heard Mary scream 'Oh, murder' before going back to sleep.

The Ripper slashed Mary's throat, almost decapitating her. As she was facing him, some of her blood must have splashed onto his clothes, which were found burnt in the stove. Then the Ripper set about his dissection work. He cut off both of her breasts and put them on the table, placing her severed nose and flesh from her thighs and legs alongside. Her forehead and legs were stripped of flesh and her abdomen was slashed open. Her liver and intestines were removed and her hand shoved into the gaping hole in her belly. (Mary was three months pregnant when she died.) There was blood around the window from which the Ripper was thought to have escaped. He would have been naked, except for a long cloak and boots.

The next day the rent man called and discovered Mary's mutilated corpse. He called the police, who were horrified and, once again, baffled.

Mary Kelly was last woman whom we know to have been a victim of the Ripper. Other murders followed that may either have been his handiwork or the work of a copycat killer. In June 1889, for example, the headless corpse of Elizabeth Jackson, a prostitute who worked in the Chelsea area, was found floating in the Thames. The following month the body of Alice McKenzie, a prostitute working in Whitechapel, was found; her throat had been cut from ear to ear and her sexual organs cut out. Frances Cole, a streetwalker known as 'Carroty Nell' because of her flaming-red hair, was also found dead in Whitechapel with her throat cut and slashes around her abdomen. Her assailant may have been planning a more thorough mutilation, but had been disturbed by a policeman, who reported having seen a man stooping over the body who had run away before the constable could get a good look at him.

The newspapers had already produced an image of the Ripper that had seized the public's imagination. It was based on a description given by the friend of Mary Kelly who had seen her with a client on the night of her death. She said that he was 5 feet 6 inches (1.65 metres) tall, about 35 and well dressed, and that he had had a gold watch chain dangling from his waistcoat pocket.

Mary had been heard in conversation with the man. 'Will you be alright for what I have told you?' he had asked. 'All right, my dear', she had replied, taking him by the arm. 'Come along, you will be comfortable.' A few hours later a roast-chestnut vendor had seen a man matching the same description, wearing a long cloak and silk hat, with a thin moustache that turned up at the ends. Ominously, he was carrying a black bag, which could have contained surgical instruments. 'Have you heard that there has been another murder?' the man had asked. 'I have', the chestnut vendor had replied. 'I know more of it than you do', the man had said as he walked away.

The Ripper was never caught, and over the past century an enormous number of theories have been put forward regarding who he was. The police alone came up with 176 suspects, of whom perhaps the most likely was a Russian physician, Dr Alexander Pedachenko, who had worked under an assumed name at a Camberwell clinic that catered to prostitutes, including four of the victims. He had died in an asylum in St Petersburg after killing a woman in the Russian town. A document naming him as the Ripper was said to have been found in the basement of Rasputin's home in St Petersburg after the monk's murder in 1916; sceptics, however, have pointed out the house did not have a basement.

Another popular suspect was a Dr Stanley, a Harley Street physician who had contracted syphilis from a prostitute called Kelly in Whitechapel. It was said that he had gone about killing prostitutes out of vengeance until he hit upon the right one. Stanley subsequently fled to Buenos Aires, in Argentina, where he died in 1929 after supposedly confessing all to a student.

At the time of the murders Jewish immigrants to the East End were blamed for having perpetrated them. It was said that they represented ritual Jewish slaughters and had been performed by a *shochet*, a butcher who kills animals according to Talmudic law. The *shochet* theory was given some credence by a strange message that was found scrawled on a wall in Whitechapel after the murder of Catherine Eddowes, which said 'The juwes are not the men that will be blamed for nothing'. It was also noted that 'juwes' was a Masonic spelling of 'Jews', which gave rise to the theory that the murders had been part of a Masonic rite. The police commissioner, Sir Charles Warren, himself a leading Mason, had the graffiti removed in order to prevent the inflammation of anti-Jewish sentiments. He resigned from the police force after the murder of Mary Kelly, admitting his utter failure to solve the case.

A Polish Jew named V Kosminski, who lived in Whitechapel and had furthermore threatened to slice up prostitutes, was a suspect, but later became insane and died in an asylum. Another Polish immigrant, Severin Klosowich – alias George Chapman – was also under suspicion. A barber and surgeon in Whitechapel, he kept sharp knives for bloodletting and the removal of warts and moles. He also poisoned three of his mistresses and went to gallows in 1903. A further suspect was Thomas Cutbush, who was arrested after the murder of Frances Cole for stabbing women in the buttocks; he died in an mental institution, too.

A newspaper reporter named Roslyn D'Onston wrote to the police in 1888 accusing Dr Morgan Davies, a surgeon at the London Hospital in Whitechapel, of being Jack the Ripper. Yet D'Onston was himself a suspect; a failed doctor and a drug addict, he was said by some to have killed the women in order to give his career a fillip. It was claimed that the stories that he published in the newspapers contained details about the murders that were never released by the police. D'Onston subsequently became a Satanist; his fellow devil-worshipper, Aleister Crowley, claimed that he had ritually murdered killed the women in an attempt to become invisible.

The insomniac G Wentworth Bell Smith, who lived at 27 Sun Street, off

Finsbury Square, became a suspect because he railed against prostitutes, saying that they should all be drowned. For his part, Frederick Bailey Deeming confessed to the Ripper's murders. Deeming had murdered his wife and children in England and had then fled to Australia, where he had killed a second wife; he had been about to murder a third when he was arrested in Melbourne. It is thought that his confession was an attempt to postpone, if not evade, his trip to gallows. Another popular suspect was the 'Lambeth Poisoner', Dr Thomas Neil Cream, who poisoned a number of prostitutes during the 1890s. Before he was hanged he told his executioner 'I am Jack the . . .', just as the trap opened.

The police's prime suspect was Montague John Druitt, an Oxford graduate and scion of a once wealthy family. After failing as a barrister, Druitt became a school teacher. Unable to keep his homosexual urges under control, he was dismissed for molesting a boy. He then moved to Whitechapel, where he was seen walking the streets. In December 1888 his body was fished out of the Thames; there were stones in his pockets and he appeared to have drowned himself.

Somewhat surprisingly, the secretary of William Booth (the latter the founder of the Salvation Army), also found himself on the list of suspects – apparently he had said 'Carroty Nell will be the next to go' a few days before the slaying of Frances Cole. Another man, the alcoholic railway worker Thomas Salder, was arrested after the murder of Alice McKenzie; he also knew Frances Cole, but was released due to lack of evidence.

Although Sherlock Holmes was not around to solve the case, his creator, Sir Arthur Conan Doyle, was, and used all of his considerable powers of reasoning to deduce that the Ripper was a woman. According to his theory, 'Jill the Ripper' was a midwife who had gone mad after having been sent to prison for performing illegal abortions.

The spiritualist William Lees staged a seance for Queen Victoria in an attempt to discover who the Ripper was, but the results frightened him so much that he fled to the Continent. The Ripper, he believed, was none other than the queen's physician, Sir William Gull. The theory that was later developed was that Prince Eddy, the Duke of Clarence – Victoria's grandson and heir to the throne – had secretly married a shop girl called Crook, who had borne him a child which was placed in the care of one Mary Kelly. Gull and some of his Masonic cronies, it was said, went about killing prostitutes until they got to Kelly and retrieved the child. Gull's papers were examined by Dr Thomas Stowell and were discovered to name Prince Eddy, who died of syphilis before he could ascend the throne, as Jack the Ripper. Another suspect was James Kenneth Stephen, the prince's tutor and possibly also his lover; the pair frequented homosexual clubs in Whitechapel together.

The painter Frank Miles, an intimate of Oscar Wilde, was named as the Ripper, too, but the truth is that the identity of Jack the Ripper will probably never be known.

2 ❖ The Boston Strangler

The man who came to personify the modern serial killer was the Boston Strangler, who terrorised the USA's Boston area for two years. No one was ever charged with the Boston Strangler killings, but a man did confess to them: his name was Albert DeSalvo.

DeSalvo was the son of a vicious drunk. When he was 11 he watched his father knock out his mother's teeth before bending back her fingers until they snapped – this was just another ordinary day in the DeSalvo household. When they were children, DeSalvo's father sold him and his two sisters to a farmer in Maine for just $9. DeSalvo escaped, and after he had found his way home his father taught him how to shoplift by taking him to a shop and showing him what to steal. His father would also bring prostitutes back to the family apartment and make the children watch while he had sex with the women.

Perhaps unsurprisingly, the young DeSalvo soon developed a lively interest in sex. He made numerous conquests among the neighbourhood girls, as well as earning a healthy living from the local gay community, members of which would pay him for his services. DeSalvo continued his sexual adventuring in the army until he met Irmgaard, the daughter of a respectable, Catholic family, in Frankfurt-am-Main, Germany. After marrying Irmgaard, DeSalvo returned to the USA with his wife, where he was dishonourably discharged from the army for sexually molesting a nine-year-old girl; he only escaped criminal charges because the girl's mother wanted to protect her daughter from publicity.

DeSalvo next became a professional thief, making his living by breaking and entering. At home he appeared to be the perfect family man, although his prodigious sexual appetite was more than his wife could cope with: his demands for sex five or six times a day annoyed, and finally repelled, Irmgaard. DeSalvo then began to hang around the campus area of Boston on the lookout for apartments shared by young, female students. He would knock on the door with a clipboard and introduce himself as the representative of a modelling agency before asking whether he could take the measurements of the women who lived there. He was a charming man and sometimes succeeded in seducing them (occasionally they would seduce him). On other occasions he would just take their measurements – either when they were clothed or, as he preferred, naked – and promise that a female representative would call later. He never assaulted any of the women, who sometimes complained that no one had made the promised, follow-up visit. The police called him 'Measuring Man'.

At around that time DeSalvo was arrested for housebreaking and was consequently jailed for two years. Prison soured him, and when he was released he began breaking into houses throughout New England, tying up women and raping them. Known as the 'Green Man' because he wore a green shirt and trousers, the police throughout Connecticut and Massachusetts guessed that his assaults numbered in the hundreds. DeSalvo himself later claimed more than a thousand, bragging that he had tied up and raped six women in one morning.

In 1962 DeSalvo began to concentrate his activities on Boston, also adding murder to his repertoire. His first victim was the 55-year-old Anna Slesters, whose body, which had been left in an obscene pose, was found in her apartment. DeSalvo had strangled her and had then tied the cord that he had used to kill her in a bow around her neck. This became his trademark. Two weeks later he murdered the 55-year-old Mary Mullen, whom DeSalvo subsequently said had reminded him of his grandmother. Then he raped and strangled an 85-year-old nurse, Helen Blake. For her part, Nina Nichols fought back, scratching some flesh from his arms before he strangled her. On 19 August the 75-year-old Ida Irga was raped and strangled and on the following day DeSalvo murdered the 67-year-old Jane Sullivan.

The Boston police force soon realised that a maniac was at work and began questioning all known sexual deviants. DeSalvo, however, had a police record for housebreaking alone – the details of his sexual deviancy appeared only in his army file.

DeSalvo took a long autumn break from his murderous activities, but by the time of his wedding anniversary – 5 December 1962 – his brain was so overheated by violent sexual images that he felt that it was going to explode. Seeing an attractive girl go into an apartment block, he followed her and knocked on the door of her apartment, pretending to be a maintenance man who had been sent by the landlord to check the pipes. She did not let him in, so he tried the same ploy at the next apartment, whose door was opened by a tall, attractive, 25-year-old African-American woman called Sophie Clark. This time DeSalvo reverted to his 'Measuring Man' routine and remarked upon her curvaceous figure. When she turned her back he pounced on her, and after he had subdued her he stripped, raped and finally strangled her. As with his other victims, before leaving he propped up her naked body, spread her legs and tied the cord that he had used to strangle her in a bow under her chin.

Three days later DeSalvo made a return call on one of the women, a 23-year-old secretary, whom he had previously visited as the 'Measuring Man'. After Patricia Bissette had invited him in for a coffee she turned her back, whereupon he grabbed her around the throat, raped her and then strangled her with her own stockings. DeSalvo's next victim, however, fought back so violently – biting, scratching and screaming – that the Boston Strangler fled and she escaped with her life, but she was so distraught that the description that she gave of her attacker was practically worthless.

The failed murder seems to have marked something of a turning point in DeSalvo's career of crime, because from then on his attacks became even more violent. On 9 March 1963, for example, he entered the apartment of the 69-year-old Mary Brown on the pretext of fixing the stove. He had brought a piece of lead pipe with him, which he used to beat in her head. When she was dead he raped her and then stabbed her breasts with a fork, which he left sticking from her flesh. Although he maintained his *modus operandi* by strangling her, this time the victim was already dead when he did so.

Two months later DeSalvo took a day off work and drove to Cambridge, Massachusetts. Spotting a pretty girl, a 23-year-old student named Beverley Samans, on University Road, he followed her back to her apartment. Once inside, he tied her to her bedposts, stripped, blindfolded, gagged and then repeatedly raped her before strangling her with her own stockings. But this was no longer enough for him and before he left the apartment he pulled a penknife from his pocket and started to stab her naked body. Once he had started he could not stop, and when her body

The Boston Strangler - Albert DeSalvo. Photographed 25th February, 1967.

was discovered it was found to bear 22 savage wounds. After his frenzy had subsided DeSalvo calmly wiped his fingerprints from the knife, dropped it into the sink and went home.

On 8 September 1963 the Boston Strangler struck again. This time it was a straightforward case of rape and strangulation, the 58-year-old Evelyn Corbin being strangled with her own nylons, which he left tied in his signature bow, but around her ankle, in a departure from his usual style.

By this time the people of Boston and the surrounding area were in a state of panic. The Strangler seemed to come and go at will. The police had no useful description of the killer and no clues – they seemed powerless. In desperation they brought in a Dutch psychic, Peter Hurkos, who had had some success in other cases, but he failed to identify the Boston Strangler.

While the USA – and particularly John F Kennedy's home state of Massachusetts – was in mourning following the assassination of the president, the Boston Strangler struck again, raping and strangling Joan Gaff, a 23-year-old dress designer, in her own apartment before tying her black leotard in a bow around her neck. DeSalvo later said that he did not know why he had killed her; 'I wasn't even excited', he commented. After he had left her apartment, he revealed, he had gone home, played with his children and watched the report of Joan's murder on television. Then, he said, he had sat down and had his dinner, without thinking of her again.

On 4 January 1964 the Boston Strangler killed for the last time. His victim was the 19-year-old Mary Sullivan. He gained access to her apartment, tied her up at knife point and raped her before strangling her with his bare hands. Her body was left sitting up in bed, with her head lolling against her right shoulder. Her eyes were closed and a viscous liquid dripped from her mouth down her right breast. Her breasts and sexual organs were exposed and a broom handle protruded from her vagina. More semen stains were found on her blanket and a New Year's greeting card that the killer had found in the apartment was placed between her toes.

Later that year a woman reported having been sexually assaulted by a man who had used the Measuring Man routine, but otherwise the Boston Strangler's activities stopped. This was because DeSalvo had again been arrested for housebreaking. In jail his behaviour became increasingly disturbed and he was transferred to a mental hospital in Bridgewater, where he was diagnosed as being schizophrenic.

Although DeSalvo was in custody, the police still had no idea that they were holding the Boston Strangler. But in the Bridgewater hospital another inmate – who had killed a petrol-station attendant and was himself a suspect in the Boston Strangler case – listened to DeSalvo's deranged ramblings and began to put two and two together. He then persuaded his lawyer to speak to DeSalvo. In his taped interviews with the lawyer DeSalvo discussed facts about the murders that the police had not revealed. He spoke of the positions in which he had left the bodies, the ligature that he had used to strangle each victim, as well as the other wounds that he had inflicted. He also admitted to two murders that had not yet been attributed to the Boston Strangler.

Despite his admissions DeSalvo was a mental patient who was plainly unfit to stand trial and whose confession was legally worthless. He was therefore not prosecuted for the rapes and murders to which he had admitted. There was no doubt, however, that he was indeed the Boston Strangler, even if he could only be charged with robbery and other sexual offences unconnected to the Strangler's activities. He was sentenced to life imprisonment and transferred to Walpole State Prison. On 26 November 1973 the 36-year-old DeSalvo was found dead in his cell, stabbed through the heart.

3 ❖ The Campus Killer

Like Albert DeSalvo, Ted Bundy also had the power to charm women, many of whom paid for their susceptibility with their lives. For three years during the 1970s Bundy preyed on young female students on college campuses across the USA, killing at least 19 young women and maybe as many as 40.

Bundy was well educated, ran his own business, had been a noted high-school athlete and worked for both the Republican Party and the Washington State Crime Commission. He even became a counsellor at a Seattle rape-crisis centre after having been screened for 'balance and maturity'. He had one significant problem, however: his sexual impulses were so strong that he could not control them. He later said that after his first attacks he had had to wrestle with his conscience, but had subsequently begun to desensitise himself to his crimes. He claimed not to have caused his victims unnecessary suffering, but said that he had had to kill them after he had raped them in order to prevent them from identifying him. He admitted deliberately terrorising his victim – or rather victims –in only one case: when he kidnapped two girls at the same time, intending to rape each in front of the other before killing them both.

From an early age Bundy had been a compulsive masturbator, and after glimpsing a girl undressing through a window he had become a Peeping Tom. He later became obsessed by sadistic pornography. His long-time girlfriend, Meg Anders, described how he liked to tie her up with her own stockings before having anal sex with her, but said that she had put a stop to this sex game when he almost strangled her. For years they maintained a normal sexual relationship while Bundy indulged his perverse cravings elsewhere. And what he craved was total control over an anonymous victim, whom he often strangled during sex. Indeed, his attitude to sex was ambivalent: although his victims were always attractive young women, he liked to defile their bodies by stuffing twigs and dirt into their vaginas or sodomising them with aerosol cans or other foreign objects. When they were discovered, some of the bodies of his victims, although partly decomposed, were found to be wearing newly applied make-up and to have freshly washed hair – he had kept them for the purposes of necrophilia.

Bundy began his murderous career in his home town of Seattle. His first victim was Sharon Clarke, into whose apartment he broke while she was asleep before hitting her around the head with a metal rod. Although she survived – albeit with a shattered skull – she could not identify her attacker; nor was there any indication of the motivation for the attack.

Soon afterwards, young women began disappearing from the nearby campus of the University of Washington. Six went missing within seven months. The clue to what may have happened to them came from the Lake Sammanish resort in Washington State, when a number of women reported having been approached by a young man calling himself Ted. He had had his arm in a sling and had asked them to help him to lift his sailing boat off the roof of his car. Once in the car park, however, they had found that there was no boat, whereupon Ted had then said that they would have to go to his house to get it. Although most of the women had declined his invitation to accompany him, it seemed that Janice Ott had agreed to go. And a few hours later Denise Naslund went missing from the same area; she had been seen with a good-looking, dark-haired young man. The remains of Janice Ott, Denise Naslund and another unidentified young woman were later found on waste ground. Their bodies had been dismembered and eaten by animals. Witnesses at the University of Washington subsequently said that they had seen a man wearing a sling, and more bodies were also found on wasteland.

The police had two suspects: Gary Taylor and Warren Forrest. Taylor, a former convict, had been arrested by the Seattle police for abducting women under false pretexts. For his part, Forrest, a park attendant, had picked up a young woman who had agreed to pose for him. He had taken her to a secluded part of the park, where he had stripped her naked and tied her up. He had then taped up her mouth and had fired darts at her breasts before raping and strangling her and leaving her for dead. His victim had survived, however, and had identified her attacker. The problem for the police was that although both men were in custody the attacks continued.

By now Bundy's girlfriend was growing suspicious of him and called the police anonymously to give them his name. But her tip-off was just one among the thousands of leads that the police had to follow up and it was overlooked.

Serial Killer Ted Bundy, who was killed by electric chair at 7am on 24th January, 1989. Before his death, he managed to escape from secure institutions on two occasions.

Nevertheless, things were becoming a bit too hot for Bundy in his home state, so on 30 August 1974 he quit his job in Seattle and moved to Salt Lake City, where he enrolled at the University of Utah's law school. On 2 October he abducted Nancy Wilcox after she had left an all-night party. On 18 October he raped and strangled the 18-year-old Melissa Smith, the daughter of the local police chief; her body was found near Salt Lake City. He abducted the 17-year-old Laura Aimee from a Hallowe'en party in Orem; her naked body was discovered at the bottom of a canyon. He tried to pick up a pretty young French teacher outside her high school, but she refused to go with him. The 17-year-old Debbie Kent did, however, disappearing on 8 November from a school playground in which the key to a pair of handcuffs was later found.

A week later he approached the 18-year-old Carol DaRonch in Salt Lake City. Bundy pretended to be a police detective and asked her for the licence number of her car, explaining that someone had been trying to break into it. He then invited her to accompany him to the police station in order to identify the suspect and she obligingly got into his car. Once they were in a quiet street he handcuffed her and put a gun to her head when she began to scream. Despite being handcuffed, Carol managed to get out of the car, whereupon Bundy chased after her with a crowbar, which he swung at her head. Carol was just able to deflect it when at that moment a car drove down the street. Seizing her chance, she threw herself in front of it, forcing it to stop; after she had jumped in the car drove away.

Carol gave a good description of her attacker to the Utah police, but shortly thereafter Bundy moved to Colorado. In January 1975 Dr Raymond Gadowsky reported that his fiancée, Carolyn Campbell, was missing from her hotel room in Snowmass Village, a ski resort. A month later her naked body was found in the snow; she had been raped and her skull smashed in. Julie Cunningham disappeared from nearby Vail, and the remains of Susan Rancourt and Brenda Bell were found on Taylor Mountain. The body of Melanie Cooley was discovered just ten miles (16 kilometres) from her home. Unlike the other victims she was still clothed (although her jeans had been undone), but the police were nevertheless convinced that the motive for her murder was a sexual one. The Colorado attacks continued: Nancy Baird vanished from a petrol station, while Shelley Robertson's naked body was found down a mine shaft.

One day a highway patrolman was cruising through Granger, Utah, which had recently been plagued by a series of burglaries. He noticed Bundy's VW driving slowly, without its lights on, and indicated that he should pull over. Instead of complying, however, Bundy sped off, causing the patrolman to give chase. On catching up with him the patrolman asked him what he had in the car, to which Bundy replied 'Just some junk'. The junk turned out to be a ski mask, handcuffs, some nylon stockings and a crowbar. Bundy was detained for having committed a traffic offence and was later released. On the following day he was arrested at his apartment in Salt Lake City and charged with possessing tools with which to commit burglary, but he was again released on bail.

The police had impounded Bundy's car, however, in which they discovered maps and brochures of resorts in Colorado, some of which coincided with the places from which the girls had disappeared. Forensic experts found a hair in the VW that matched that of Melissa Smith. A witness recognised Bundy from Snowmass Village. Furthermore, Carol DaRonch picked him out of a line-up.

Bundy was charged with kidnapping and was subsequently tried, found guilty and sentenced to a period in jail of from one to fifteen years. Then he was extradited to Colorado to stand trial for the murder of Carolyn Campbell. In court Bundy came across as an intelligent and person-able young man – the sort who could have had any girl whom he wanted – and it seemed unlikely to many that he could have been responsible for the terrible sex attacks.

In Aspen, Colorado, Bundy was given permission to conduct his own defence, even being allowed to use the law library. It was there that he managed to give his guard the slip, jump from a window and escape. He was recaptured eight days later. Bundy continued to protest his innocence and was able to spin out the pre-trial hearings by using skilful, legal, stalling tactics. In the meantime he had lost weight. One day, while stand-ing on a stack of legal books in his cell, he managed to cut a hole under the light fitting with a hacksaw blade. He then squeezed through the 1-foot-square (30-centimetre-square) hole, stole a police car and got clean away.

Bundy made a murderous tour of the USA before settling in Tallahas-see, Florida, a few blocks from the sorority houses of Florida State Univer-sity. On the evening of 15 January 1977 Nita Neary saw a man lurking in front of her own sorority house. She was about to phone the police when a fellow student, Karen Chandler, staggered from her room, blood streaming from her head, screaming that she had just been attacked by a madman. Her room-mate, Kathy Kleiner, had also been attacked and her jaw broken. The 21-year-old Margaret Bowman had been sexually assaulted and stran-gled with her own tights. The 20-year-old Lisa Levy had also been sexually assaulted: Bundy had bitten off one of her nipples and had sunk his teeth into her buttocks before beating her around the head. She died on the way to hospital. Cheryl Thomas had been viciously attacked in another build-ing, too, but survived. The police could elicit only a sketchy description of the attacker from his victims.

On 8 February, in Lake City, Florida, Bundy abducted the 12-year-old Kimberley Leach, sexually assaulted and strangled her, mutilated her sexual organs and dumped her body in a pig shed.

Bundy was now short of money, so he stole some credit cards, along with a car, and did a moonlight flit from his apartment, on which he owed rent. But the stolen car was a giveaway and he was stopped by a highway patrolman, whereupon Bundy attacked him and tried to escape. The patrolman caught up with him, however, and clubbed him unconscious. At the police station Bundy admitted that he was wanted in Colorado. For their part the Florida police had begun to link him to the Tallahassee attack. When they tried to take an impression of his teeth he went berserk and it took six men to hold his jaw open. The impression was subsequently found to match the teeth marks on the buttocks of the murdered student, Lisa Levy, as well as those on the body of Kimberley Leach.

Bundy was charged with the murder of the child. At his trial he again conducted his own defence, cannily using points of law with which to prolong the court case and charming the jury with his personality. The evidence against him was too strong, however, and Bundy was found guilty of murder and sentenced to death. All the while protesting his innocence, he managed to postpone his execution for another ten years. Eventually, when all the legal avenues had been exhausted, he broke down and confessed to nearly 40 murders. 'I deserve to die', he said.

At 7am on 24 January 1989 Bundy went to the electric chair. He is said to have died with a smile on his face. On death row Bundy had made a detailed confession, thereby aiding a number of academics who were studying serial killers. He had also received sacks full of mail from young women whose letters dwelt on various cruel and painful ways in which to make love – it seems that even on death row he had not lost his charm.

4 ◆ Ten Rillington Place

John Reginald Christie got his kicks by murdering women and sexually abusing their corpses. He went about his grisly business in his shabby house in Notting Hill Gate, London, whose address – 10 Rillington Place – has since become infamous.

Christie was born on 8 April 1898 in Halifax, Yorkshire. His father, Ernest, a designer for Crossley Carpets, was a pillar of local society, being a leader of the Primrose League (an organisation intended to promote morality among the working classes) and a founder member of the Halifax Conservative Party. He was also a stern disciplinarian and his son was terrified of him. 'We almost had to ask if we could speak to him', he later wrote. Christie also had other problems within his family: one of seven children, he was completely dominated by his older sisters.

Christie did well at school and sang in the choir. He was first a boy scout and then an assistant scout master. But there were other, deeper, tides flowing within Christie. When he was eight, for example, his grandfather died and Christie reported having felt a trembling sensation of both fascination and pleasure on seeing the body.

After leaving school Christie started work at the Gem Cinema in Halifax. One day he was part of a gang of boys and girls who went down to the Monkey Run, as the local lovers' lane was known. They paired off and Christie found himself with a girl who was much more sexually experienced than he was. Intimidated, he could not rise to the occasion and when word of it got around his friends started taunting him, calling him 'Reggie-no-dick' and 'Can't-do-it-Reggie'.

At the age of 17 Christie was caught stealing at work and sacked, whereupon his father kicked him out of the house; he had to sleep on the family's allotment and his mother took him food. He then drifted from job to job until he was called up to serve as a soldier during World War I. He was gassed in France before being sent home and discharged from the army with a disability pension.

On 20 May 1920 Christie married the long-suffering Ethel Waddington. He got a job as a postman, but was caught stealing money from letters. In 1921 he was jailed for nine months. Two years later he was bound over for posing as a former officer. Following a violent incident he was put on probation, and when he was sent down for another nine months for theft Ethel left him. In 1929 he was sentenced to six months' hard labour for assaulting a prostitute. A Roman Catholic priest befriended him, but Christie stole his car, which earned him another spell in prison.

On his release Christie wrote to Ethel asking her to come back to him and she foolishly did so. They moved to London, and on a visit to Ethel's family in Leeds Christie boasted of his 'big house in London' and his servants. In fact, he and Ethel lived in a shabby little flat in North Kensington, with no servants. He never earned over £8 a week, which was the going rate for a junior clerk.

On the outbreak of World War II in 1939 Christie became a special constable in the War Reserve Police. No checks were carried out to see if he had a criminal record, but in any case he seemed to be a reformed character. He was never much liked, however, because of his petty-mindedness – indeed, Christie and another special constable were known as the 'rat and the weasel'.

Although he was balding, Christie still regarded himself as a charmer. Deep down, however, he feared and hated women. 'Women who give you the come-on wouldn't look nearly so saucy if they were helpless and dead', he thought. He took pride in hiding his violent intentions from the women whom he took back to 10 Rillington Place, and by the time that they arrived there it was too late for them to save themselves.

His first victim was an Austrian refugee, the 17-year-old Ruth Fuerst. Ruth worked in a munitions factory, but because the pay was poor she supplemented her income with the proceeds of a little prostitution. Christie had met her while he was trying to trace a man who was wanted for theft; she had asked him to lend her ten shillings and Christie had invited her home. On one hot, August afternoon in 1943, while Ethel was in Sheffield, she called again at 10 Rillington Place. At first Christie refused to engage in sexual intercourse, but Ruth encouraged him. Once the sex was over he strangled her. Christie said that he had felt a great sense of peace after he had killed Ruth. He had been fascinated by the beauty of her corpse and had wanted to keep it, but his wife had returned home unexpectedly that night and he had had to bury Ruth's body in the garden. He compared his début in murder to an artist's first painting. 'It was thrilling because I had embarked on the career I had chosen for myself, the career of murder. But it was only the beginning', he later said.

Christie left the police force at the end of 1943 and went to work at the Ultra Radio Works in west London, where he met an attractive, 31-year-old woman, Muriel Eady. Muriel suffered from catarrh and Christie claimed that he had a remedy for it. On one afternoon in October 1944 she therefore went to see him at 10 Rillington Place and he showed her what he claimed was his patent inhaler. In fact, it was nothing more than a jar containing perfumed water that had two holes in its lid with rubber tubes leading from them. Christie then persuaded Muriel to inhale his remedy through one of them; unbeknownst to her the other tube was connected to the gas pipe. The perfume in the jar concealed the smell of gas and when Muriel lapsed into unconsciousness Christie had sex with her and then strangled her. He was thrilled by the notion that his second murder was much cleverer than the first.

In 1948 Timothy Evans, a lorry driver, and his wife, Beryl, moved into the top-floor flat at 10 Rillington Place. Born in Merthyr Vale on 20 November 1924, Evans was educationally challenged and also had a speech impediment (when he was a child he could not even pronounce his own name). His schooling had been held back further by a foot injury which caused him to spend long spells in hospital. Evans' father had walked out on his mother before Timothy was born (his mother subsequently procured a certificate saying that he was presumed dead). She later remarried and the family moved to Notting Hill Gate, where Timothy married a local girl, Beryl Thorley, in 1947.

Evans was 24 when he saw the 'To Let' sign outside 10 Rillington Place. He and the pregnant Beryl were still living with his mother and stepfather and because the young couple desperately needed a place of their own they took the cramped attic flat. Charles Kitchener, a railway worker with failing eyesight, lived on the floor below. He kept himself to himself and was often in hospital. The ground floor was occupied by John and Ethel Christie. Shortly after the Evanses moved in Beryl gave birth to a baby daughter, whom they named Geraldine. The Evanses and Christies were soon getting on well and Ethel, who was fond of the baby, looked after Geraldine when Beryl was working part-time.

In the summer of 1949 Beryl became pregnant again. There was little money coming in and the Evanses were behind on their hire-purchase payments. Beryl, who was still only 19, wanted an abortion, but Timothy, a Roman Catholic, forbade it. The adamant Beryl then discovered that there was a back-street abortionist on the Edgware Road who would do the job for £1. When Christie heard of her plan he told Beryl that he could help her out by performing the abortion himself. She in turn told Timothy of Christie's offer, who said that he had not realised that Christie knew anything about medical procedures. In order to reassure him Christie showed him the St John's Ambulance Brigade's first-aid manual; Evans, who was illiterate, knew no better.

On 8 November 1949 Evans came home to find Christie waiting for him with bad news: the operation had not been a success, Christie explained, and Beryl had died. Christie begged Evans not to go to the police, saying that he would be charged with manslaughter because Beryl had died during an illegal abortion. Evans' first concern was who would look after Geraldine and therefore suggested his mother, but Christie said that he would find someone else to care for the baby. When Evans returned from work on 10 November Christie said that he had delivered the child to a couple in East Acton, and that evening Evans assisted Christie in disposing of Beryl's body down the outside drain.

Christie helped Evans to sell off his furniture and Evans then returned to Wales with £40 in his pocket. He was plagued by guilt, however, believing that as a Catholic he should have stopped Beryl from having the abortion; if he had done so, he reasoned, she would still have been alive. So he walked into Merthyr Vale's police station and confessed. Evans thought that he could take the blame for Beryl's death without implicating Christie, whom he considered to be his friend. He therefore told the police that he had obtained a bottle that contained something that would make his wife miscarry from a man whom he had met in a transport café. He had not intended to give it to his wife, he said, but explained that she must have found it while he was out at work. When he returned he had found her dead and had opened a drain outside the front door into which he had dropped her body.

The Merthyr Vale police contacted their counterparts at Notting Hill Gate, who sent police officers to 10 Rillington Place. It took three of them to lift the manhole cover over the drain, only to find that it was empty. Back in Merthyr Vale the police then challenged Evans' statement: he could not possibly have lifted the manhole cover himself, they said. Unable to continue the pretence, Evans made a second statement, this time telling the truth: Christie, he said, had performed an illegal abortion on his wife, who had consequently died; together he and Christie had disposed of the body.

The police had searched 10 Rillington Place, but not very thoroughly – they did not even notice Muriel Eady's thighbone, which was propped up against the garden fence. Christie made a statement saying that he had overheard the Evanses quarrelling; Beryl had complained that her husband had grabbed her by the throat, he elaborated. The police believed Christie – after all, the man had been policeman.

The house was searched again and this time Beryl's corpse was found. It had been wrapped in a green tablecloth and hidden behind a stack of wood in a downstairs washroom. Beside it was the body of the 14-month-old Geraldine. Both had been strangled. An autopsy revealed that there was bruising in Beryl's vagina and that her right eye and upper lip were swollen. In the police view this evidence confirmed their belief that Beryl's murder had been a simple 'domestic'.

Evans' trial took place at the Old Bailey in the January of 1950. Standing in the witness box, Christie apologised to the judge for speaking softly, explaining that this was the result of having been gassed during World War I. The court was also told of his service as a special constable. His long record of petty crime was not mentioned and the impression was given that he was a solid citizen whose word was not to be doubted. When he was asked if he had performed an illegal abortion on Beryl Evans he denied it, saying that he had been lying ill in bed on the day of Beryl's death.

Evans cut a much shabbier figure. He was out of his depth in the court-room and gave his evidence poorly. His allegation that his wife had died during an illegal abortion performed by Christie held no water with the court as the evidence proved that she had been strangled. Furthermore, he could not explain the death of the baby. The jury deliberated for just 40 minutes before returning a verdict of guilty. The sentence imposed by the judge was death by hanging.

Evans maintained to the end that Christie had killed both his wife and daughter. There was some public disquiet about the verdict and a petition bearing nearly 2,000 signatures was presented to the home secretary appealing against the verdict. It did no good and Evans was hanged on 9 March 1950.

Christie later said that on 14 December 1952 he had been woken when his wife, Ethel, went into convulsions. She seemed to have overdosed on phenobarbital and Christie decided that it was too late to get help. It would be kindest to put her out of her misery, he reasoned, so he put a stocking around her neck and strangled her. Unsure of what to do with it, he then left his wife's body in the bed for two days before pulling up the floor-boards in the front room and burying her under them. The couple had been married for 32 years.

Over the next four months Christie sold his furniture to fund a sex-and-murder spree. The 25-year-old prostitute Rita Nelson had just discov-ered that she was pregnant when, on 12 January 1953, she visited 10 Rillington Place, where Christie strangled her, subsequently shoving her body into an alcove in the kitchen. The 26-year-old Kathleen Maloney was lured into his flat to pose nude while he photographed her. Instead she was gassed and sexually abused, her body then also being placed in the alcove.

Christie had more trouble with his final victim, Hectorina MacLennan. He had met her in the café in which he picked up prostitutes and had offered her somewhere to stay. She had turned up at 10 Rillington Place with her boyfriend, however. After they had been there for three nights Christie at last found her alone on 6 March 1953. He gave her a drink and offered her a whiff of his inhaler, which she did not enjoy. Following a struggle Christie strangled her and had sex with her corpse. He then bun-dled her body into the alcove, joining those of Rita Nelson and Kathleen Maloney, propping her up into a sitting position, with her bra hooked to Maloney's leg.

After that Christie built a false wall in front of the alcove and papered over it. He sublet the flat to a couple called Reilly, took his dog to the vet to be put to sleep and moved out. The landlord subsequently evicted the Reillys and gave Beresford Brown, who was living in the flat that had previously been occupied by the Evanses, permission to use the kitchen in the ground-floor flat provided that he cleared it out. After Brown had removed the clothes, rubbish and filth that Christie had left behind him, he started to redecorate the kitchen. He had wanted to put up some brackets on the rear wall, but when he tapped it he found that it was hollow. Pulling away some of the wallpaper, he saw a papered-over, wooden door. On opening it he discerned a partially clothed woman's body sitting on a pile of rubbish. Brown promptly called the police.

The police soon discovered that there was more than one body at 10 Rillington Place. A thorough search of the alcove revealed a second, wrapped in a blanket, and then a third, whose ankles had been tied together with plastic flex. All three had been strangled. Next, the corpse of Ethel Christie was found under the floorboards in the front room.

The police quickly realised that John Reginald Christie was the man for whom they should be searching and issued his description to the press. His picture appeared in every national newspaper and appeals for information regarding his whereabouts were made over the loudspeaker systems at football matches. Soon the whole country was looking for a slight, balding, middle-aged multiple murder. There were numerous reported sightings of Christie, but few were genuine.

Meanwhile, in the tiny garden of 10 Rillington Place, the police had unearthed the skeletons of two more women, which, they estimated, had lain buried for about ten years. Both women had been strangled and the skull of one was missing.

On the day that he left 10 Rillington Place Christie had moved into a hotel in King's Cross Road. He had soon moved on, however, tramping back and forth across London homeless and alone. At around 11pm on the night of 19 March 1953, at the height of the biggest manhunt that the country had ever known, Norman Rae, the chief crime reporter of the Sunday newspaper the *News of the World*, received a phone call. 'Do you recognise my voice?' the caller asked. Rae did: he had met Christie during the trial of Timothy Evans. 'I can't stand any more', said Christie. 'They're hunting me like a dog.' In return for a meal, some cigarettes and a warm place in which to sit, Christie promised that he would give the *News of the World* an exclusive. They arranged to meet at 1.30am, outside Wood Green's town hall, and as Rae parked outside it two policemen walked by. It was pure chance, but Christie ran off, thinking that he had been double-crossed.

Two days later PC Thomas Ledger stopped a man near Putney Bridge, who, in response to the constable's questioning, said that he was John Waddington, of 35 Westbourne Grove. The young policeman then asked him to turn out his pockets, one of which proved to contain a newspaper cutting from 1950 concerning Timothy Evans' murder trial. The hunt for Christie was over.

Christie made a detailed confession, providing a separate – and self-serving – explanation for each killing. The prostitutes had forced themselves upon him, he said, and things had got out of hand. His wife had had to be put out of her misery. The murders of Muriel Eady and Beryl Evans had been mercy killings, too.

At his trial Christie pleaded insanity, but could not disguise the fact that he had carefully planned the killings (which he described with a chilling lack of contrition as 'those regrettable happenings'). He had even constructed a special apparatus with which to gas four of his victims. Christie was found guilty and sentenced to death. There was no appeal and he was hanged at Pentonville Prison at 9am on 15 July 1953.

There remained a legal problem, however, in that Timothy Evans had been convicted of the murder of his wife, Beryl, and their daughter, Geraldine – murders to which Christie had subsequently confessed. A formal inquiry was therefore set up, which concluded that two murderers had been operating at 10 Rillington Place; Christie had told the truth at Evans' trial, it reasoned, but had lied at his own. It was not until 1966 that Evans received a royal pardon, after which his body was exhumed from the grounds of Pentonville Prison and was reburied in consecrated ground.

5 ❖ Jerry Brudos

On 10 May 1969 a fisherman angling from a bridge across the Long Tom river in Oregon, in the USA, saw what he took to be a large package floating in the water. On looking closer, however, he realised that it was the bloated body of a young woman, which had been weighed down by a car's gearbox. The body was identified as being that of the 22-year-old

Linda Salee, who had vanished two weeks earlier. The corpse had been in the water for too long to determine whether Linda had been raped, but it was noted that curious burn marks surrounded puncture wounds a few inches below her armpits.

Police frogmen searching the area then found another body, which had been anchored in the water by means of a cylinder head. It belonged to the 19-year-old Karen Sprinkler, who had disappeared on 27 March; it was estimated that her corpse had been in the water for six weeks. The dead woman was fully clothed and was wearing a black bra that was plainly too big for her. Her breasts were missing and the bra had been padded out with screwed-up paper. Both Karen and Linda had been strangled.

The skeleton of the 16-year-old Stephanie Vilcko was later washed up in a creek along the same river. She had disappeared from her home in Portland, Oregon, the year before. The Oregon state police also had two other missing girls on their books: the 19-year-old encyclopaedia seller Linda Slawson, who had gone missing during a sales trip in the Portland area; and the 23-year-old Jan Whitney, whose broken-down car had been discovered on a highway near Lebanon, Oregon.

Linda Salee and Karen Sprinkler's bodies had both been tied up with electrical flex and the police therefore thought that the murderer might be an electrician. But the corpses had been weighed down with car parts, too, so it was equally possible that he might be a mechanic. As Oregon was full of electricians and car mechanics, these speculations did not take them further forward.

Karen Sprinkler had been a student who lived on the Corvallis campus of Oregon State University. Several of the other girls there now reported that they had received phone calls from a man who claimed to be a psychic, as well as a veteran of the Vietnam War. He had used a variety of names and had always ended the conversations by asking the girls for a date; when they had refused he seemed offended. However, one of the more daring girls had indeed met him for a date. He had been fat and freckled, she said, and she had thought that there was something odd about him. During their conversation he had told her that she should be sad. When she asked why he replied 'Think of those two girls whose bodies were found in the river'. When she declined his invitation to go for a drive with him he said that she was right to be circumspect, asking 'How do you know I wouldn't take you to the river and strangle you?'

A week later the man phoned the girl again, whereupon she called the police, who seized him when he arrived at the college to pick her up. His name was Jerry Brudos and he was a 30-year-old electrician who lived in Salem, which lies between Corvallis and Portland. The police did not have any evidence on which to hold Brudos, so they had to release him, but while investigating his background they soon discovered that he had a history of violence towards women and had spent time in a state mental hospital because of his sexual deviancy.

Brudos' deviant behaviour had begun when he was five and had taken home a pair of women's patent-leather shoes that he had found in a rubbish dump. He was trying them on when his mother discovered him. She was furious and told him to throw the shoes away, but he nevertheless kept them and wore them secretly. When his mother learned of this she burnt them and beat him. At school he became obsessed with women's high-heeled shoes and even stole a pair of his teacher's. When he was caught and made to confess he was asked why he had done it, but he responded that he did not know and ran from the room.

At 16 he lured his neighbour's daughter to his bedroom. While Brudos was out of the room a masked man burst in brandishing a knife and forced the girl to strip, after which he took pictures of her nude. When the masked man left Brudos reappeared. The masked man had locked him in the barn, he said. At 17 he had taken another girl for a drive when he stopped on a deserted road, dragged her from the car and forced her to undress. She was saved by a passer-by who had heard her screams. This time the police were called and Brudos lamely protested to them that this girl had been attacked by a weirdo. When the police searched his bedroom, however, they found a box of women's shoes and underwear. Brudos was sent to Oregon State Mental Hospital for treatment and was discharged after nine months.

His condition did not improve and he began attacking young women and stealing their shoes. Members of his family were afraid that he was well on his way to becoming a rapist, but then, to their great relief, he fell in love with a 17-year-old girl called Darcie and married her. They had their first child eight months later. Married life seemed to calm Brudos. His wife even indulged his obsession with photographing her in the nude, but later became concerned about the increasingly disturbing poses that he wanted her to adopt. Then, when his wife was in hospital having their second child, Brudos saw a young woman in the street who was wearing attractive shoes. He followed her home and choked her until she was unconscious before raping her.

As well as being an electrician, Brudos was also a mechanic who ran a one-man car-repair business from the garage of his home. He had furthermore been working in Lebanon, Oregon, close to the place where Jan Whitney's car had been discovered. The police found lengths of rope in Brudos' home, too, one of which was tied in the same kind of knot that the killer had used when trussing up the corpses.

Although the police were convinced that they had identified the right man they still did not have enough evidence with which to make an arrest. Then they discovered that they had a potential eyewitness to Brudos' criminal activities: a 15-year-old schoolgirl had been attacked by a fat, freckled man with a gun in Portland just two days before Linda Salee had disappeared. She had screamed, but the man had grabbed her around the neck, whereupon she had bitten his thumb and he had beaten her unconscious. When a car had fortuitously approached he had run off.

The girl identified Brudos from his mug shot and the police were on their way to arrest him when they saw his station wagon driving towards Portland. When it was stopped by highway patrolmen Brudos' wife was found to be driving; Brudos himself was hiding under a blanket in the back

**Jerome Brudos
with his wife.**

of the car. When he was made to change into prison overalls at the police station it was revealed that he was wearing women's underwear.

Brudos withstood questioning for five days. After that he began to talk about his interest in women's shoes and admitted tailing a pretty girl before breaking in to her home in order to steal her shoes. Next he shared his obsession with women's underwear; his favourite fetish, he said, was a large, long-waisted, black bra that he had stolen from a washing line. It was the type of bra that had been found on the body of Karen Sprinkler.

Then Brudos confessed everything, including the murder of the two missing women whose bodies had not been found. In January 1968, he revealed, Linda Slawson had come to his house selling encyclopaedias and wearing high-heeled shoes that he had found irresistible. Brudos had told her that his wife had visitors and asked her if she would mind discussing the encyclopaedias in his workshop. Having agreed, she was sitting on a stool running through her sales patter when he knocked her unconscious with a lump of wood. Then he strangled her. His mother and children were upstairs in the house at the time, so he gave them money and told them to go to a local hamburger joint. When they had gone he rushed back to the workshop and undressed the corpse, discovering to his delight that Linda was wearing attractive underwear. Making use of a box full of women's underwear that he had stolen from clothes lines he began to dress and undress the corpse as if it were a doll. That night he also chopped off Linda's foot, which he kept in the freezer and used to try on women's shoes. He dumped the rest of her body in the river, using a cylinder head with which to weigh it down.

Ten months later he was driving home from his job in Lebanon when he noticed that a car had broken down on the motorway. Brudos stopped and explained to the driver, Jan Whitney, that although he was a car mechanic they would have to drive to Salem to get his tool box. On arriving at his house together, he then ran inside alone, ostensibly to get his tools. Instead, however, he went in to check that his wife was not at home. Having ascertained that Darcie was not in he slipped silently into the back seat of the car, threw a leather strap around Jan's neck and strangled her. He then sodomised her corpse before beginning his game of dressing and undressing the body. This time he took photographs, breaking off from time to time in order to violate the body. Brudos then decided to prolong his pleasure by leaving Jan's body hanging from a hook in the locked garage. In that way he could come and play with it whenever he felt the need. He later cut off one of her breasts to make into a paperweight.

Two days after the murder his perverted secret was almost discovered when a car crashed through his garage wall. Although a policeman looked into the garage he did not spot Jan's body hanging there, shrouded as it was by dust and gloom. That night Brudos weighed down the corpse with scrap iron and dumped it in the river.

Four months later, while Brudos was driving past a department store, he spotted a young woman wearing a miniskirt and high-heeled shoes. He parked the car and chased after her, but she vanished into the crowd. On his way back to his car he saw Karen Sprinkler in the car park, pulled a gun and forced her to get into his station wagon. Brudos' family was away, so he knew that he was in no danger of being disturbed. Karen begged for her life, saying that she would do anything he wanted if he did not kill her. He asked if she was a virgin, to which she replied that she was and also told him that she was having her period. It made no difference, for he made her lie on the garage floor and raped her. Next he forced her to pose in high-heeled shoes and sexy underwear while he took pictures of her. After that he tied her hands behind her back, put a rope around her neck and threw the end of it over a beam, pulling it slowly until she suffocated. 'She kicked a little and died', Brudos said. He then violated Karen's corpse, cut off her breasts and dumped her body in the river.

Linda Salee was buying her boyfriend's birthday present when Brudos flashed a fake police badge at her and told her that he was arresting her for shoplifting. He then drove her to his garage. When they arrived Brudos' wife came out the house on to the porch, so Brudos ordered Linda to stand still in the darkness. At that moment a single scream could have saved her life, but instead Linda meekly did as she was told. After Darcie had gone back inside Brudos took Linda into the garage and tied her up before going to have his dinner. When he returned he found that she had freed herself. Although there was a telephone in the garage she had not called the police – 'She was just waiting for me, I guess', Brudos told his interrogators with a smile. Linda then tried to fight back, but the petite 22-year-old was easily subdued by Brudos, who put a leather strap around her neck. 'Why are you doing this to me?' she gasped. Pulling the rope tight, he raped her as she died. Brudos then strung up her corpse and jabbed two syringes into her sides, through which he ran an electric current intended to make her dance, but only succeeding in burning her flesh. On the following day he raped her corpse again. He considered cutting off her breasts, but did not like her pink nipples, preferring brown ones; he nevertheless made a mould of her breasts before throwing her body into the river.

On searching Brudos' garage the police found his lingerie collection, along with photographs of his victims either posing in the underwear or hanging from the ceiling. Brudos had incriminated himself in one shot by capturing on film his own reflection in the mirror. A female breast, hardened with epoxy, was also found on the mantelpiece in the living room.

After pleading guilty to four counts of murder, Brudos was sentenced to life imprisonment. Utilising his gift for all things electrical, he set up a computer system in jail, being permitted to order shoe and underwear catalogues from the outside world in return.

The police could not believe that Darcie Brudos was unaware of her husband's murderous activities. She was charged with abetting the murder of Karen Sprinkler, but was subsequently found not guilty.

A year after Brudos was sent to jail the body of Jan Whitney surfaced. It was so badly decomposed that it could only be identified by means of dental records. Linda Slawson's body was never found.

6 ✦ Brides in the bath

The notorious 'Brides in the Bath' killer, George Joseph Smith, discovered that murdering women could prove a lucrative occupation, provided that he had enough sex appeal in order to get them to the altar first. Although far from good-looking and poorly educated, the petty criminal from east London found that he had what it took to become a lady-killer. His formula was simple: he married his victims and then dispatched them when they were naked and at their most vulnerable.

By the age of 25 Smith had spent most of his adult life in jail for petty thieving. In an effort to go straight he opened a baker's shop in Leicester, under the alias George Oliver Love. It was there that he met a friend of one of his shop assistants, the 18-year-old Caroline Thornhill. Within weeks he had wooed and wed her. Then his shop failed, and with it his plan to pursue a legitimate career. With his young wife acting as his accomplice, he embarked upon a new life of crime. Caroline would take a job as a housemaid with a wealthy family and steal their valuables; Smith would sell

'Brides in the Bath' murderer George Joseph Smith, posing with a female companion.

them and the pair would then move on. They got away with it for nearly two years, but when Caroline tried to pawn some silverware the pawn-broker smelt a rat. She was arrested and Smith did a runner. After being sent to prison for a year Caroline resolved to rid herself of her cowardly husband.

While Caroline was in jail Smith made his way to London. Unable to afford the rooms that he rented, he resolved his plight by means of the simple expedient of marrying his landlady – bigamously. On her release Caroline also went to London, where she by chance bumped into Smith on Oxford Street. She called a policeman, who arrested him; he was subsequently sentenced to two years' hard labour.

By the time that he got out of jail Caroline had emigrated to Canada. Smith moved back in with his second 'wife', but things did not work out between them, so he set out on a career as a swindler and serial bigamist. In 1908, with £90 that he had conned out of an unsuspecting spinster, he opened an antiques shop in Bristol. He took on a housekeeper, the 28-old Edith Pegler. Within a month she had become wife number three.

Leaving Edith in charge of the business, his antique-dealing cover gave him the perfect excuse for travelling the country in search of new victims to marry. The wooing-and-winning process sometimes took months rather than weeks. In order to explain his unduly long absence to her, he once claimed to have been abroad and told the unsuspecting Edith that he had sold a Chinese figure for £1,000.

Edith occasionally accompanied her husband on his travels and was with him in Southampton when he spotted Sarah Freeman, whereupon Edith was promptly sent home while Smith went about his business. Sarah initially resisted his advances, however, and it took him four months to get her up the aisle. After being married by special licence they set off for London – Sarah had just £90 in cash. Then, in their lodgings in Clapham, Smith spotted his new wife's bank book and lost no time in suggesting that she take out all of her money and hand it over to him. Soon he was £300 the richer. For a treat, he later took her to the National Gallery, where he sat her down on a bench and said that he was going to the lavatory. When he had not returned after about an hour, Sarah asked an attendant to go into the gents and look for him, but he was not there. When she eventually returned to their lodgings she found that her jewellery, clothes and other belongings had gone, along with Smith.

Florence Wilson, a widow from Worthing, married Smith in 1908. Her dowry was twenty gold sovereigns and two large, white, £5 notes. After Smith had pocketed the money he suggested that they visit the Anglo-French Exhibition at London's White City. He left her sitting on a bench while he went to buy a newspaper, but did not come back.

Bessie Mundy, a handsome woman in her mid-thirties, fell for a similar trick. She had married Smith believing him to be called Henry Williams. After a few weeks she had returned home to find her husband, as well as her life savings, gone. He had left a note accusing her of having given him venereal disease. Eighteen months later she saw him on the promenade at Weston-super-Mare. 'Henry?' she enquired tentatively. 'My dearest Bessie', he exclaimed, 'I have been searching the country for you. It was all a terrible mistake.' He then sat her down on a bench and explained that when he thought that he had contracted venereal disease he had decided to do the honourable thing: leave home rather than risk passing it on to her. The £150 that he had 'borrowed' from her had been used to pay back a loan. By the time that he had discovered that he did not have VD after all he had lost track of her and had since been combing the country trying to find her. He was only in Weston-super-Mare, he said, because he had heard that she was there. Soon they were locked in a tearful embrace. Back at her lodgings, Bessie announced to her landlady that she had been reunited with her husband. The landlady was suspicious and wired Bessie's aunt, but by the time that she arrived the lovebirds had flown.

To seal their new-found happiness, the reconciled couple went to a solicitor and had wills drawn up, each naming the other as the sole beneficiary. Bessie had £2,500; Smith was, as always, penniless. They then moved to Herne Bay, in Kent, where he set himself up as an art and antiques dealer. Because the house that they were renting did not have a bath Smith ordered a £2 tub from the local ironmonger; since it did not come with taps or fittings Bessie was sent to the ironmonger to bargain two shillings and six pence off the price. Despite the reduction, Smith omitted to pay for it when the bath was delivered on the next day.

On the day after that Smith took Bessie to their doctor, saying that his wife had had a black-out during a fit. Bessie seemed well enough, but the doctor nevertheless prescribed bromide of potassium, a sedative. Two days later the doctor was woken in the early hours by Smith beating on his door – Bessie had had a second fit, Smith said. Although she was hot and clammy when the doctor examined her, it was a humid July night and she showed no other signs of having had a fit. Even so, he provided another bottle of bromide of potassium.

Bessie seemed to be in good health on the following day, but on the morning after that the doctor received a note from Smith asking him to come at once because Bessie was dead. Once at Smith's house the doctor found Bessie's naked body floating face upwards in the bath; her right hand was clutching a bar of soap and her mouth and nose were under the water. Smith said that he had left the house to buy herrings for breakfast and that he had found her dead upon his return.

The inquest returned a verdict of accidental death. Smith sobbed decorously throughout and then buried his wife in a pauper's grave. The bath was returned to the ironmonger (Smith had still not paid for it). After the reading of Bessie's will and receiving his legacy Smith sold up and moved on.

In the following year Smith married the 25-year-old Alice Burnham, the buxom daughter of a rich fruit farmer, in Southend; this time he used his real name. Money soon found its way out of her account into his and he used it to insure her life for £500. She also made a will in his favour. They then set off for a belated honeymoon in Blackpool. The first boarding house that they inspected had a piano, but no bath. They took a room – with a bath – at a second boarding house for ten shillings.

Within days Alice became ill. She complained of headaches and a doctor prescribed some tablets. Soon afterwards the landlady was having dinner when she noticed a damp patch on the ceiling, which seemed to be growing bigger. Smith then came in saying that he had just bought some eggs for their breakfast the next morning and disappeared upstairs. Moments later he cried out, asking for a doctor to be called. When the doctor arrived he found Smith in the bathroom. His wife was in the bath, naked and dead. The inquest returned a verdict of accidental death. Like Bessie, Alice was buried in a pauper's grave, Smith inheriting her estate of £600.

A few weeks after the outbreak of World War I Alice Reavil was listening to a band in Bournemouth when she was picked up by Smith. This time he was masquerading as Charles Oliver James, a gentleman with a private income from land in Canada. They were married within less than a week.

On the pretext of opening an antiques shop Smith persuaded Alice to hand over the £76 that was in her post-office savings account. She also gave him the £14 that she had made from selling her furniture. (They were moving to new accommodation, he had said, and the rest of her belongings had been loaded onto a barrow and taken away.) Then Alice's husband took his new bride for a walk in a nearby park. After sitting her down on a bench he went off to find a lavatory, never to return. All that she had left was a few shillings and the clothes that she stood up in, but at least she had escaped Smith's clutches with her life.

In December 1914 Smith married Margaret Lofty, a clergyman's daughter, in Bath. He called her Peggy and she thought that his name was John Lloyd. After the marriage service they took a train to London and rented rooms in Bismarck Road, Highgate. On the following evening, after the landlady had boiled up water for Mrs Lloyd's bath, she heard a splashing sound, a sigh and then the front door slamming. A few minutes later Mr Lloyd entered with a bag of tomatoes, which, he said, were for his wife's dinner. Announcing his intention to ask her whether she was ready for them, he went upstairs and found Peggy lying dead in the bath.

After haggling with the undertaker, Smith had Margaret Lofty interred in a common grave for £1 off the standard burial price. He then returned to Bristol to spend Christmas with Edith, bringing her a present of Margaret Lofty's dresses, from her bridal trousseau.

Smith had made a fatal mistake in the murder of Margaret Lofty, however. Until then his killings had taken place in seaside resorts, where details of the inquests only appeared in the local papers. But Margaret had drowned in a bath in London and the mass-circulation Sunday newspaper the *News of the World* picked up on the story. Its headline, 'Bride's tragic fate on the day of her wedding', attracted the attention of Alice Burnham's father, who alerted Scotland Yard to the similarities between the deaths of Margaret Lofty and his daughter.

Although the inquest into Margaret Lofty's death in Highgate had returned a verdict of accidental death, the police began to keep an eye on 'Mr Lloyd'. A month later police detectives arrested him at a lawyer's office in Shepherd's Bush as he was trying to speed up the probate procedure on Margaret's will. He was charged with making a false declaration on his marriage certificate, whereupon 'Mr Lloyd' admitted that his name was really George Joseph Smith.

While Smith was being held in Bow Street police station, officers from Scotland Yard set off to follow his trail, their investigations taking them to 40 seaside resorts. After interviewing over 150 witnesses the police compiled 13 points of similarity between the untimely deaths of Bessie Mundy, Alice Burnham and Margaret Lofty.

The dead women were then exhumed and the Home Office pathologist Dr Bernard Spilsbury quickly established that they had died neither as the result of an accident nor of suicide, but had been murdered by Smith. Each of the women had been quite relaxed when Smith had entered the bathroom, he believed. Smith had then knelt by the bath, putting one arm under the victim's knees and then pulling them upwards. Next he had put his other hand on top of her head and had pushed it under the water. The whole thing would have happened so fast, Spilsbury thought, that the woman would have died of shock rather than of drowning.

On 23 March 1915 Smith was formally charged with the murders of the three women. Even though Britain was fighting the Great War at the time there was still intense public interest in the 'Brides in the bath' case. Caroline Thornhill – Smith's first and only legitimate wife – risked attack by German U-boats to make the two-week trip from Saskatchewan to attend the committal hearings. As Smith was committed for trial at the Old Bailey Caroline burst into tears, along with half-a-dozen other women in the courtroom.

Throughout his trial Edith Pegler stood by Smith (who protested his innocence), as did a flock of female fans, who queued around the block for seats in the courtroom. In a private room a nurse in bathing dress played the victim in a staged demonstration of Spilsbury's theory. The jury watched as Inspector Neil of Scotland Yard grasped her feet and pulled them upwards, simultaneously forcing her head under the water. Although the nurse was submerged for only a matter of seconds she had to be revived by means of artificial respiration.

Smith was found guilty of murder and sentenced to death. He wrote to Edith Pegler from Pentonville Prison, calling her 'his one true love'. The last words on his lips when he went to the gallows on 13 August 1915 were 'I am innocent'.

The day after Smith was executed his only legal wife, Caroline Thornhill, married a Canadian soldier. Soon afterwards Bismarck Road was renamed Waterloo Road as a result of anti-German sentiment. The bath in which Margaret Lofty had died was bought by Madame Tussaud's for display in its chamber of horrors. One of the other baths used by Smith to murder his 'brides' is kept in Scotland Yard's Black Museum.

7 ❖ Bluebeard

The legendary Bluebeard – Gilles de Rais – was a distinguished French soldier who saw battle against the English at the side of Joan of Arc. After she was captured and burnt at the stake (a punishment in which some say de Rais took great pleasure) he returned to his estate, where he kidnapped, tortured and killed perhaps as many as 140 children. His servant, Poitou, lured de Rais' victims to his castle, where his master sodomised them while simultaneously strangling them or cutting off their heads; he also enjoyed disembowelling them and then masturbating over their entrails. Some 50 dismembered bodies were found in a disused tower in the castle when he was arrested, although he later confessed under torture that he and his followers had murdered over 800 children.

France produced a second Bluebeard in the person of the notorious lady-killer Henri Desiré Landru, who, the French police estimated, killed nearly 300 women. Despite his small stature, bald head and pointed beard his strong powers of attraction enabled him to seduce almost any woman that he pleased.

As a young conscript Landru had impregnated his attractive young cousin, Mademoiselle Remy, and had been forced to marry her. On leaving the army he decided to become a con man, but was not a very successful one, being arrested four times between 1900 and 1908. Landru had fathered three illegitimate children and maintained a love nest for his assignations, but that had strictly been a matter of pleasure and he now decided that he would use his seductive skills to make a living. In 1914, using a number of aliases, he therefore placed advertisements in the lonely hearts' columns of various newspapers, saying that he was a wealthy bachelor who was seeking the companionship of a respectable woman. His plan was simple: when women answered his advertisements he would seduce them, marry them, take their money and then murder them.

His first victim, Madame Izoré, vanished shortly after replying to his advertisement, along with 15,000 francs. A 39-year-old widow, Madame Cuchet, was the next to respond to one of his advertisements. When she announced that she was going to marry Landru some suspicious members of her family went to visit him; on arriving, however, they found that he was out. They seized the opportunity to search the villa that he was renting in Vernouillet and found a huge bundle of love letters, but when they alerted Madame Cuchet to their discovery she did not believe them. Soon afterwards she, as well as her 16-year-old son, disappeared.

In 1915 a widow named Madame Laborde-Line, who was originally from Buenos Aires in Argentina, left Paris saying that she was going to live with a wonderful man whom she had met in Vernouillet. After her subsequent disappearance Landru cashed in her securities and sold her furniture, piece by piece, from a garage in Neuilly. Madame Guillin, along with 22,000 francs, was the next to vanish; her furniture also ended up in a garage sale in Neuilly. When Landru forged Madame Guillin's signature in an attempt to withdraw 12,000 francs from her account he was questioned at the bank. Claiming that he was Madame Guillin's brother-in-law, he explained that she had suffered a stroke and was no longer able to handle her own financial affairs.

Moving on to the village of Gambais, he enticed another widow to his villa with the promise of marriage. She, too, disappeared, and the residents of Gambais began to notice that black smoke belched from the chimney of Landru's villa at odd hours.

Landru then placed another advertisement in the lonely hearts' columns, which said that he was a 'widower with two children, aged forty-three, with a comfortable income' who wanted to meet a 'widow, with a view to matrimony'. The 45-year-old Madame Collomb, who worked as a typist and had saved 10,000 francs, answered it and Landru quickly proposed to her. Although her mother disliked Landru and warned her against marrying him the lovesick Madame Collomb took no notice and joined her fiancé at his villa in Gambais, never to be seen again.

On 11 March 1917 the 19-year-old Andrée Babelay told her mother that she was going to be rescued from her life of poverty: she had met a rich man on the Paris underground-railway system, the Métro, and they would soon be on their way to his villa in Gambais to get married, she said. Madame Babelay never saw her daughter again. (Andrée was the only one of Landru's known victims who yielded him no financial profit, although she briefly satisfied his almost incessant need for sex.)

His next conquest was Madame Buisson, a 47-year-old widow who was worth around 10,000 francs. She disappeared after informing her relatives that she was getting married. Landru later appeared at her apartment bearing a note that had ostensibly been signed by Madame Buisson authorising him to take her furniture. It went straight to his garage sale in Neuilly.

Gille De Rais. Also known as Bluebeard, he fought with Joan of Arc.

A matrimonial agency introduced Madame Jaume to Landru. She was last seen on 25 November 1917, leaving her apartment with him. A few days later Landru withdrew 1,400 francs from her account.

The 36-year-old Madame Pascal had very little money, but Landru kept her in an apartment in Paris and saw her on and off for a year. Then he grew tired of her sexual charms and took her to Gambais.

Although Madame Marchadier did not have much money either, she did have a large house on the rue St Jacques. After escorting her and her two dogs on a trip to Gambais Landru sold her house and all of her belongings.

Although Landru tried to avoid the relatives of his victims, nearly two years after the disappearance of Madame Buisson her sister, Madame Lacoste, recognised Landru as he was walking with an attractive young woman down the rue de Rivoli in Paris. She followed the pair into a china shop, where he ordered a delivery of crockery using the name Lucien Guillet and giving an address in the rue de Rochechouart. Madame Lacoste went to the police, who visited 'Guillet's' apartment on the rue de Rochechouart, where they found Landru lying naked in bed with Fernande Segret, a 27-year-old clerk. The lovers were planning a trip to Gambais.

The police discovered a notebook in Landru's pocket in which were written the names of some of his victims. On searching the villa at Gambais they found the personal effects of a large number of unknown women. They also discovered Landru's voluminous correspondence. His letters were sorted into seven groups, headed 'No reply'; 'Without money'; 'Without furniture'; 'To be answered *poste restante*'; 'To be answered to initials *poste restante*'; 'Possible fortune'; and 'In reserve for further investigation'. In all, Landru had written to 283 women, of whom almost none could be located. The police then dug up the garden, exhuming the corpses of three dogs, but no human remains. However, in the villa's stove they found ashes and tiny fragments of bone.

At his trial the prosecution said that Landru had drugged and then strangled his victims, after which he had chopped up the corpses into tiny pieces and burnt them. But Landru taunted them with the challenge 'If I am a murderer produce your bodies'. For its part the defence maintained that Landru was no mass murderer, but rather a white-slaver who had abducted and sold his victims to brothels in South America. The prosecution, however, pointed out that most of the missing women were in their fifties and that Landru had kept their false teeth, hair and breasts.

Landru remained cool throughout the proceedings. When the presiding judge asked him if he was a liar Landru replied 'I am not a lawyer'. The women of Paris flocked to see Bluebeard in court and Landru played to the gallery. When he left the court after the death sentence had been pronounced he turned and enquired of his female devotees 'I wonder if there is any lady present who would care to take my seat?' On the day of his execution a priest asked Landru if he wanted to make his confession; in response Landru pointed to the guards who were about to escort him to the guillotine and said 'Sorry, but I do not want to keep those gentlemen waiting'.

Landru maintained his innocence to the end. Yet he had drawn a picture for his defence attorney while awaiting execution, and when the daughter of the lawyer in question had the picture cleaned in 1963 a full confession was found on the back in Landru's handwriting.

8 ◆ Carl Panzram

During the early years of the twentieth century the German-American Carl Panzram went on a life-long campaign of murder and mayhem. He claimed to have killed 21 people, to have committed thousands of burglaries, robberies and arson attacks and to have sodomised more than 1,000 men.

Born in 1891 to a family of immigrant Prussian farmers in Warren, Minnesota, Panzram became a criminal as a young boy. His father had deserted his family soon after Panzram's birth and his mother could not control him. When he was just eight years old he was brought before a juvenile court for being drunk and disorderly. Then, after burgling the house of a well-to-do neighbour, he was sent to reform school, where the discipline was rigid, if not sadistic. Panzram burned the place down.

Released in 1906, he began his war against the world in earnest, starting in the west, where he committed a string of robberies and assaults. While travelling the country he was raped by four hoboes, which instilled a new mode of revenge in him: 'Whenever I met a hobo who wasn't too rusty looking,' he later wrote in his autobiography, 'I would make him raise his hands and drop his pants. I wasn't very particular either. I rode them old and young, tall and short, white and black'. Having ended up in Montana State Reformatory, he quickly escaped from jail, robbing and burning down several churches over the next couple of months. Then he joined the army, only to be court-martialled on 20 April 1907 for insubordination and pilfering US-government property. Three years spent at Fort Leavenworth, where he crushed rocks under the blistering Kansas sun, honed his meanness to the sharpness of a razor's edge.

After his release in 1910 Panzram headed for Mexico, where he joined up with the rebel leader Pascaul Orozco, who fought alongside Pancho Villa and Emiliano Zapata during the Mexican Revolution. He later returned to the USA, leaving a trail of murder, robbery, assault and rape in his wake as he moved north through California and the Pacific Northwest region.

Arrested in Chinook, Montana, for burglary, he was sentenced to a year in prison, but escaped after eight months. A year later Panzram was arrested again, this time while using the alias Jeff Rhoades; he was given a two-year jail sentence. Paroled in 1914, he immediately resumed his life of crime. In Astoria, Oregon, he was once more arrested for burglary and was offered a minimal sentence if he revealed the whereabouts of the goods that he had stolen. Although he kept his side of the bargain he was sentenced to seven years' imprisonment. Outraged at this injustice, Panzram escaped from his cell and wrecked the jail. After the guards had beaten him up he was sent to Salem's correctional facility, the toughest prison in the state. Almost as soon as he arrived there he flung the contents of a chamber pot into a guard's face, for which he was beaten unconscious and chained to the floor of a darkened cell for 30 days. This punishment did not break his spirit, however, and he spent his time in the hole screaming words of defiance.

The facility's warden was shot dead during an escape attempt, and although the new warden was even tougher Panzram still managed to burn down the prison's workshop, as well as a flax mill. He also went berserk with an axe and incited a prison revolt, for which he was given another seven years in jail. By now, however, the atmosphere in the prison was so tense that the guards would not venture into the yard, so the warden was dismissed. The next warden was an idealist who believed that Panzram might respond to kindness. When Panzram was next caught trying to escape the warden told him that he was the 'meanest and most cowardly degenerate' that the prison authorities had ever seen. Panzram agreed with this description, but to his astonishment instead of punishing him the warden let him leave the jail on condition that he returned that evening. Although Panzram walked through the prison gates with no intention of going back he did, in fact, return that evening. The liberal regime was maintained and Panzram continued to respond to it, that is until he got drunk with a pretty nurse one night and absconded, only to be recaptured after a gunfight. He was returned to a punishment cell, where he was fed a diet of bread and water, also being beaten and sprayed with a fire hose. Finally, the ever resourceful Panzram constructed his own tools and hacked his way out of the prison in May 1918.

He headed east, stealing $1,200 from a hotel in Maryland and then boarding a merchant ship bound for South America. He jumped ship in Peru, where he worked in a copper mine. In Chile, he became a foreman for an oil company, later, for no apparent reason, setting fire to an oil rig. Back in the USA he stole $7,000 from a jewellery shop and $40,000 in jewels and liberty bonds from the New Haven home of the former US president, William Howard Taft. With the money he bought a yacht, and after hiring sailors to help him to refit it he raped and shot them before dropping their bodies in the sea. He killed ten in all.

Panzram served a six-month jail sentence in Bridgeport for petty theft before being arrested again for inciting a riot during a labour dispute. Jumping bail, he headed for western Africa, where he continued his murder spree. On one occasion he was approached by a 12-year-old boy who was begging for money. 'He was looking for something. He found it, too', wrote Panzram later. 'First I committed sodomy on him and then I killed him.' He smashed in the boy's head with a rock: 'His brains were coming out of his ears when I left him and he will never be deader', Panzram enthused. Panzram once decided to go crocodile-hunting and hired six black porters to guide him through the backwaters, later shooting them in their backs and feeding them to the crocodiles.

Back in the USA Panzram raped and killed three more boys. In June 1923, while he was working as night watchman for the New Haven Yacht Club, he stole a boat, killing a man who clambered aboard and tossing the body into New York's Kingston Bay. He was eventually caught attempting to rob an office in Larchmont, New York, and was sentenced to five years in Sing Sing. The guards there were unable to handle him, however, and he was sent to Clinton Prison in Dannemora, which was considered to be the end of the line for hard cases such as he. There he received savage beatings and also smashed his leg after falling from a high gallery. He spent his days plotting his revenge against the whole human race, amongst other things planning to blow up a railway tunnel when there was a train in it; to poison an entire city by putting arsenic in its water supply; and to start a war between Britain and the USA by blowing up a British battleship in US waters.

When he tried to escape from Clinton Prison he was tortured by having his hands tied behind his back and then being suspended by a rope from a beam. He could endure this for 12 hours on end, all the while screaming and cursing his mother for having brought him into the world. Despite his horrendous treatment at the hands of the guards, one of them, Henry Lesser, sympathised with Panzram and persuaded him to write his autobiography. Panzram did so, making no excuses for himself in it, saying that he had broken every law of God and humanity and furthermore commenting that if there had been more laws in existence he would have broken those, too.

Released yet again in 1928, Panzram hit the Washington-Baltimore area like a one-man crime wave, committing eleven robberies and one murder. He was soon arrested. At his trial he addressed the jury, saying 'While you were trying me here, I was trying all of you. I have found you guilty. Some of you I have already executed. If I live, I'll execute some more of you. I hate the whole human race'. The judge sentenced him to 25 years in jail. 'Visit me', Panzram retorted.

At Fort Leavenworth Panzram told his guards 'I'll kill the first man that bothers me'. True to his word, he murdered the mild-mannered, civilian prison-laundry supervisor Robert G Warnke with an iron bar. After a hasty trial Panzram was sentenced to death by hanging. Meanwhile, Lesser had been hawking Panzram's autobiography around the literary establishment, which included the legendary newspaperman H L Menken. People were impressed by it, but when Panzram heard that they were thinking of starting a movement to work for his reprieved he protested, saying 'I would not reform if the front gate was opened right now and I was given a million dollars when I stepped out. I have no desire to do good or become good'.

The Society for the Abolition of Capital Punishment also stepped in to try to save his neck, but he told it to forget it. Hanging would be a 'real pleasure and a big relief' for him, he said. 'The only thanks you or your kind will ever get from me for your efforts is that I wish you all had one neck and I had my hands on it. I believe that the only way to reform people is to kill them. My motto is: "Rob 'em all, rape 'em all and kill 'em all."' He even turned on Lesser in the end, writing in his last letter 'What gets me is how in the heck any man of your intelligence and ability, knowing as much about me as you do, can still be friendly towards a thing like me when I even despise and detest my own self'.

The end could not come soon enough for Carl Panzram. He was standing on the gallows on 11 September 1930 when the hangman, a son of Indiana, asked him if he had any last words. Panzram replied 'Yes, hurry it up, you Hoosier bastard. I could hang a dozen men while you're fooling around'.

9 ❖ Harvey Glatman

The *Los Angeles Times* journalist Robert Dull had separated from his pretty, young, blonde wife, Judy, because he objected to her modelling in the nude for other men, but the bust-up had not been acrimonious. She had invited him to her flat on 1 August 1957 to talk about a divorce, but when he arrived she was not at home. Her flatmate, Lynn Lykles, said that she had left several hours earlier with a photographer called Johnny Glynn. Over the next two hours two other photographers called, saying that the 19-year-old Judy had failed to turn up for a session. No one answered the phone number that Glynn had left, so Dull called Judy's family and friends. After ascertaining that none of them had seen her he called the police.

Lynn gave the Los Angeles Police Department (LAPD) a description of Glynn: he was short, with jug-handle-like ears, she said, and looked rather scruffy and dishevelled. He had visited the flat two days earlier, when another of her flatmates, Betty, had showed him Judy's portfolio, which had captivated him. He had phoned that morning, she continued, saying that he had a rush assignment and asking Judy to act as his model. Judy had been reluctant to do so, however, as she had a busy schedule ahead of her; Betty's description of him had made her rather suspicious, too. But when Glynn had said that his studio was being used for another assignment and that they would therefore have to shoot the pictures in her flat she had agreed. When he had turned up at the flat he had brought no photographic gear with him because, he explained, a friend had lent him his studio. He had agreed to the fee that Judy asked and the two of them had then left. That was the last time that anyone saw Judy alive.

Descriptions of both Judy and the mysterious photographer were circulated, but there was little else that the LAPD could do. However, Judy's disappearance did make the newspapers and for weeks Police Sergeant David Ostroff was kept busy following up potential leads. Ostroff also studied the file on a beautiful young actress named Jean Spangler, who had vanished eight years earlier.

Five months after Judy's disappearance a rancher and his dog discovered a skull lying in the desert near the Interstate 60 motorway, over 100 miles (161 kilometres) east of Los Angeles. When the police arrived they unearthed a half-buried skeleton clad in women's underwear and the remains of a brown dress like the one that Judy was wearing when she was last seen. Tufts of hair attached to the skull showed that the dead woman had been a blonde; furthermore, the skeleton measured 5 feet 4 inches (1.6 metres), the same height as Judy.

Eight months after Judy Dull went missing another woman in the Los Angeles area disappeared. A divorcée and mother of two, the 24-year-old Shirley Ann Bridgeford had gone on a blind date with a short, dishevelled man with prominent ears called George Williams. Police Sergeant Ostroff soon came to believe that Johnny Glynn and George Williams were the same man. Three months later Ruth Rita Mercado, a 24-year-old stripper and nude model who used the stage name Angela, also vanished. Although Ostroff added her file to his dossier he was still no nearer to catching the culprit. Then, however, the police got lucky.

On the evening of Monday, 27 October 1958, Officer Thomas F Mulligan, of the California Highway Patrol, turned into a dark street in the dusty town of Tustin, 35 miles (56 kilometres) south of Los Angeles. The light thrown by his motorcycle headlamp revealed a couple struggling, so he stopped and called out to them. Seeing that the woman was holding a gun and that her clothes were in a state of considerable disarray, Officer Mulligan pulled out his own pistol and ordered them to stop, whereupon they put up their hands. The woman, who identified herself as Lorraine Vigil, claimed that the man had tried to rape and kill her. The man did not deny her allegations.

Lorraine was a secretary who was determined to break into modelling, she later explained. A friend, who ran a modelling agency, had called her that evening and had asked her if she wanted to undertake a photographic assignment. Although her friend knew the photographer, who was called Frank Johnson, she had warned Lorraine to be a little wary of him. Lorraine had accepted the job and the photographer had later picked her up from her flat on Wiltshire Boulevard. Heading downtown, he had driven past the modelling studio on Sunset Strip that the agency had said would be the venue for the session. When Lorraine had mentioned this he had said that he was taking her to his studio in Anaheim, but then he had driven through Anaheim as well.

He had stopped on the dark road in Tustin and had pulled out a gun. Having ordered her to keep quiet, he had then produced a length of rope. Seeing this, Lorraine had said that she did not want to be tied up and would do anything that he wanted. At that moment a car had driven by and Lorraine had made a lunge for the door handle, whereupon the gun had gone off, the bullet grazing her thigh. In the resultant split second of confusion she had thrown herself at her assailant, causing the car door to fly open. They had fallen out of the car on to the road, and Lorraine had bitten her attacker as hard as she could. He had then dropped the gun, which she grabbed. She was in the process of trying to shoot the fake photographer who had attacked her when Officer Mulligan arrived.

At Santa Ana police station the photographer who called himself Frank Johnson revealed that he was, in fact, Harvey Murray Glatman, aged 30. It was furthermore discovered that Glatman lived no more than a few streets from Ruth Rita Mercado's San Pico Boulevard flat. When they visited the address that he had given the police found a run-down, white-shingle bungalow. Inside, the walls were covered with nude pin-ups, some of which featured bound and gagged young women. Among Glatman's meagre possessions were found a number of lengths of rope.

Glatman agreed to take a lie-detector test; when the name Angela – Ruth Rita Mercado's professional name – was mentioned the stylus leapt, and within minutes Glatman had confessed to killing Ruth. Then he said 'I killed a couple of other girls, too'. It turned out that he had quite a story to relate.

Harvey Glatman was born in Denver, Colorado, in 1928. He was a mummy's boy who did not get on well with other children. When he was 12 his parents noticed red welts encircling his neck and after persistent questioning forced him to admit that tightening a rope around his neck gave him sexual satisfaction. The family doctor told his worried parents that he would grow out of it. At school Glatman was unattractive to girls and would instead gain their attention by grabbing their purses. This was not a very effective method of courtship, however, and at 17 he therefore took more direct action by pointing a toy gun at a girl and ordering her to undress. After she had screamed and run away Glatman was arrested, fleeing to New York on being released on bail.

In New York Glatman turned his perverted urges into a way of life, robbing women at gunpoint and later graduating to burglary, for which he spent five years in Sing Sing. He seemed to respond to psychiatric help in prison and became a model prisoner. On his release he went back to Colorado and began working as a television repairman – a job that allowed him to enter other people's homes quite legitimately (he would sometimes sneak into their bedrooms). His mother then lent him the money with which to set up a television-repair business in Los Angeles.

Glatman confessed everything to the police. Judy Dull, he said, had been the girl of his dreams. After he had picked her up he had driven her to his makeshift studio, where he had asked her to take off her dress and put on a pleated skirt and cardigan instead. He had then produced a length of rope and had tied her up. The shots that he was taking, he had explained to her, were for the cover of a true-life crime magazine, which was why she had had to be bound and gagged.

He had taken some pictures of her, but the sight of the helpless Judy had been too much for him; bound as she was, she could not resist as he had slowly undressed her. After that he had put a gun to her head and had told that he would kill her if she cried out for help; she had nodded, whereupon he had untied her gag. Glatman had next made her pose on the sofa for more explicit bondage photographs and had then raped her twice. When he had finished he told her that he would take her to a remote spot in the desert, where he would release her.

He had let Judy put on her brown dress and had then driven her into the Nevada Desert. After spreading a blanket on the ground in a lonely spot he had again made her pose for erotic photographs, some with a noose around her neck. When Glatman had grown tired of taking pictures he had tied the loose end of the noose around her ankles and had pulled it until she was dead. Glatman had apologised to Judy's corpse before burying it in a shallow grave and had kept her shoes as a keepsake. Although he had originally intended to get a thrill from photographing and raping a beautiful woman – naked, bound and gagged – Glatman found that the killing had given him the greatest satisfaction of all and was determined to do it again.

Glatman had then registered in the name of George William with a dating agency and the agency had fixed him up with a date with Shirley Ann Bridgeford. When he had picked up Shirley he could see by her reaction that she found him a disappointment, but she had nevertheless gone with him.

Glatman had driven her south, out of Los Angeles towards San Diego. He had stopped in the Anza Desert and had tried to put his arm around her, to which she had responded that she did not feel that this was appropriate behaviour on a first date. He had then suggested that they went for a meal and she had seemed relieved. He had driven with one hand on the steering wheel while trying to fondle her with the other. She had again tried to fend him off and he had soon grown angry. He had stopped the car and had pulled out his automatic pistol, ordering her to get into the back of the car and undress. She had refused, so he had torn off her clothes and then raped her.

That had not been the end of Shirley's hideous blind date, however. Next he had driven her into the desert, where, after unpacking his photographic gear, he had made her pose on the same blanket on which he had killed Judy Dull. After having forced her to lie on her front he had tied a rope around her neck and garrotted her. He had taken her red knickers as a memento and had left her body where it lay, covered with brushwood because the ground was too hard to dig a grave in.

Five months later Glatman had spotted an advertisement in the newspaper offering the services of a nude model called Angela. He had called her before visiting her on the evening of 23 July 1958. She had taken one look at him, however, and had refused to let him in, but because he had liked her appearance he had pulled out his gun and had forced his way into her flat.

He had ordered Angela to undress at gunpoint and had then tied her up and raped her. After that he had announced that they were going for a little picnic, whereupon he had driven her to a deserted spot about 30 miles (48 kilometres) from where he had murdered Shirley Ann Bridgeford. Much as he had enjoyed killing Shirley and Judy, he had later thought that those murders had been over too quickly and had decided that in this instance he would take his time. The two of them had accordingly spent the day together, eating, sleeping and drinking. Glatman had also occasionally forced Angela (or Ruth Rita Mercado, as she was known when she was not at work) to pose for him. He had furthermore repeatedly raped her. Ruth had been very compliant, he said, clearly having decided that her only chance of surviving was to try to please him. After 24 hours spent toying with his victim, however, Glatman had garrotted her in the same manner in which he had dispatched his previous two victims.

After making his detailed confession Glatman helped the police to find the remains of Ruth Rita Mercado and Shirley Ann Bridgeford. Although his lawyers suggested that he plead guilty but insane, Glatman pleaded guilty without caveat, thus opting for a quick execution rather than a life spent in a mental institution. He died in the gas chamber on 18 September 1959.

10 ❖ The Vampire of Düsseldorf

Peter Kürten terrorised the German city of Düsseldorf during the year of 1929. He was sexually aroused by blood and flames, as well as by the notoriety that his monstrous crimes bestowed upon him.

Kürten's childhood was a catalogue of abuse. His father was a violent drunk who physically and sexually abused his wife and 13 children. At the age of nine Kürten drowned two of his playmates in the river Rhine, a dog-catcher who shared the Kürtens' house furthermore encouraging Peter to torture animals. Peter was also sexually precocious and began indulging his enormous sexual appetite with farm animals, soon discovering that stabbing the animal during the act increased his satisfaction. (He later took up with a prostitute.)

Convicted for theft, he was sent to jail, where his sexual longings became sublimated into gruesome fantasies. On his release he strangled a young woman in a wood while they were having sex. Subsequently finding himself back in prison, Kürten deliberately flouted prison rules in order to be put into solitary confinement, where he worked on developing his erotic fantasies. After being released again he next added arson to his repertoire of crime. He was then called up, but later deserted from the army, an action which landed him in prison once again. He was in the process of breaking into a house in 1913 when he discovered a 13-year-old girl asleep in bed; on raping and strangling her it was then that he discovered murder as a pleasure in its own right. Soon afterwards he attacked two strangers in the street with an axe, achieving orgasm at the sight of their blood.

Kürten spent World War I in jail for burglary. When he was released he wooed his future wife with a mixture of sweet talk and threats of appalling violence. His intended was stoical: a former prostitute, she had spent four years in jail for shooting a man who had failed to fulfil his promise to marry her and she put up with Kürten's strange ways as a form of atonement. He was physically gentle with his wife, although he admitted that he could only have sex with her by fantasising about being violent to someone else. During the early years of their marriage they lived in the small town of Altenburg. Kürten worked hard and was a political activist, but from time to time he sought out women for brutal sexual encounters. They later moved back to Düsseldorf, where Kürten again took up arson. 'I got pleasure from the glow of the fire, the cries for help', he later said. 'It gave me so much pleasure that I got sexual satisfaction.' He also attacked four or five women, strangling them to the point of unconsciousness.

On 3 February 1929 his assaults assumed a new ferocity when he attacked a woman in the street, stabbing her 24 times with a pair of scissors. A week later he stabbed a workman to death, subsequently also raping and strangling an eight-year-old girl before mutilating her body with a knife. He half-strangled four women during his attacks and also murdered two children. He killed and buried the 20-year-old Maria Hann, later returning to her grave and digging up her corpse because he wanted to frighten people by nailing her body to a tree in a perverted form of mock crucifixion. He murdered two women with a hammer, severely injuring two others. Then he killed a five-year-old girl, buried her and sent a map of the grave site to the newspapers; Kürten joined the crowd that rushed to the scene, discovering a fresh source of sexual pleasure in the fear and outrage of the people around him. Kürten continued his attacks, assaulting ten more women. After having been battered or half-strangled, those who escaped gave a description of their attacker to the police.

By this time the police had interviewed more than 9,000 people and had investigated 2,000 clues in connection with Kürten's crimes. His name had even come up during the investigation, but the woman who had accused him of being her attacker was eventually fined for wasting police time. When a woman whom Kürten had raped bumped into him on the stairs outside his flat, however, Kürten knew that his time was up. He accordingly confessed everything to his wife and urged her to go to the police to collect the reward for identifying him. She did not believe his story at first, and it was only when he started relating every detail of his assaults with evident relish that she was convinced.

Kürten had planned one more act of mass murder, but was prevented from carrying it out when his wife went straight to the police and arranged for him to give himself up. In custody, Kürten made a full confession, admitting many crimes that the police had not yet heard about. He often did not even know his victim's name. 'I went out with my scissors', ran one typical confession. 'At the station a girl spoke to me; I took her to have a glass of beer and we then walked towards the Grafenberg woods. I seized her by the throat and I held on for a bit . . . I threw her down the river and went away.'

After having been found guilty in court Kürten was studied by Professor Karl Berg, who described him as the 'king of the sexual perverts'. 'I have no remorse', Kürten told Berg. 'As to whether recollection of my deeds makes me feel ashamed, I will tell you. Thinking back to the details is not at all unpleasant. I rather enjoy it.'

Kürten received a huge amount of mail while he was being held in prison. Around half of the letters that were sent to him spelt out the cruel and unusual punishments that the writers would have liked to have inflicted upon him. The other half consisted of fan mail, including a large number of love letters from women.

The death penalty was very unpopular in Germany at that time and there was therefore widespread protest when Kürten was sentenced to death. Kürten himself was unconcerned about the sentence, however – indeed, when he heard that he would be able to experience the ultimate pleasure of hearing the blood gush from his neck for the split second during which his head was being severed he relished the prospect. And on 2 July 1930, after a final meal of Wiener schnitzel, fried potatoes and white wine, Peter Kürten went eagerly to the guillotine.

11 ❖ The Moors murderers

Ian Brady and Myra Hindley still rank as perhaps the world's most infamous killers. Their bizarre and deviant sexual relationship drove them to torture and murder defenceless children for pleasure in a case of serial killing that appalled the world. The idea that Hindley may one day be released from prison elicits howls of protest from the public. Nobody – least of all himself – however, has ever contemplated freeing Brady.

When Hindley met Brady he was already deeply warped: a 21-year-old stock clerk at Millwards (a chemical company in Manchester), his mind was full of sadistic fantasies. He had a collection of Nazi memorabilia and listened to recordings of Nazi rallies, while in his lunch hour he read Adolf Hitler's autobiography *Mein Kampf* ('My Struggle') and studied German grammar. He believed in the Nazi cause and regretted that he had not been part of its terrible excesses.

For her part, Hindley was known as a loner. Her first boyfriend had died when she was 15; she had not been able sleep for days afterwards and had turned to the Roman Catholic Church for consolation. At school it was noted that she was tough, aggressive and rather masculine, and that she enjoyed contact sports and judo, none of which suited her to the genteel life of 1950s' Britain. At the age of 19 she became a typist at Millwards, where she met Brady. He impressed her immediately: she considered most of the men whom she knew to be immature, but Brady dressed well and rode a motorbike. 'Ian wore a black shirt today and looked smashing . . . I love him', she confided to her diary.

For nearly a year Brady took no notice of her, however: 'The pig. He didn't even look at me today', she wrote more than once. Finally, in December 1961, he asked her out. 'Eureka!' her diary says. 'Today we have our first date. We are going to the cinema.' (The film that they saw was *Judgement at Nuremberg*, which was about the trial of Germany's leading Nazis following World War II.) Hindley rapidly surrendered her virginity to Brady, later writing 'I hope Ian and I love each other all our lives and get married and are happy ever after'. Yet their relationship would not be as innocent as her hopeful worlds suggest, for Hindley soon became Brady's

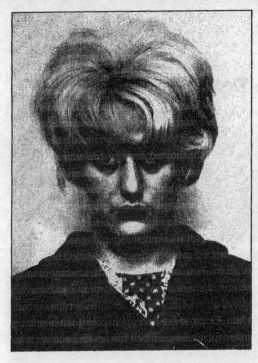

Moors Murderer Myra Hindley. This picture was taken during her trial.

sex slave. He introduced her to sexual perversion and urged her to read his books on Nazi atrocities. They also took pornographic photographs of each other and kept them in a scrapbook; some showed weals across Hindley's buttocks that had been left by a whip.

Hindley subsequently gave up babysitting and going to church. Within six months she and Brady were living together at her grandmother's house; because her grandmother was a frail woman who spent most of her time in bed they had the run of the place. Brady persuaded Hindley to bleach her brown hair a Teutonic blonde and dressed her in leather skirts and high-heeled boots. He often called her Myra Hess – or 'Hessie' – after a sadistic, Nazi, concentration-camp guard.

Life with Brady made Hindley hard and cruel. She did anything that Brady asked of her and did not balk at procuring children for him to abuse, torture and kill. Their first victim was the 16-year-old Pauline Reade, who disappeared on 12 July 1963 on her way to a dance. They persuaded Pauline to go for a walk on the nearby Saddleworth Moor, where they killed and buried her. Four months later Hindley hired a car and abducted the 12-year-old John Kilbride; when she returned the car it was covered

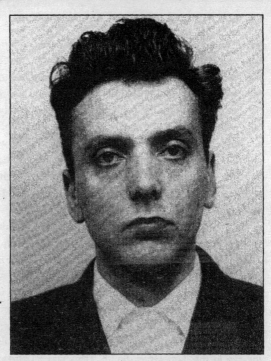

Ian Brady, who along with Myra Hindley, killed and buried children on Saddleworth Moor.

with mud from the moors. Brady and Hindley laughed when they read about the massive police hunt that was being undertaken to find the missing boy.

In May 1964 Hindley bought a car of her own, a white Mini van. During the following month the 12-year-old Keith Bennett went missing; like their other victims, Hindley and Brady had buried him on Saddleworth Moor. At Brady's behest Hindley then joined a local gun club and bought pistols for them both, which they practised firing on the moors. While they were there they visited the graves of their victims, photographing each other kneeling on them.

On 26 December 1964 they abducted the ten-year-old Lesley Ann Downey. This time they were determined to derive the utmost perverted pleasure from their defenceless victim. They accordingly forced her to pose nude for pornographic photographs and then tortured her, recording her screams, before strangling her and burying her with the others on Saddleworth Moor.

Brady now wanted to extend his sphere of evil influence, aiming to recruit Myra's 16-year-old brother-in-law, David Smith, to their perverted circle. Brady showed Smith his guns and talked to him about robbing a bank. He also lent him books about the Marquis de Sade (from whose name the word 'sadism' is derived) and persuaded him to write down quotations dictated by Brady. 'Murder is a hobby and a supreme pleasure' or 'People are like maggots, small, blind, worthless fish-bait', Smith obediently wrote in an exercise book under Brady's guidance.

Brady believed that he could lure anyone into his world of brutality and murder and bragged to Smith about the murders that he had committed. They were drinking at the time and Smith thought that Brady was joking, so Brady decided to prove his capacity for murder and simultaneously ensnare Smith by making him party to a killing.

On 6 October 1965 Brady and Hindley picked up Edward Evans, a 17-year-old homosexual, in a Manchester pub. They then called Smith and asked him to come to their house at midnight. When he arrived he heard a cry coming from the sitting room. 'Help him, Dave', said Hindley, and Smith rushed into the room to find a youth in a chair with Brady sitting astride him. Brady held an axe in his hands which he brought down on to the boy's head, hitting him at least 14 times. 'It's the messiest', Brady said with some satisfaction. 'Usually it takes only one blow.' Brady then handed the axe to the dumbstruck Smith. (This was an attempt to incriminate Smith by putting his fingerprints on the murder weapon.)

Although Smith was terrified by what he had seen he helped to clean up the blood while Brady and Hindley wrapped the boy's body in a plastic sheet; the couple made jokes about the murder as they carried the corpse downstairs. After that Hindley made a pot of tea and they all sat down. 'You should have seen the look on his face', said Hindley, who was flushed with excitement; she then started reminiscing about the murders that she and Brady had previously committed. Although Smith could not believe what was happening he realised that he would be their next victim if he showed any signs of disgust or outrage. After a decent interval he made his excuses and left; when he got back to his flat he was violently ill.

Smith told his wife what had happened, who urged him to go to the police. At dawn, armed with a knife and screwdriver, the couple went out to a phone box and reported the murder. A police car picked them up and took them to the police station, where Smith told his lurid tale to incredulous policemen. When the police visited Hindley's house at 8.40am to check out Smith's story, however, they found Edward Evans' body in the back bedroom.

Brady admitted killing Evans during an argument and then tried to implicate Smith in the murder. Hindley merely said 'My story is the same at Ian's . . . Whatever he did, I did'. The only emotion that she showed was when she was told that her dog had died: 'You fucking murderers', she screamed at the police.

The police found a detailed plan that Brady had drawn up for the removal from the house of all clues to Evans' murder. Curiously, one of the items listed was Hindley's prayer book; when the police examined it they discovered that a left-luggage ticket from Manchester Station had been stuck down its spine. On following up the lead at the left-luggage office the police found two suitcases containing books on sexual perversion, as well as coshes and photographs of a naked and gagged Lesley Ann Downey. The tape that had recorded her screams – which was later played to the stunned courtroom at Chester Assizes – was also discovered. Other photographs showed Hindley posing beside graves on Saddleworth Moor, and it was these that subsequently helped the police to locate the bodies of Lesley Ann Downey and John Kilbride.

At Brady and Hindley's trial the truly horrific nature of the murders was revealed. The pathologist disclosed that Edward Evans' fly had been undone and that dog hairs had been found around his anus; John Kilbride's body was discovered with his trousers and underpants around his knees. Hindley, it seemed, had been turned on by watching Brady perform homosexual acts on his victims. Later Brady let it slip that both he and Hindley had been naked when they had photographed Lesley Ann Downey in the nude, but otherwise the pair refused to talk about their crimes.

They were sentenced to life imprisonment. Brady did not bother to appeal against the sentence; Hindley did, but her appeal was rejected. They were refused permission to see each other in jail, although they were allowed to exchange letters.

Brady showed no contrition in prison and refused to allow his spirit to be broken, regarding himself as a martyr to his own perverted cause. He gradually became insane. Hindley, however, broke down and petitioned to be released. When her appeal was refused a warder (who was Hindley's lesbian lover) organised an abortive escape attempt, for which Hindley was sentenced to an additional year in jail.

She took an Open University degree and gave additional information about the whereabouts of her victims' graves to the police in a bid for mercy. Brady, however, countered her every move by revealing more of her involvement in the crimes, considering any attempt on her part to go free as an act of disloyalty to him. 'The weight of our crimes justifies permanent imprisonment', Brady told the Parole Board in 1982. 'I will not wish to be free in 1985 or even 2005.'

Hindley still hoped for parole, but public opinion was resolutely against it: after all, the families of their victims were still suffering.

12 ◆ Henry Lee Lucas

Henry Lee Lucas holds the record for being the USA's most prolific serial killer. He confessed to over 360 murders, of which 157 were investigated by the authorities and proved to have been committed by him – as for the rest, they took his word for it.

Lucas' mother, a half Native American Chippawa, was drunk for most of the time on the corn liquor that she bought with the proceeds of prostitution. Known to be 'as mean as a rattlesnake', she sent the seven children from her first marriage to a foster home. Lucas' natural father worked on the railways and lost both of his legs in an accident; Lucas himself was brought up by one of his mother's lovers, Andrew Lucas. His mother beat her children constantly and after one beating he was unconscious for three days and suffered brain damage; another such incident resulted in a glass eye. Lucas was also made to grow his hair long and to wear a dress.

Lucas was introduced to sex at the age of ten by the educationally challenged Bernard Dowdy, another of his mother's lovers. Dowdy would slit the throat of a calf and have sex with the carcass, encouraging the boy to do the same. Lucas enjoyed the experience and from childhood onwards associated sex with death. Throughout his childhood he continued to have sex with animals, sometimes skinning them alive for his sexual pleasure. At 14 he turned his perverted attention to women, beating a 17-year-old girl unconscious at a bus stop and raping her; when she came to and started to scream he choked the life out of her.

Convicted of burglary, he was sent to a reformatory when he was 15. Two years of hard labour on a prison farm did nothing to reform him, however, and on his release he resumed housebreaking, again being caught and sent back to jail. He escaped from prison, whereupon he met and fell in love with a young woman called Stella. They stayed together for four years and she agreed to marry him. Then his mother turned up demanding that her son take care of her and after a violent row Lucas killed her. This time he was sentenced to 40 years' imprisonment.

By 1970 the authorities considered Lucas to be a reformed character and released him. He killed a woman within hours of getting out of jail. In 1971 he was arrested for attempting to rape two teenage girls at gunpoint; the only excuse that he gave at his trial was that he craved women all the time. Released again in 1975, he then married Betty Crawford, but the marriage broke up when Betty discovered that he was having sex with her nine-year-old daughter, as well as trying to force himself on her seven-year-old child. Lucas then moved in with his sister, only to be thrown out when he started to have sex with her daughter, too.

In 1978 he met another sex-murder freak in a soup kitchen in Jacksonville, Florida. Ottis Toole was a sadist with homosexual tendencies who often dressed as a woman and picked up men in bars – he had even started to take a course of female hormones in furtherance of his ambition to have a sex change. Toole was also a pyromaniac who had an orgasm at the sight of a burning building.

Lucas and Toole became lovers and together embarked upon a series of violent robberies which frequently involved murder – often for the sheer pleasure of it. In Toole's confession he admitted that at around that time they had seen a teenage couple walking along a road because their car had run out of petrol. Toole had shot the boy while Lucas had forced the girl into the back of the car. After he had finished with her he had shot her six times and they had then dumped her body by the side of the road. (This was one of the cases that the police would later confirm.) Another incident had occurred outside Oklahoma City, when they had picked up a young woman called Tina Williams whose car had broken down. Lucas had shot her twice and had then had sex with her corpse.

Later in 1978 Lucas and Toole were in Maryland when a man asked them if they would help him to transport stolen cars. This was much too tame a sport for such hardened criminals, they explained, so he enquired whether they would be interested in becoming professional killers instead. They answered that they would, to which the man replied that the one condition was that they joined a Satanic cult.

Lucas and Toole subsequently claimed to have been inducted into the

Hand of Death sect in Florida by a man named Don Meteric. As part of the initiation ceremony Lucas had had to kill a man. He had lured his victim to a beach and had given him a bottle of whisky; when the man had thrown back his head to take a swig of it Lucas had cut his throat. As part of the cult's activities Lucas and Toole kidnapped young prostitutes, who were forced to perform in pornographic videos which often turned out to be 'snuff movies' in which the prostitutes were killed. The pair also abducted children, taking them across the border into Mexico where they were sold or used as sacrifices in Satanic ceremonies.

At around that time Toole introduced Lucas to his 11-year-old niece, Becky Powell, who was slightly educationally challenged. Becky was then living in Toole's mother's house in Florida, where they were also staying. Toole – who had been seduced by his older sister, Druscilla, before he became a homosexual – enjoyed watching the men whom he picked up make love to Becky or her older sister, Sarah. After Druscilla committed suicide, however, Becky and her brother, Frank, were put into care. Lucas then 'rescued' them and by January 1982 they were all on the run together, living off the money that they stole from small grocery shops. Becky called Lucas 'Daddy', but one night, when he was tickling her innocently at bedtime, they began to kiss; Lucas then undressed her before stripping off himself. Becky may have been only 12 at the time, he said, but she looked 18.

During his time with Becky Lucas continued his murderous rampage in conjunction with Toole. Lucas later outlined a typical two weeks in Georgia. In that short space of time they had kidnapped and murdered a 16-year-old girl before raping her dead body, as well as abducting, raping and mutilating a blonde woman. Another woman had been taken from a car park and stabbed to death in front of her children. During the course of one robbery the shop's owner had been shot; another man had died in a second robbery; in a third the owner of the shop had been stabbed; and in a fourth a woman had been tied up before being stabbed to death. Toole had also tried to force his sexual attentions upon a young man, whom he had shot after being spurned. Becky and Frank had often taken part in the robberies, also witnessing several of the murders.

Lucas and Toole eventually parted company, Toole taking Frank back to Florida while Lucas and Becky were given work with a couple named Smart who ran an antique shop in California. After five months the Smarts sent Lucas and Becky to Texas to look after Mrs Smart's 80-year-old mother, Kate Rich. A few weeks later Mrs Smart's sister visited her mother, only to find the house filthy. Lucas, it transpired, had been taking Mrs Rich's money in order to buy beer and cigarettes. On finding him drunk, in bed with Becky, the pair was fired.

They were trying to hitch a lift out of town when they were picked up by the Reverend Reuben Moore, who ran a religious community nearby called the House of Prayer. Lucas and the 15-year-old Becky quickly became converts and joined the community, living in a converted chicken barn. Becky then seems to have had a genuine change of heart and to have become homesick. She wanted to go back to Florida, she told Lucas, who reluctantly consented, whereupon the two set off to hitchhike to her home state. They settled down with their blankets in a field at nightfall. It was a warm, June night. A row then broke out about Becky's decision to return home and she struck Lucas in the face. He retaliated by knifing her through the heart, after which he had sex with her corpse, cut up her body and scattered the dismembered pieces in the woods. Becky was, Lucas later claimed, the only woman whom he had ever loved.

Lucas returned to the House of Prayer, where he, too, then seems to have had some sort of change of heart. One Sunday he dropped in at Mrs Rich's house to give her a lift to church. During the journey she asked him where Becky was, whereupon Lucas pulled out a knife and stabbed her; she died instantaneously. He then drove to a piece of waste ground, where he undressed and raped her corpse before stuffing it into a drainage pipe that ran underneath the road. He subsequently returned, placing her body in a dustbin bag and then burning it in the stove at the House of Prayer.

Sheriff Bill F 'Hound Dog' Conway, of Montague County, Texas, had begun to have his suspicions about Lucas when he reappeared without Becky. Now it seemed that he was linked to the disappearance of another woman, Mrs Rich, and Lucas was accordingly hauled into the sheriff's office for questioning. Lucas was both a chain smoker and a caffeine addict, so Conway deprived him of cigarettes and coffee, but still Lucas refused to break, saying that he knew nothing about the disappearance of Kate Rich and that Becky had run off with a lorry driver who had promised to take her back to Florida. Conway finally had to release him.

Soon afterwards Lucas told Reverend Moore that he was going to look for Becky. While heading for Missouri he saw a young woman standing beside her car at a petrol station; holding a knife against her ribs he forced her into her car. They then drove south, towards Texas. When she dozed off

Lucas pulled off the road, intending to rape her. She awoke suddenly to find a knife at her neck, whereupon Lucas stabbed her in the throat, pushed her out of the car on to the ground and cut her clothes off her body. After he had raped her corpse he dragged it into a copse and took the money from her handbag. He abandoned her car in Fredericksburg, Texas, and then returned to the House of Prayer.

While he had been away Reverend Moore had told Sheriff Conway that Lucas had given Becky a gun for safekeeping. Because Lucas was a convicted felon who had therefore forfeited his right to bear arms under US law this was enough to justify his arrest. After taking him into custody Conway again deprived him of coffee and cigarettes and this time Lucas began to crack; he was later found hanging in his cell with his wrists slashed.

After having been patched up in the prison hospital Lucas was put in a special observation cell in the women's wing. On the next night he cracked completely, starting to yell in the early hours of the morning. When his jailer arrived Lucas claimed that the light in his cell was talking to him. The prison officer, Joe Don Weaver, who knew that Lucas had already smashed the bulb in his cell, told him to get some sleep. Later on during the night Lucas called the jailer again and confessed that he had done some pretty bad things. Weaver advised him to get down on his knees and pray, but instead Lucas asked for a pencil and paper.

Lucas spent the next half an hour writing a note to Sheriff Conway, which read 'I have tried to get help for so long and no one will believe me. I have killed for the past ten years and no one will believe me. I cannot go on doing this. I have killed the only girl I ever loved'. Lucas then pushed his confession through the peephole in the door of his cell. After reading it Weaver called Sheriff Conway, who plied Lucas with coffee and cigarettes upon his arrival and asked about the murders. Lucas said that he had seen a light in his cell that had told him to confess his sins and then told the sheriff that he had killed Kate Rich. Sheriff Conway and Phil Ryan, a Texas Ranger, later asked Lucas what had happened to Becky Powell. Tears flowed from his one good eye as Lucas told of how he had stabbed, raped and dismembered her. The story left the two hardened law officers feeling sick and wretched. 'Is that all?' asked Ryan wearily, half hoping that it was. 'Not by a long way', replied Lucas. 'I reckon I killed more than a hundred.'

On the next day the Montague County police began to investigate Lucas' story. Near the drainage pipe in which Lucas had temporarily hidden Mrs Rich's body they discovered some of her underclothes, as well as her broken glasses. At the House of Prayer they found burnt fragments of human flesh, along with charred bones. Lucas himself took them to the field in which he had killed Becky. There they found her suitcase, which was full of women's clothing and make-up. Her skull and other parts of her body were discovered in an advanced stage of decomposition in nearby woodland.

Lucas began to confess to other murders, too – often in breathtaking detail. These were also investigated and confirmed. A week after he had begun to confess Lucas appeared in court, where he was charged with the murders of Kate Rich and Becky Powell. When he was asked whether he understood the seriousness of the charges against him Lucas replied he did, then admitting to about a hundred other murders. The shocked judge could scarcely credit this behaviour and asked Lucas whether he had ever had a psychiatric examination. Lucas replied that he had, but commented 'They didn't want to do anything about it . . . I know it ain't normal for a person to go out and kill girls just to have sex'.

Lucas' sensational testimony made the headlines in every newspaper in the country. Police departments in each US state and county began to check their records, while Lucas' confession was also run through the computer at the newly formed National Center for the Analysis of Violent Crime.

Toole, it was discovered, was already in prison: he had been sentenced to 15 years' imprisonment for arson and was currently incarcerated in Springfield, where he had been regaling a cell mate with the gruesome tale of how he had raped, murdered, beheaded, barbecued and eaten a child named Adam Walsh. The police were now forced to take his lurid stories seriously. Indeed, both Toole and Lucas now began to admit their crimes freely. They confessed to a series of robberies of convenience stores, for example, saying that at one they had tied up a young girl who had had wriggled free, so Lucas had shot her in the head and Toole had had sex with her dead body.

Lucas was next taken on a 1,000-mile- (1,609-kilometre-) long tour of his murder sites. In Duval County, Florida, he confessed to eight unsolved murders. The victims had been women ranging in age from 17 to 80; some had been beaten, some strangled, some stabbed and others shot (Lucas claimed that the Hand of Death had said that he should vary his coup de grâce.) Near Austin, Texas, Lucas pointed to a building and asked whether it had once been a liquor store; on being told that it had Lucas confessed to having murdered its former owners during a robbery in 1979. Lucas then led the police to a field in the same county in which he had murdered and mutilated a girl called Sandra Dubbs – he even pointed out where her car had been found.

It transpired that Lucas and Toole had cruised the Interstate 35 motorway murdering tramps, hitchhikers, men who were also robbed of their money and old women who had been abducted from their homes. Over a period of five years they had killed more than 20 people up and down that highway alone. One of their victims was a young woman whose corpse was later found naked, except for a pair of orange socks, near Austin. She had been hitchhiking along Interstate 35 when Lucas had picked her up; according to Lucas she had refused to have sex with him, so he had strangled her and taken what he wanted. Although she was never identified it was for her murder that Lucas was sentenced to death.

Despite his subsequent withdrawal of his confession to the murder of Becky Powell and his plea of not guilty, Lucas was found guilty of the crime and sentenced to life imprisonment, in addition receiving four further life sentences, two sentences of 75 years each and one of 67 years, all for murder.

During his confession Lucas had told the police that Toole had poured petrol over a 65-year-old man before setting him alight; the pair had then hidden so that they could watch the fire engines arrive. The police identified the man as being George Sonenberg, who had died four days later. Until then they had assumed that the fire was an accident, but Toole freely admitted to the killing and furthermore claimed to have started hundreds of other fires. It was for this particularly horrific murder, however, that Toole was also sentenced to death.

Both Lucas and Toole enjoyed their brief period of notoriety and relished revealing the ghoulish details of their shocking crimes. Further information about the Hand of Death was not forthcoming, however.

13 ❖ Dennis Nilsen

Dennis Nilsen was Britain's most prolific serial killer. Sadly, of all of his 15 victims only one – a Canadian tourist – was missed; the rest were homosexual drifters who were looking for money, love or just a place to stay for the night.

Nilsen was born in Fraserburgh, a small town on the bleak, north-eastern coast of Scotland, on 23 November 1945. His father was a Norwegian soldier who had escaped to Scotland following the German invasion of his country in 1940 and had married Betty Whyte, a local girl, in 1942. The marriage did not work out, however, and Betty continued to live with her parents before the couple divorced a few years later.

Dennis grew up living with his mother, elder brother and younger sister, but the strongest influence on his young life was that of his stern and pious grandparents. Their faith was so strict that they banned alcohol from the house and regarded the radio and cinema as instruments of the devil. Nilsen's grandmother would furthermore not cook on Sunday – the Lord's day – and their dinner therefore had to be prepared on Saturday.

The young Nilsen was sullen and intensely withdrawn. The only person who could penetrate his private world was his grandfather, Andrew Whyte, Nilsen's hero. A fisherman, he would regale the little boy with tales of the sea and of those of his ancestors who had been lost beneath its churning waves. When Whyte died of a heart attack at sea in 1951 he was brought home and laid out on the dining-room table. Dennis, aged six, was invited to view his grandfather's body and thus got his first sight of a corpse. From that moment on the images of death and love were fused in his mind.

He left school at 15 and joined the army. After basic training he was transferred to the catering corps, where he was taught how to sharpen knives and to dissect a carcass. During his time in the army Nilsen had only one close friend, whom he persuaded to pose for photographs sprawled on the ground, as if he had been killed in battle. On one night in Aden the drunk Nilsen fell asleep in the back of a taxi. He woke to find himself naked and locked in the boot of the car. When the taxi driver appeared Nilsen played dead, but as the Arab manhandled him out of the boot Nilsen grabbed a jack and beat him around the head with it. Nilsen never knew whether he had killed the man, but after that he began having nightmares about being raped, tortured and mutilated.

After spending 11 years in the army Nilsen left to join the police force. Part of his training included a visit to a mortuary; the partially dissected corpses that he saw there fascinated him. Although he did well in the police force his private life was gradually disintegrating. Death became an obsession with him, and he liked to masturbate while pretending to be a corpse, lying naked in front of a mirror with blue paint smeared on his lips and his skin whitened with talcum powder. His incipient homosexuality also began to bother him. After 11 months in the police force he caught two men committing an act of gross indecency in a parked car; because he could not bring himself to arrest them he decided to resign.

He then went to work interviewing unemployed applicants for benefit at the Jobcentre in London's Charing Cross Road, becoming the branch secretary of the civil-service union and developing increasingly radical political views. His work was nevertheless good enough to earn him promotion to the position of executive officer at the Jobcentre in Kentish Town, north London.

Despite his professional progress Nilsen was lonely and yearned for a lasting relationship. He had been aware of his attraction towards other men since his teens, but had somehow managed to repress it while in the army and police force. In 1975 he met a young man called David Gallichen outside a pub, with whom he later moved into a flat at 195 Melrose Avenue, in the Cricklewood district of London, along with a cat and a dog called Bleep. Gallichen, or 'Twinkle', as Nilsen called him, stayed at home and decorated the flat while Nilsen went to work. They made home movies together and spent a lot of time drinking and talking. The relationship did not last, however, and when Gallichen moved out Nilsen was again plunged into a life of loneliness.

On New Year's Eve in 1978 Nilsen met a teenage Irish boy in a pub and invited him back to Melrose Avenue. They had been too drunk to have sex and when Nilsen woke in the morning the boy was lying fast asleep beside him. He was afraid that when the boy woke up he would leave, and Nilsen wanted him to stay.

Their clothes were thrown together in a heap on the floor. Nilsen lent over and grabbed his tie, wrapping it around the boy's neck and pulling it

Dennis Nilsen, who was infatuated with the corpes of his victims.

tight. The boy immediately awoke and began to struggle. They rolled on to the floor while Nilsen kept on pulling the tie. Although the boy's body went limp about a minute later, he was still breathing. After going into the kitchen and filling a bucket with water Nilsen took the bucket to the bedroom and held the boy's head under water until he drowned. Now he had to stay with Nilsen. He carried the dead boy into the bathroom and gave him a bath. He then dried the corpse lovingly, before dressing it in clean socks and underpants. For a while he lay in bed holding the dead boy; after that he put him on the floor and went to sleep.

On the following day he decided to hide the body under the floorboards, but *rigor mortis* had stiffened its joints, making it hard to handle. He therefore left the body as it was while he went to work. After the corpse had loosened up Nilsen undressed it and washed it again, this time masturbating beside it. He found that he could not stop playing with, and admiring, the boy's body. All the time that Nilsen was playing with the corpse he expected to be arrested at any moment, but no one came: it seemed that the dead boy had not been missed by anyone. After a week of living happily with the corpse Nilsen hid it under the floorboards; seven months later he cut it up and burnt it in the garden.

Nilsen's first experience of murder had frightened him. He was determined that it would not happen again and decided to give up drinking. But because he was lonely and liked to go to pubs to meet people he soon slipped off the wagon. Nearly a year later, on 3 December 1979, Nilsen met Kenneth Ockenden, a Canadian tourist, in a pub in Soho. Nilsen took the afternoon off work to join Ockenden on a sightseeing tour of London, after which Ockenden agreed to go back to Nilsen's flat for something to eat. After a visit to the off-licence they sat in front of the television eating ham, eggs and chips and drinking beer, whisky and rum. As the evening wore on disturbing feelings began to grow inside Nilsen. He liked Ockenden, but realised that he would soon be leaving to go back to Canada. A feeling of desolation swept over him – it was the same feeling that he had had when he killed the Irish boy.

Late that night they were both very drunk. Ockenden was listening to music through earphones when Nilsen wrapped the flex of the earphones around Ockenden's neck and dragged him struggling across the floor. When he was dead Nilsen took off the earphones and put them over his own ears. He then poured himself another drink and listened to records. He stripped the corpse in the early hours of the morning and carried it over his shoulder into the bathroom. When the body was clean and dry he placed it on the bed and went to sleep next to it.

Later that morning he put the body into a cupboard and went to work. In the evening he took out the corpse and dressed it in clean socks, underpants and a vest. He then took some photographs of it before arranging it next to him on the bed. For the next two weeks Nilsen would watch television in the evening while Ockenden's body was propped up in an armchair next to him. Last thing at night he would undress it, wrap it in some curtains and place it under the floorboards.

Because Ockenden had gone missing from a hotel his disappearance made the news for a few days. Nilsen was again convinced that he was about to be arrested at any moment – after all, people in the pub, on the bus and in the off-licence had seen them together. But when there was still no knock on the door Nilsen felt that he could pursue his macabre hobby unfettered. He began deliberately to seek out his victims, going to pubs where lonely, young homosexuals hung out, where he would buy them drinks, offer advice and invite them back to his flat for something to eat. Many accepted.

One of those who did was Martin Duffey, who, following a disturbed childhood, had run away from home and had ended up sleeping in railway stations in London. He went home with Nilsen and crawled into bed after drinking two cans of beer. When he was asleep Nilsen strangled him and then dragged his unconscious body into the kitchen, filling up the sink and holding his head under water for four minutes. After that Nilsen went through his now standard procedure of stripping and bathing the corpse before taking it to bed. He talked to it, complimenting it on its physique, kissing it and masturbating over it. Nilsen kept the corpse in a cupboard for a few days; when it started to swell he put it under the floorboards.

The 27-year-old Billy Sutherland, on the other hand, died because he was a nuisance: Nilsen hadn't fancied him, but after meeting him on a pub crawl Sutherland had followed him home. Nilsen later said that he vaguely remembered strangling him – there was certainly a dead body in the flat on the following the morning.

Nilsen did not even know the names of some of his victims. Indeed, he was not that interested in them – only in their bodies, their dead bodies. To him, their seduction and murder were sad, mechanical processes, but once they were dead they really turned him on: just touching a corpse would give him an erection.

Nilsen would go out to work as if all was perfectly normal, but when he got home in the evening he would retrieve his latest corpse from its hiding place and play with it. To him it was a thrill to own such a beautiful body and he would engage the corpse in a passionate embrace and talk to it. When he was finished he would stuff it under the floorboards again.

Some of his murders were terrifyingly casual. Nilsen came across one of his victims, the 24-year-old Malcolm Barlow, for example, after he had collapsed on the pavement on Melrose Avenue. Barlow was an epileptic and said that the pills that he was taking made his legs give way, so Nilsen carried him home and called an ambulance. When he was released from hospital the next day Barlow returned to Nilsen's flat. Nilsen prepared a meal and Barlow began drinking, even though Nilsen warned him not to mix alcohol with the new pills that he had been prescribed. When Barlow indeed collapsed Nilsen could not be bothered to call the ambulance again and therefore strangled him, after that carrying on drinking until it was bedtime. By now the space under the floorboards was full of corpses, so the following morning Nilsen stuffed Barlow's body into the cupboard under the sink.

As the place was full up Nilsen decided that it was time to move. There were six corpses under the floorboards; several others had been dissected and stored in suitcases. He decided that he had better dispose of the bodies first and after a stiff drink pulled up the floorboards and began cutting up the corpses. He hid the internal organs in the garden, where birds and rats dealt with them. The other body parts were wrapped in a carpet and thrown onto a bonfire; a tyre was placed on top to disguise the smell.

Nilsen then moved to an attic flat at 23 Cranley Gardens, in the London district of Muswell Hill, in a deliberate attempt to put a halt to his murderous career – he could not kill people, he reasoned, if he had no floorboards under which to hide their corpses and no garden in which to burn them. Indeed, although he had several casual encounters at his new flat, when he picked up men at night he let them go in the morning, unmolested. He was elated because he believed that he had finally broken the cycle of killing.

When, however, John Howlett – or 'Guardsman John', as Nilsen called him – came back to Cranley Gardens Nilsen could not help himself and strangled Howlett with a strap before drowning him. A few days later he strangled Graham Allen while he was eating an omelette. The death of his

Dennis Nilsen, being transported by maximum security.

final victim, Stephen Sinclair, a drifter and a drug addict, upset Nilsen. When they met Nilsen felt sorry for him and bought him a hamburger. Having gone back with Nilsen to Cranley Gardens, Sinclair slumped in a chair in a stupor and it was then that Nilsen decided to relieve him of the pain of his miserable existence. He first got a piece of string from the kitchen, but finding that it was not long enough he instead used his one remaining tie to choke the life out of his unconscious victim.

Killing at Cranley Gardens presented Nilsen with a problem: how to get rid of the bodies of his victims. With no floorboards or garden he was forced to dispose of the corpses by dissecting them, boiling the flesh from the bones, dicing up the remains and flushing them down the toilet. Unfortunately, the drains in Muswell Hill were not built to handle bodies and those at 23 Cranley Gardens had been blocked for five days when, on 8 February 1983, the drain-clearance company Dyno-rod sent Michael Cattran to investigate.

Cattran quickly determined that the problem was not inside the house, but on the outside. Locating the manhole that led to the sewers at the side of the house, he removed its cover and climbed in. At the bottom of the access shaft he saw a glutinous, grey sludge, which smelled awful. As he was examining it more sludge came out of the pipe that led from the house. He called his manager and told him that he thought that the substance that he had found had originally been human flesh.

On the following morning Cattran and his boss returned to the manhole, only to find that the sludge had vanished. No amount of rainfall could have flushed it away, which meant that someone must have gone down there and removed it. Cattran put his hand inside the pipe that connected the sewer to the house and pulled out some meat and four small bones. One of the tenants living in the house told them that they had heard footsteps on the stairs during the night and that they suspected that the man who lived in the attic flat had been down to the manhole. They then called the police.

Detective Chief Inspector Peter Jay took the flesh and bones that Cattran had recovered to Charing Cross Hospital, where a pathologist confirmed that the flesh was indeed human. The tenant of the attic flat was still at work when Jay visited Cranley Gardens, but when Nilsen returned at 5.40pm Jay met him at the front door and introduced himself, saying that he had come about the drains. Nilsen remarked that it was odd that the police should be interested in drains, prompting Jay to explain that the drains contained human remains. 'Good grief! How awful', exclaimed Nilsen. Jay told him to stop messing about and asked 'Where's the rest of the body?' After a short pause Nilsen replied 'In two plastic bags in the wardrobe next door. I'll show you'. He then pointed out the wardrobe to Jay, the smell that emanated from it confirming what he was saying. 'I'll tell you everything', Nilsen said. 'I want to get it off my chest, not here, but at the police station.'

The police could scarcely believe their ears when Nilsen admitted killing 15 or 16 men. In the wardrobe in Nilsen's flat, however, they found two large, black, dustbin bags, one of which held a shopping bag containing the left side of a man's chest, including the arm; a second shopping bag contained the right side of a chest and an arm. A third held a torso which had no arms, legs or head, while a fourth was full of human offal. The unbearable stench indicated that the bags had been closed for some time. In the second dustbin bag were two heads – one whose flesh had been boiled away, the other largely intact – and a torso, whose arms were still attached to it although the hands were missing. One of the heads belonged to Stephen Sinclair (Nilsen had severed it four days earlier and had started to simmer it in a pot on the kitchen stove). The police found Sinclair's pelvis and legs under a drawer in the bathroom. There was another torso in a tea chest in Nilsen's bedroom, along with a skull and more bones. The police also examined the garden at 195 Melrose Avenue, where they identified human ash and enough fragments of bone to determine that at least eight people, and probably more, had been cremated there.

Nilsen was eventually charged with six counts of murder and three of attempted murder. His solicitor had one simple question for Nilsen: 'Why?' 'I'm hoping you will tell me that', Nilsen replied.

Nilsen had intended to plead guilty, in order to spare the jury and the victims' families the details of his horrendous crimes, but his solicitor instead persuaded him to claim diminished responsibility. He was sentenced to life imprisonment, with the recommendation that he serve at least 25 years.

14 ❖ Jeffrey Dahmer

Like Dennis Nilsen, the Milwaukee mass murderer Jeffrey Dahmer kept the corpses of his victims lying around his home. He went one step further than Nilsen, however: in an effort to possess them more completely he began eating their flesh, reasoning that they would thus become a part of him and therefore stay with him forever.

Dahmer began his murderous career at the age of 18, at a time when his parents were going through an acrimonious divorce. Dahmer's father had already left home, his mother was away on holiday and Dahmer was alone in the house, feeling very neglected. He therefore went out to look for company and picked up a hitchhiker, a 19-year-old youth named Stephen Hicks who had spent the day at a rock concert. They got on well and Dahmer took Hicks back to his parents' house, where they had a few beers and talked about their lives. When Hicks said that he had to go Dahmer begged him to stay, but Hicks was insistent, so Dahmer made him stay by picking up a heavy dumbbell, clubbing him around the head with it and then strangling him.

Dahmer dragged Hicks' body into the crawl space under the house and dismembered it with a hunting knife (he had had plenty of practice because his childhood hobby had been dissecting animals). Even though he had wrapped Hicks' body parts in plastic bags the stench of rotting flesh soon permeated the house, so that night Dahmer buried them in a nearby wood. Becoming afraid that local children would find the grave, he then dug up them up again, stripped off the flesh and pulverised the bones with a sledgehammer before scattering the remains around his garden and the neighbouring property. It would be ten years before Dahmer would kill again.

After that Dahmer moved to Milwaukee to live with his grandmother. A loner, he hung out in gay bars. If another customer chatted him up he would slip drugs into their drink and they would often fall into a coma. Dahmer made no attempt to rape them – he was simply experimenting – but when the owner of the Club Bar ended up in hospital Dahmer was barred from it. In 1986 Dahmer was sentenced to a year's probation for exposing himself and masturbating publicly in front of two twelve-year-old boys. He claimed that he had been urinating and promised the judge that it wouldn't happen again.

Six days after the end of his probation period he picked up the 24-year-old Stephen Tuomi in a gay club and went to the Ambassador Hotel with him to have sex. When Dahmer awoke he found Tuomi lying dead; there was blood surrounding his mouth and bruising around his neck. Dahmer had been drunk the night before and realised that he must have strangled Tuomi; now he was alone with a corpse in a hotel room and at any moment a porter would be checking to see whether the room had been vacated. In a controlled state of panic he rushed out and bought a large suitcase, into which he stuffed Tuomi's body before taking it back by taxi to his grandmother's house, the taxi driver even helping him to drag the heavy case inside. Dahmer then cut up the corpse and put the pieces into plastic bags, which he left outside for the refuse collectors. (He performed this task so well that he left no traces at all: when police investigating the disappearance of Tuomi called at the house there was no sign of the body. Dahmer had got away with his second murder.)

Companionship, sex and death were now inextricably linked in Dahmer's mind. Four months later he picked up a young, male prostitute and went back with him to his grandmother's house to have sex in the basement. Dahmer then gave the boy a drink laced with a powerful sedative and when the young man was unconscious he strangled him. He then dismembered the corpse, stripped off the flesh, crushed the bones to powder and scattered the remains. Two months later Dahmer met an impoverished, 22-year-old homosexual and offered him money to perform in a video. Having agreed, the man had oral sex with Dahmer in his grandmother's basement. When it was over Dahmer offered him a drink, drugged and strangled him and finally disposed of the corpse.

Dahmer's grandmother began to complain about the terrible smell that persisted even after the rubbish had been collected; she also found a patch of blood in the garage. By way of explanation Dahmer said that he had been skinning animals there, an excuse that she accepted, although she made it clear that she wanted him to move out. Dahmer consequently found himself a small flat in a run-down, predominantly black, area. On his first night there he lured Keison Sinthasomphone, a 13-year-old Laotian boy, to the flat and drugged him. The boy managed to escape, however, and Dahmer was arrested. Charged with sexual assault and enticing a minor for immoral purposes, he spent a week in jail before being released on bail.

Dahmer could not control his compulsion to kill and while out on bail picked up Anthony Sears, a handsome, 26-year-old bisexual. Fearing that the police were watching his flat, he took Sears to his grandmother's basement instead. After they had had sex Dahmer drugged Sears and dismembered his body, disposing of his corpse in the rubbish, but keeping his skull as a souvenir.

In court the district attorney pushed for a sentence of five years' imprisonment for Dahmer's assault on Sinthasomphone. For his part, Dahmer's attorney argued that the attack was a one-off offence, continuing that his client was a homosexual and a heavy drinker who needed psychiatric help, not punishment. Dahmer was sentenced to five years on probation, as well as a year on a correctional programme. It did not help, however, for Dahmer was now set in his murderous ways.

After picking up a young stranger in a club he offered him money to pose for nude photographs. Back in Dahmer's flat the youth accepted a drink, which Dahmer had drugged. When he lapsed into unconsciousness Dahmer strangled and stripped him before performing oral sex on the corpse. He then dismembered the body, again keeping the skull, which he

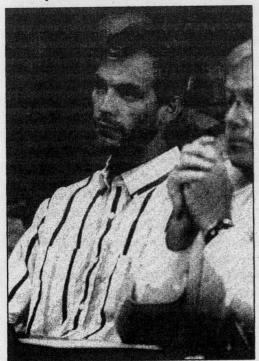

Cannibalistic serial killer Jeffrey Dahmer during his trial.

painted grey. He picked up another notorious homosexual, known as the 'Sheikh', and did the same to him, except that this time he engaged in oral sex before drugging and strangling him.

His next victim, a 15-year-old boy who had accepted Dahmer's offer of $200 for posing in the nude, was luckier. Although the boy undressed Dahmer had neglected to drug him before attacking him with a rubber mallet; Dahmer then tried to strangle him, but the boy fought back. Eventually Dahmer calmed down, and after the boy had promised not to inform the police he let him go, calling him a taxi. When he went to hospital for treatment the next day, however, the boy broke his promise and told the police what had happened. But because he begged them not to let his foster parents find out that he was a homosexual they dropped the matter.

The next time that Dahmer picked up a victim, a few weeks later, he craved more than his usual formula of sex, murder and dismemberment, having decided to keep the skeleton and to bleach it with acid. Although he dissolved most of his victim's flesh in acid he left the biceps intact and stored them in the fridge. When his neighbours began to complain about the smell of putrefying flesh that was coming from Dahmer's flat he apologised, saying that his fridge was broken and that he was waiting to have it fixed.

Dahmer's next victim, the 23-year-old David Thomas, was not gay. Although he had a girlfriend and a three-year-old daughter he nevertheless accepted Dahmer's offer to come back to his flat for money. After drugging him Dahmer realised that he did not fancy his latest pick-up, but killed him anyway, fearing that Thomas might otherwise cause trouble when he woke up. This time he took more pleasure in the dismemberment process, photographing it step by step.

The 19-year-old Curtis Straughter, an aspiring model, was engaged in oral sex with Dahmer when the sleeping potion took effect. Dahmer strangled him and again photographed his dismemberment; his skull was also kept as a trophy. The 19-year-old Errol Lindsey's murder proceeded along exactly the same lines, Dahmer offering him money to pose for nude photographs before drugging, strangling and dismembering him. The grisly process was once again recorded photographically and his skull was added to Dahmer's collection. The 31-year old deaf-mute Tony Hughes also accepted $50 to pose in the nude and was duly murdered, but by this time Dahmer had become so blasé about the whole procedure that he kept Hughes' body in his bedroom for several days before cutting it up.

Dahmer's next victim was Keison Sinthasomphone's older brother, the

14-year-old Konerak. As in Keison's case, things went badly wrong for Dahmer, who, after drugging, stripping and raping the boy, went out to buy some beer instead of strangling him. On his way back to the flat Dahmer saw a naked and bleeding Konerak talking to two girls on the street. When Dahmer tried to grab him the girls hung on to Konerak; one of them had called the police and two patrol cars soon arrived.

The police wanted to know what the trouble was about and Dahmer claimed that he and Konerak had had a lover's tiff. He managed to convince them that the 14-year-old Konerak was really 19, and after taking them to his flat showed them Polaroids of Konerak in his underwear which seemed to back up his story that they were lovers. The police, however, did not realise that the photographs had been taken earlier that day, while Konerak was drugged. Throughout all of this Konerak sat passively on the sofa thinking that his ordeal was over. In fact, it had only just begun: the police accepted Dahmer's story and left, whereupon Dahmer immediately strangled and then dismembered the boy. (The three policemen in question were later dismissed.)

On one occasion Dahmer was returning home after attending Gay Pride Day in Chicago when he picked up another would-be model, Matt Turner. Turner was also strangled and dismembered at Dahmer's flat. On meeting Dahmer in a gay club the 23-year-old Jeremiah Weinberger asked his former roommate whether he should go with him, to which the roommate replied 'Sure, he looks okay'. Dahmer seems to have liked Weinberger, for they spent the whole of the next day together having sex. Then, when Weinberger looked at the clock and said that it was time that he went, Dahmer asked him to stay for just one more drink. His head ended up next to Turner's in the freezer.

When Dahmer lost his job he knew that one thing alone would make him feel better. He accordingly picked up a 24-year-old man called Oliver Lacy and took him back to his flat, where he strangled him and sodomised his corpse. Four days later the 25-year-old Joseph Bradeholt – who was married, with two children – accepted Dahmer's offer of money for nude photographs and willingly engaged in oral sex with him. His dismembered torso was left to soak in a dustbin filled with acid.

By the time that Dahmer had killed 17 men – all in much the same way – he was becoming so casual about murder that it was perhaps inevitable that he would be caught. On 22 June 1991 Dahmer met Tracy Edwards, a young man who had just arrived from Mississippi. He was with a number of friends, so Dahmer invited them all to his flat for a party. He and Tracy would go ahead in a taxi to buy some beer, he said, instructing the others to follow later. Edwards went along with this plan, but did not realise that Dahmer was giving his friends the wrong address.

When he got there Edwards found that he did not like Dahmer's flat: it smelled funny and there was also a fish tank in which Dahmer kept some Siamese fighting fish. As Dahmer told lurid tales about the fish fighting each other to the death Edwards glanced nervously at the clock as he sipped his cold beer. After he had finished the beer Dahmer gave Edwards a drugged drink of rum and coke. When Edwards became drowsy Dahmer put his arms around him and whispered that they would go to bed. Within an instant Edwards was wide awake and telling Dahmer that it was all a mistake and that he had to be going. Before he knew it, however, his hands had been handcuffed and Dahmer was poking a butcher's knife at his chest while ordering him to undress. Realising the seriousness of the situation, Edwards knew that he had to humour the man, to make him relax, and slowly unbuttoned his shirt.

Dahmer then suggested that they go into the bedroom, and escorted Edwards there at knife point. The room was decorated with Polaroid photographs of naked young men; there were also pictures of dismembered bodies and chunks of meat. The smell in the room was sickening; the putrid aroma seemed to be coming from a plastic dustbin under the window. Edwards thought that he could guess the rest.

Dahmer wanted to watch a video with his captive friend, so they sat on the bed and watched *The Exorcist*. The gruesome film made Dahmer relax, while Edwards was frantically thinking of ways in which to escape. If Edwards did not comply with his requests, Dahmer then threatened, he would rip out his heart and eat it. Next he told Edwards to strip so that he could photograph him in the nude. As Dahmer reached for the camera Edwards seized his opportunity and punched Dahmer in the side of the head. When Dahmer crumpled up Edwards kicked him in the stomach and ran for the door. Dahmer managed to catch up with him and offered to unlock the handcuffs, but Edwards ignored him, wrenching open the door and running for his life.

Halfway down 25th Street Edwards spotted a police car and ran over to it, yelling for help. Once inside the car he explained to the policemen that a maniac had tried to kill him and directed them to Dahmer's flat. The door was answered by a well-groomed man who seemed calm and composed; the police began to have doubts about the story that Edwards had told them – that is, until they noticed the strange smell.

A contrite-looking Dahmer admitted that he had threatened Edwards, explaining that he had just lost his job and had been drinking. But when the police asked for the key to the handcuffs he refused to hand it over and became violent, whereupon the policemen pushed him into the flat and forced him to lie face down on the floor while they read him his rights. Then they began to look around the flat, one of them opening the fridge door. 'Oh my God,' he exclaimed, 'there's a goddamn head in here.' Dahmer began to scream like an animal and the police rushed outside to get some shackles with which to restrain him. After that they began their search of the flat in earnest.

They ascertained that the fridge contained meat – including a human heart –in plastic bags. There were three human heads in the freezer. A filing cabinet contained grotesque photographs, three human skulls and a collection of bones. Two more skulls were found in a pot on the stove. Another pot contained male genitals and severed hands, while the remains of three male torsos were found in the dustbin in the bedroom.

At the police station Dahmer seemed almost relieved that his murderous spree was over. He made a detailed confession and admitted that he had now reached the stage at which he was cooking and eating his victims' bodies.

Dahmer's cannibalism and necrophilia were the cornerstones of his plea of insanity, but the district attorney pointed out to the jury that if Dahmer were found to be insane and sent to a mental hospital his case would be reviewed in two years' time, further explaining that if he was then found to be sane he could be released. The jury found Jeffrey Dahmer guilty of 15 murders, for which he received 15 life sentences.

15 ❖ The Candy Man

The Texan town of Houston's Candy Man, the killer Dean Corll, did not realise that he was homosexual until he was drafted into the army at the age of 25. After being discharged 11 months later he went back to work in his mother's sweet factory. Although he was late in recognising the true nature of his sexuality he quickly learnt how to exploit his personal situation and began giving sweets to local boys, also being in a position to hire any boys that he fancied. Furthermore, his mother covered up for him; when one boy complained about Corll's sexual advances she sacked him. For their part, the other teenagers on the workforce made sure that they were never left alone with Corll.

At around that time Corll met a 12-year-old boy called David Brooks, who had a deeply insecure background. Brooks liked Corll, considering him to be good and generous (Corll paid him $5 a time for oral sex.) By the time that Brooks was 15 he was using Corll's flat as his second home. Corll lived in the run-down Heights area of Houston, in which children were always short of money and often high on drugs, making things easy for a predatory homosexual like Corll. Even after the sweet factory closed down Corll continued to be known as the kind man who gave sweets to children; the boys also knew that he gave away money in return for oral sex.

Corll seems to have committed his first murder during this period, for it is thought that he picked up and took home Jeffrey Konen, a 21-year-old student at the University of Texas who disappeared while hitchhiking. Konen's body was discovered three years later on High Island Beach (which later became one of Corll's favourite body-dumping grounds). It was so badly decomposed that forensic experts were unable to determine the cause of death. It was certainly murder, however, because the body was found bound hand and foot.

In 1970 Brooks visited Corll's flat, where he found two dead, naked boys strapped to a board. Corll, who was also naked, explained that he had killed the boys during sex and offered Brooks a car if he kept quiet. From then on Brooks, who was soon seen driving around in a green Corvette, acted as Corll's accomplice, helping to lure boys to Corll's flat, where Corll would rape and kill them while Brooks looked on. Brooks found the whole business highly lucrative, for Corll seemed to have an insatiable desire for young boys and penetrated them anally before strangling them. 'He killed them because he wanted to have sex and they didn't want to', Brooks later explained.

Corll developed a taste for double murders. In December 1970, for example, he picked up the 14-year-old James Glass and the 15-year-old Danny Yates when they were on their way back from church. Glass already knew and liked Corll and had visited his flat before. On this occasion, however, he and his friend ended up being tied to the board before being raped and strangled. Six weeks later the same fate befell the 17-year-old Donald Waldrop and his 13-year-old brother, Jerry.

Then, on 29 May 1971, the 13-year-old David Hilligiest and his friend, the 16-year-old George Winkie, vanished while on their way to the swimming pool. They had been seen together getting into Corll's white van. Although their disappearance was reported the police showed no interest in following up these cases and – like the others who had disappeared before them – listed the two missing boys as runaways. This was not good enough for David Hilligiest's parents, however, who had posters printed offering a $1,000 reward for information about their son's whereabouts. One of the boys who distributed the posters was Wayne Henley, a lifelong friend of David Hilligiest.

Later that summer the Hilligiests' younger son, the 11-year-old Greg, revealed that he had once played an exciting game called poker with David, Wayne Henley and David Brooks, who had once worked at the neighbourhood's sweet factory. David Hilligiest had gone missing once before, his parents then recalled. On that occasion they had found his bike outside the sweet factory and had discovered David inside with the manager, Dean Corll, a nice man who had given him sweets. They still did not put two and two together, however.

It later transpired that sometime before David Hilligiest went missing David Brooks had taken Wayne Henley to meet Corll, guessing that he could be potential victim. Corll, however, had quickly realised that Henley was a popular boy, and also that he would do anything for money. He soon began paying Henley $200 a time to deliver his friends to him. Henley would sit in the car while Corll cruised the district offering young boys a lift. With one teenager in the car already they felt that it was safe to get in, but would then be driven to Corll's flat to be raped and killed.

Henley soon took over from Brooks as Corll's major source of supply. He subsequently admitted to being present at the murders of at least nine boys and furthermore confessed to killing one himself. Henley had shot the boy in the head, he said, but his victim had not died immediately. When he had looked up at Henley and had said 'Wayne, why did you shoot me?', Henley had pointed the gun at him and had shot him again. Henley had also played an active role in the murder of the 18-year-old Scott Mark, who, unlike the younger boys, was no pushover. Mark had grabbed a knife and had tried to stab Corll, but Corll had disarmed him. Henley had then seized Corll's pistol and had aimed it at Mark while Corll strangled him.

Between them Henley and Brooks regularly supplied Corll with victims aged between nine and twenty. Corll continued to rape and kill the boys singly, as well as in pairs; he sometimes also castrated his victims. The local people were becoming increasingly concerned about their missing children, but still the police did nothing. Indeed, Corll's killing spree only came to an end when Henley made a near-fatal mistake and brought Corll a girl instead of a boy.

Henley had comforted the 14-year-old Rhonda Williams after her boyfriend, the 18-year-old Frank Aguirre, had gone missing (he was another of Corll's victims). She soon considered herself to be Henley's girlfriend and the two decided to run away together. This suited Corll, who was becoming tired of murder and was planning to go straight.

Corll now had a regular boyfriend, Guy, whom he had picked up in a public lavatory before taking him back to his flat, where they had become lovers. When Guy had expressed interest in a locked room in the flat Corll had vowed that he would never take Guy into it and nothing more was said. Corll also had a girlfriend called Betty Hawkins, whom he had been dating on and off for five years; she had two children, who called Corll 'Daddy'. Corll promised Betty that he would finish with Guy and they then planned to move to Colorado together.

Henley and Rhonda had planned to run away together on 17 August 1973, but Rhonda could not wait and left home nine days early, on 8 August, to join Henley. Henley had invited a friend named Tim Kerley to a paint-sniffing party that was being held at Corll's flat on that night and had no choice but to take Rhonda along. When they arrived Corll was furious: 'You weren't supposed to bring a girl', he yelled.

Corll eventually calmed down and they soon began to get high by sniffing acrylic paint that had been sprayed into a paper bag. Within an hour they had all passed out. When Henley awoke he found that he had been handcuffed and bound; the other two youngsters had been tied up as well, and Kerley was naked. Corll was now furious again: 'I'm going to kill you,' he told Henley, 'but first I'm going to have my fun'. He then dragged Henley into the kitchen, holding a .22 pistol against his stomach. This was the moment that Henley had long feared would happen: he had always believed that Corll would kill him one day, in order to get his hands on Henley's 14-year-old brother, Ronnie.

Having procured victims for Corll for two years Henley understood him well and knew how to sweet-talk him. He therefore said that he would be willing to participate in the rape and murder of the other two: Henley would rape Rhonda while Corll had Kerley. Corll agreed to this suggestion and released Henley. They then carried their bound victims into the bedroom, where Corll turned up the radio in order to drown the sound of any screams. Next he gave Henley a knife and ordered him to cut away Rhonda's clothing. After that Corll set about raping Kerley, but when Kerley began to struggle Rhonda grew distressed. 'Why don't you let me take her out of here?' Henley asked Corll. 'She doesn't want to see that.' But Corll ignored him, so Henley grabbed Corll's pistol and told him that they were going. 'Go on Wayne, kill me, why don't you?' taunted Corll, whereupon Henley pulled the trigger and hit Corll in the head with a bullet, causing him to stagger forward a few paces. When Henley fired again Corll fell through the bedroom door and Henley then emptied the clip full of bullets into his back.

After he had untied the other two they called the police. When they arrived Henley admitted to killing Corll and the others vouched for him – after all, he had done it to save them, they believed. A chance remark of Henley's alerted the police to the true story, however: he had told Kerley that if he hadn't been his friend he would have got $1,500 for him. The police then found a 17-inch- (43-centimetre-) long dildo in Corll's flat, along with other tools of the sadist's trade. Inside his white Ford van they also discovered rings, hooks and lengths of rope.

When questioned about all of this Henley confessed that he had taken money from Corll in return for procuring boys for him, furthermore admitting that he and Corll had also killed boys. There were a lot of them buried in a boat shed that Corll had hired three years earlier, Henley volunteered, later helpfully taking the police to it. Inside they found some possessions belonging to the missing boys, as well as bags of lime. They then started digging up the floor and soon the naked bodies of 17 boys were revealed. They had been bound and gagged; their genitals had sometimes been buried separately; and there were also body parts that did not belong to any of the 17 victims. Henley then told the police that more bodies were buried around Lake Sam Rayburn, as well as to the south, at High Island Beach. Twenty-three bodies were found in all; although Henley said that two more bodies were buried on the beach they were never located.

Brooks was surrendered to the police by his father. When Henley saw him he told him that he had confessed and warned him that if he, Brooks, did not do the same he would recant and blame everything on him. Brooks then admitted everything, too.

Twenty-seven bodies had been discovered by the time that the police abandoned the search, but both the extra body parts and the frequency of killing indicated that there were probably at least six or seven more. Forty-two boys were missing from the district in all, although some of them may have been genuine runaways.

The trials of Wayne Henley and David Brooks took place in San Antonio, Texas, in June 1974. Their insanity pleas were rejected and Henley was found guilty of nine murders – not including that of Dean Corll – and sentenced to 594 years' imprisonment. Brooks was found guilty of just one count of murder and was given a life sentence.

16 ❖ Wayne Gacy

Like Dean Corll, John Wayne Gacy, Jr also discovered that he was a homosexual relatively late in life. He was 22, and a married man, when, in 1968, he lured a youth into the back room of the fast-food franchise that he was operating. After handcuffing him he tried to bribe him to perform oral sex; when the youth refused Gacy tried to sodomise him, but his victim escaped. The young man reported Gacy to the police, who arrested him. After having been sentenced to ten years' imprisonment he became a model prisoner, who, because he had no history of serious crime, was released after 18 months. He then moved to Chicago, where he set up a construction firm.

Within a year of his release Gacy picked up another youth and tried to force him to have sex. Although he was again arrested the case against him was dropped when the young man did not turn up in court. Gacy then pulled a gun on another youth, who had approached him asking for work, and threatened to shoot him if he did not consent to sex. The youth called his bluff, even though Gacy had said that he had killed people before (this was true), and managed to leave unmolested. In fact, Gacy had already taken a number of teenage boys back to his home, where he had held them captive and sexually abused them over a number of days. When he had tired of them he had murdered them.

US mugshot of
John Wayne
Gacy.

In 1977 Gacy was accused of having sexually abused a youth at gunpoint. Although Gacy admitted having engaged in brutal sex with the boy he claimed that the youth had been a willing participant who was now trying to blackmail him. The police accepted his story and Gacy was released with a caution.

By this time Gacy was both a successful contractor and a leading light in the local Democratic Party who furthermore provided entertainment at children's parties by dressing up as a clown. He also hung out at notorious gay bars and in 1978 met the 27-year-old Jeffrey Rignall at one of these hangouts. Having invited the young man to share a joint with him in his car, once inside the Oldsmobile Gacy held a chloroform-soaked rag soaked over Rignall's face.

Rignall awoke to find himself naked in Gacy's basement, strapped to a device that resembled a pillory. Gacy, who was also naked, then showed Rignall a number of whips, along with more sinister sexual devices, and explained how he intended to use them. Gacy furthermore told Rignall that he was a policeman and that he would shoot him if he raised any objections. Gacy's subsequent abuse and torture of Rignall went on for hours. At times it was so painful that Rignall begged to die, but Gacy would then chloroform him again and wait until he had come round before starting again. Eventually Rignall promised that he would leave town without telling anyone what had happened to him.

Having blacked out again, Rignall later woke up to find himself fully dressed and lying in Chicago's Lincoln Park. Although there was money in his pocket his driver's licence was missing. He checked into a hospital, where it was discovered that he was not only bleeding from the anus, but also that his face and liver had been damaged by chloroform. Although sympathetic, the police had nothing to go on: Rignall could not give them the name, address or licence-plate number of his abuser.

Rignall remained determined to exact his retribution on his attacker. Renting a car, he followed the route along which he thought Gacy had driven him, which he vaguely remembered having registered through a haze of chloroform. On identifying the motorway exit that Gacy had taken he waited patiently there until he eventually saw Gacy's black Oldsmobile sweep by. Having noted down its licence-plate number he then followed the car, which Gacy parked in the driveway of 8213 West Summerdale Avenue. Rignall subsequently checked the land-registry records and discovered that the house in question belonged to John Wayne Gacy, Jr. He then took everything that he had uncovered to the police.

When they followed up Rignall's leads the Chicago Police Department ascertained that Gacy's suburban home was outside their jurisdiction, which therefore meant that they could not press felony charges against Gacy. For his part, Gacy agreed to give Rignall $3,000 towards his medical bills and the matter was then dropped.

Later that year Mrs Elizabeth Piest made a report to the local police saying that her 15-year-old son, Robert, had gone missing. He had been looking for a summer job and had said that he was going to visit a contractor who lived nearby. The neighbourhood pharmacist had then ventured that the contractor concerned must be Gacy, who had recently given him an estimate for the refurbishment of his shop.

The police phoned Gacy, who denied all knowledge of the missing boy. (In fact, Robert Piest was lying dead on Gacy's bed as they spoke.) On checking their records the police then discovered Gacy's earlier conviction for sodomy and went to see him. However, when Gacy refused to accompany them to the police station to discuss the matter they realised that they had no charge on which to hold him. After his house was put under 24-hour surveillance Gacy nevertheless managed to place Piest's body in a trunk and smuggle it into his car. He then jumped behind the wheel and raced off at top speed, leaving the police standing. Having lost his tail Gacy drove to the nearby Des Plaines river and dropped Piest's body into it. The police then obtained a search warrant, but the only potential clue that they found in Gacy's house was a receipt from a chemist that had been made out to Robert Piest. It wasn't much, but it was enough to justify continuing their surveillance of Gacy.

Gacy, however, was becoming cocky and one morning invited two of the policemen who had been stationed outside his house to join him inside for breakfast. As they sat down to eat the policemen noticed a peculiar smell, which they investigated. It turned out that Gacy had inadvertently switched off the pump that drained the basement and that the water that had flowed under the house as a result had disturbed the soil in which Gacy had buried 29 of his victims, which, armed with another warrant, the police subsequently disinterred. Another four bodies – including that of Robert Piest – were found in the Des Plaines river. The youngest of his victims had been nine, while the oldest had been fully grown men.

John Wayne Gacy, Jr was convicted of mass murder in 1980. Despite his known homosexuality, when he was on death row Gacy received fan mail from women who said that they admired him because he was a deviant and that they loved the excitement of a wild fight. Gacy died by lethal injection in 1994.

17 ❖ The Butcher of Hanover

The Butcher of Hanover – who was also known as the Werewolf of Hanover and the Vampire of Hanover – killed at least 27, and possibly as many as 50, young boys. He killed them by biting out their throats, after that selling their flesh to unwitting consumers on the black market that flourished in Germany following the end of World War I. When one woman grew suspicious about the origins of the joint of meat that she had bought she was told by the police that she should be grateful for finding such a fine piece of pork in these difficult times.

The Butcher of Hanover was a degenerate homosexual named Fritz Haarmann. Haarmann had had a difficult upbringing: his mother, whom he adored, had become an invalid soon after he was born, while his father was a mean and moody locomotive stoker, nicknamed 'Sulky Olle', who had tried to have his son committed to a mental institution on the grounds that he was feeble-minded.

Like many other serial killers, Haarmann started out as a petty criminal. As a youth, he wandered around Germany supporting himself by means of petty theft, swindling and picking pockets. For pleasure, however, he took to child-molesting. Other crooks regarded him as a simpleton who tried hard to please, and he developed a reputation among policemen for laughing when he was arrested.

Haarmann sat out World War I in jail. Following the crushing defeat of Germany, when the war ended he was released into a country that had been broken by the ravages of four years' war: families had been destroyed, the cities were full of homeless refugees and the country was in a state of near famine. To a man like Haarmann, this desperate situation presented a business opportunity that was not to be missed.

Posing as a policeman, Haarmann preyed upon the rootless young drifters who congregated around Hanover's main railway station. He would be there every night, offering cigarettes and chocolate to the new arrivals and then luring them back to his grim lodgings on the Kellerstrasse with the promise of a mattress for the night. Here Haarmann seduced or raped his victims before killing them.

Unaware of the fate of the boys who ended up in his care, the welfare workers at the station began to regard Haarmann as one of their team. The police were aware of his history of petty crime, but Haarmann was proving himself to be a useful informer. No one questioned the source of the second-hand clothes that he sold and his keenly priced joints of meat were sought after.

In September 1918 the parents of a 17-year-old youth reported that their son had gone missing and that he had been seen in the company of Haarmann. The police reluctantly questioned their useful informant, only to eliminate him from their inquiries. Six years later, at his trial, Haarmann boasted 'When the police examined my room the head of the boy was lying wrapped in newspaper behind the oven'.

This close shave with exposure merely served to convince Haarmann that he was unstoppable, and in September 1919 he teamed up with another homosexual degenerate, Hans Grans. Together they transferred their expanding operation to a flat on Neuestrasse. Although he was 20 years Haarmann's junior, Grans was nevertheless the dominant partner in the relationship, treating Haarmann little better than he would a servant and making sure that he took all the risks. It was Grans who picked out the pair's victims, once even instructing Haarmann to murder a boy 'because I like the clothes he's wearing'. (It has been calculated that during this period they were disposing of two victims every week through the black-market trade in meat.)

They executed their grisly business undetected for six years, a period that may well have lasted longer, for many of their victims were homeless and no one reported them missing. Furthermore, because of the economic chaos that existed in Germany at the time, the authorities were obliged to turn a blind eye to the black market. Haarmann and Grans became amazingly lax, however, carting around buckets of blood in front of their neighbours, for example, or chopping up bodies within earshot of other people before dumping the remains in the river Leine.

On 17 May 1924 some children found a human skull on the banks of the Leine. It would be the first of many, but at the time the police issued a statement saying that it had been put there by medical students as a sick joke; the statement did little to quell public fears. A pile of human remains was then discovered by a group of children playing in a meadow, and more than 500 human bones were subsequently found in the river. The newspapers now began writing about the 'Werewolf of Hanover' and one writer went so far as to claim that 600 people had disappeared in the city in the course of that year.

On 22 June 1924 Haarmann was arrested for trying to molest a boy in the street, whereupon the police searched his flat. Although its walls were spattered with blood and it was full of his victims' belongings, Haarmann protested that he was a butcher who also traded in second-hand clothes. The parents of children who had gone missing were invited to the flat to examine the clothes that had been found there, but no one recognised anything until one mother noticed that the son of Haarmann's landlady was wearing a coat that used to belong to her boy. It was only then Haarmann broke down and confessed everything.

Haarmann and Grans were jointly charged with the murders of 27 boys aged between 12 and 18. During their 14-week-long trial one newspaper wrote

Nearly two hundred witnesses had to appear in the box, mostly parents of the unfortunate youths. There were scenes of painful intensity as a poor father or mother would recognise some fragment or other of the clothing or belongings of their murdered son. Here it was a handkerchief, there a pair of braces, and again a greasy coat, soiled almost beyond recognition, that was shown to the relatives and to Haarmann. And with the quivering nostrils of a hound snuffling his prey, as if he were scenting rather than seeing the things displayed, did he admit at once that he knew them.

When the picture of one young boy was held up by the prosecution Haarmann revealed the depth of his callousness by turning to the boy's father and saying 'I should never have looked twice at a boy as ugly as your son'.

In court, Haarmann admitted to killing 30, or possibly even 40, youths – 'I really can't remember the exact number', he said. When the counsel for the prosecution asked how he had killed his victims Haarmann replied 'I bit them through their throats'. It was then that the newspapers began calling him the 'Vampire of Hanover'.

When he was found guilty, on 19 December 1924, Haarmann screamed at the judge and jury

Do you think I enjoy killing people? I was ill for eight days after the first time. Condemn me to death. I ask only for justice. I am not mad. It is true I often get into a state when I do not know what I am doing, but that is not madness. Make it short, make it soon. Deliver me from this life, which is a torment. I will not petition for mercy, nor will I appeal. I want to pass just one more merry evening in my cell, with coffee, cheese and cigars, after which I will curse my father and go to my execution as if it were a wedding.

Haarmann got his wish and was beheaded on the following day. His accomplice, Grans, however, served only 12 years in jail.

18 ❖ The Yorkshire Ripper

Peter Sutcliffe, the Yorkshire Ripper, picked up where his namesake, Jack, left off, like him (or her) specialising in killing prostitutes. By the time that he was caught 20 women had been savagely attacked, 13 brutally murdered and a whole community was living virtually under siege. During a reign of terror that spanned nearly six years he managed to elude the biggest police squad that has ever been assembled in Britain to date with the aim of capturing one man.

It started on 30 October 1975, when a Leeds milkman on his rounds saw a shapeless bundle lying on a bleak recreation ground. He went over to investigate and found a woman sprawled on the ground, her hair matted with blood and her body exposed. Her jacket and blouse had been torn open, her bra was rucked up and her trousers had been pulled down, below her knees. There were 14 stab wounds in her chest and stomach. The milkman did not see the massive wound on the back of her head that had actually caused her death. Having been attacked from behind, two vicious blows had been delivered with a heavy hammer, smashing her skull; the stab wounds had been inflicted after she was dead.

The body belonged to a twenty-eight-year-old mother of three, Wilma McCann, who had regularly hitchhiked home after spending nights on the town. She had died just 100 yards (91 metres) from her home, a council house in Scott Hall Avenue. Post-mortem blood tests showed that she had consumed 12 to 14 measures of spirits on the night of her death. Although her clothes had been interfered with, her knickers were still in place and she had not been raped. There therefore seemed to have been no overt sexual motive for her murder. Her purse, however, was missing, so in the absence of any other discernible motive the police regarded her murder as a callous by-product of robbery.

This opinion was reassessed, however, when a second killing occurred in Chapeltown (the red-light district of Leeds) three months later. Not all of the women who worked in the area were professional prostitutes: some women sold sex in order to earn some extra cash; others, such as the 42-year-old Emily Jackson, were enthusiastic amateurs who sold their bodies primarily for fun. Emily lived with her husband and three children in the respectable Leeds suburb of Churwell. On 20 January 1976 she and her husband went to the Gaiety pub on Roundhay Road, a popular venue with both Chapeltown irregulars like Emily and their prospective clients. After leaving her husband in the main lounge she went searching for business. An hour later she was seen in the car park getting into a Land Rover. At closing time her husband finished his drink and took a taxi home alone; his wife, he assumed, had found a client for the night.

Emily Jackson's body was found the next morning huddled under a coat on open ground. Like Wilma McCann, although her breasts had been exposed she was still wearing her knickers. She, too, had been killed by two massive blows to the head that had been inflicted by a heavy hammer. Her neck, breasts and stomach had been stabbed over 50 times, her back had been gouged with a Phillips screwdriver and the impression of the heavily ribbed sole of a size 7 Wellington boot was stamped on her right thigh (this was the only real clue). The post mortem indicated that Emily had had sex before the attack, although not necessarily with her murderer. Once again, there seemed to be no clear motive for the killing.

Over a year later, on 5 February 1977, the 28-year-old part-time prostitute Irene Richardson left her tawdry rooming house in Chapeltown half an hour before midnight in order to go dancing. On the following morning a jogger running through Soldier's Field, a public playing field a short car ride from Chapeltown, saw a body lying slumped on the ground. It turned out to be that of Irene Richardson. Because she was lying face down the three massive blows that had shattered her skull were obvious. Her skirt and tights had been torn off, her coat had been draped over her buttocks and her calf-length boots had been removed from her feet and lay neatly across her thighs. Her neck and torso were studded with knife wounds. The post mortem indicated that she had not had sex before her death and that she had died only 30 minutes after leaving her lodgings.

Following the murder of Irene Richardson the police were able to link the three cases: they were plainly the work of a serial killer. Parallels with the Jack the Ripper quickly sprang into the public imagination, and the murderer of Wilma McCann, Emily Jackson and Irene Richardson soon became known as the 'Yorkshire Ripper'.

It was obvious that the Yorkshire Ripper was preying on prostitutes in Leeds, so the working women of Chapeltown moved in droves to Manchester, London and Glasgow, while those who could not afford to travel so far from home began plying their trade in nearby Bradford. The York-shire Ripper's next victim, Patricia 'Tina' Atkinson, however, was a Brad-ford girl who lived in Oak Lane, just around the corner from the city's thriving red-light district. On the evening of 23 April 1977 Tina went to her local pub, The Carlisle, for a drink with friends and reeled out shortly before closing time. When nobody saw her the next day it was assumed that she was at home, sleeping off the effects of the previous night.

The following evening some friends visited her flat and found the door unlocked. Inside, they discovered her covered with blankets lying dead on her bed. It seemed that she had been attacked as she had entered the flat. Four hammer blows had smashed in the back of her head and she had then been flung on to the bed, after which her clothes had been pulled off. She had been stabbed in the stomach seven times and the left side of her body had been slashed to ribbons. There was also a size 7 Wellington-boot print on the sheet.

The footprint belonged to Peter Sutcliffe, who believed that he was on a moral crusade to rid the streets of prostitutes. The eldest of John and Kathleen Sutcliffe's six children, he was born in Bingley, a dour-looking town 6 miles (10 kilometres) north of Bradford. A timid child and later an inscrutable young man, he had always been regarded as something of an outsider. Being small and weedy he had been bullied at school and clung to his mother's skirts. Although his younger brothers had inherited their father's appetite for life, the opposite sex and the consumption of large quantities of beer, Peter liked none of these things. Despite taking no inter-est in girls, as an adolescent he spent hours preening himself in front of the bathroom mirror and later took up body-building.

After leaving school at 15 he took a job as a grave-digger at a cemetery in Bingley and regularly joked about having 'thousands of people below me where I work now'. During his three years as a grave-digger he devel-oped a macabre sense of humour. He once pretended to be a corpse, for example, lying down on a slab, throwing a shroud over himself and making moaning noises when his workmates appeared. For their part they called him 'Jesus', because of his biblical-looking beard. At his trial Sutcliffe claimed that he had heard the voice of God while working at the cemetery. He said that he had been digging a grave when he had heard a voice ema-nating from a cross-shaped headstone telling him to go out on to the streets and to kill prostitutes.

Despite the youthful Sutcliffe's good looks girls were not attracted to him. His first proper girlfriend was Sonia, a 16-year-old schoolgirl whom he had met in his local pub who suffered from the same type of introversion as Sutcliffe. On Sundays they would sit lost in conversation in the front room of her house. She would speak to other members of the Sutcliffe family only when it was absolutely unavoidable.

As a devout Catholic Sutcliffe was devastated when he learned that his mother was having an affair with a neighbour, a local policeman. His father arranged for all of his children – including Sutcliffe, who was accompanied by his bride-to-be, Sonia – to be present at a Bingley hotel to witness a humiliating confrontation with his wife. Having arrived at the bar believing that she was meeting her boyfriend, only to be greeted by her husband and children, Kathleen was then forced to show the family the new nightdress that she had bought for the tryst. This incident was particularly painful for Sutcliffe, who had earlier discovered that Sonia also had a secret boyfriend. Later in the same year, 1969, Sutcliffe carried out his first-known attack, following a row over a £10 note hitting a Bradford prostitute over the head with sock containing a stone. Psychiatrists later said that the discovery of his mother's affair had triggered his psychosis.

After a courtship lasting eight years Sutcliffe and Sonia were married. After spending the first three years of their married life living with Sonia's parents they then moved to a large, detached house in Heaton (a middle-class suburb of Bradford), which they kept immaculate.

On the evening of Saturday, 25 June 1977 Sutcliffe gave his wife a lift to the Sherrington nursing home where she worked at nights. With his neighbours, Ronnie and Peter Barker, he then went on a pub crawl around Bradford, ending up at the Dog in the Pound. At closing time they went to get some fish and chips. It was well past midnight when Sutcliffe dropped the Barker brothers at their front door, but instead of parking his white Ford Corsair outside his house Sutcliffe drove off down the main road, towards Leeds. At around 2am, illuminated by the street lights of Chapeltown Road, he saw a young woman wearing a gingham skirt. As she passed the Hayfield pub and turned left, down Reginald Terrace, Sutcliffe parked his car, got out and began to follow her down the quiet side street.

The next morning a girl's body was found lying next to a wall by a group of children on their way to a nearby adventure playground. She had been struck on the back of the head, dragged for 20 yards (18 metres) and then hit twice more. She had also been stabbed once in the back and repeatedly through the chest – the trademarks of the Yorkshire Ripper were unmistakable. But the victim had not been a prostitute: Jayne McDonald was only 16 and had just left school to work in the shoe department of a local supermarket. On the night of her death she had been out with friends in Leeds and was on her way back to her parents' home (which was just a few hundred yards from where her body was found) when she was attacked.

The murder of a teenage girl gave the investigation new impetus. By the September of 1977 the police had interviewed almost 700 local residents and had taken 3,500 statements, many of them from prostitutes who worked in the area.

Two weeks after the killing of Jayne McDonald the Yorkshire Ripper savagely attacked Maureen Long on some waste ground near her home in Bradford. By some miracle she survived, but her description of her assailant was too vague to be of help to the inquiry.

The investigation's staff was subsequently increased to 304 full-time officers, who had soon interviewed 175,000 people, taken 12,500 statements and checked out 10,000 vehicles. Their main problem was that they had no idea of the type of man for whom they were looking. It is furthermore doubtful whether anyone would have suspected the long-distance lorry driver Peter Sutcliffe. The 31-year-old was a polite and mild-mannered neighbour, a hard-working and trusted employee, a good son and a loyal husband. He was the sort of man who did jobs around the house or tinkered with his car at weekends. Nothing about him suggested that he was a mass murderer, and those who knew him would even have been surprised if they had seen him picking up prostitutes, although that was what he regularly did.

On Saturday, 1 October 1977 Jean Jordan climbed into Sutcliffe's new, red Ford Corsair near her home in Moss Side, Manchester. She took £5 in advance and then directed him to some open land 2 miles (3 kilometres) away that was used by prostitutes when entertaining their clients. They were a few yards from the car when Sutcliffe smashed a hammer on to Jean's skull, hitting her again and again – 11 times in all. He then dragged her body into some bushes, but before he could proceed further another car arrived and he made a quick getaway.

As he drove back to Bradford Sutcliffe realised that he had left a vital clue on his victim's body: the £5 note that he had given Jean was brand new; it had come directly from his wage packet and could therefore link him to the dead woman. He waited nervously for eight long days. During that time, however, nothing appeared in the press about Jean's body having been found, so he risked returning to Moss Side to try to recover the £5 note. Despite a frantic search he could not find Jean's handbag, and in his frustration he started to mutilate her body with a broken pane of glass. He even tried to saw off her head in an attempt to remove his hammer-blow signature, but the glass was not sharp enough to sever her spine. In the end he gave up, kicked the body several times and then drove home.

On the following day an allotment-owner discovered Jean's naked body. The damage to her head had rendered her unrecognisable and there was no evidence among her scattered clothing with which to identify her. (She was eventually identified from a fingerprint on a lemonade bottle that she had handled before leaving home for the last time.) The police did, however, find the £5 note and immediately set about tracing it. Over the next three months they interviewed five-thousand men, one of whom was Sutcliffe, but when the detectives saw Sutcliffe's well-appointed house they discounted him from their inquiries.

Sutcliffe's next victim was the 18-year-old Helen Rytka, who shared a miserable room next to a flyover in Huddersfield with her twin sister, Rita. Both were prostitutes who worked as a pair in the red-light district around Great Northern Street. Because the Yorkshire Ripper's murders had scared them they had devised a system which they hoped would keep them safe. Basing themselves outside a public lavatory, when one sister was picked up separately the other wrote down the number of the client's car; after giving their clients precisely 20 minutes they then returned to the lavatory. Ultimately, however, this system went terribly wrong.

On the snowy night of Tuesday, 31 January 1978 Helen returned to their usual rendezvous five minutes early. At 9.25pm a bearded man in a red Ford Corsair offered her the chance of making a quick £5, which she accepted, thinking that she could perform her services quickly and be back at the rendezvous before Rita returned.

Helen took her client to the nearby Garrard's timber yard. Because two men were already there Sutcliffe could not kill her straightaway and instead had sex with her in the back of the car. By the time that they had finished the men had gone, so as Helen got out of the back seat to return to the front of the car Sutcliffe swung at her with his hammer, but missed, hitting the door of the car. His second blow, however, struck her on the head and he then hit her five more times until the walls of the foreman's shed, which was just a few feet away, were spattered with blood. After that Sutcliffe dragged Helen's body into a woodpile and hid it. Her bra and black, polo-neck pullover had been pushed above her breasts; although she was still wearing her socks the rest of her clothes were scattered over a wide area. Her black-lace knickers were found pinned to the shed door by a lorry driver the next day.

Rita, who had waited for her sister at the lavatory, was desperately worried when she did not appear, but her fear of the police prevented her from reporting Helen's disappearance for three days. It was a police Alsatian that found the hidden body; Helen had been horribly mutilated and there were three gaping wounds in her chest, where she had been repeatedly stabbed.

The Yorkshire Ripper's latest victim had disappeared from a busy street, and the police later traced over a hundred passers-by, eliminating all but three cars and one stocky, fair-haired man from their inquiries. Although they appealed on the radio to any wife, mother or girlfriend who suspected that they were living with the Ripper to come forward no one did.

A few weeks later a passer-by spotted an arm sticking out from under an overturned sofa on wasteland in Bradford's red-light district. After initially thinking that it belonged to a tailor's dummy the putrid aroma that emanated from it sent him rushing to a telephone. The body was that of the 22-year-old Yvonne Pearson, a high-class prostitute who serviced the rich-businessmen trade in most of Britain's cities. She had been murdered two months earlier, ten days before Helen Rytka, and the killing bore all of the hallmarks of the Yorkshire Ripper. A hammer blow to the head had smashed her skull. Her bra and pullover had been pulled up, exposing her breasts, and her chest had been repeatedly jumped on. Her black, flared trousers had been tugged down and some of the sofa's horsehair stuffing had been rammed into her mouth.

Friends reported that Yvonne had spoken of her fear of the Yorkshire Ripper only days before she had disappeared. On the night of her death she had left her two daughters with a neighbour and was seen climbing into a car driven by a bearded man with black, piercing eyes shortly after 9.30pm. Sutcliffe had killed her with a hammer on wasteland in nearby Arthington Street and had then dragged her body to the abandoned sofa, jumping on her corpse until her ribs cracked. Although he had hidden her body the police deduced that the killer had become concerned when it had not been found because he had later returned in order to make it more visible, tucking a copy of the *Daily Mirror*, dated four weeks after her death, under her arm.

Two months after Yvonne Pearson's body was found the Yorkshire Ripper attacked the 41-year-old Vera Millward. A Spanish-born mother of seven children, Vera had come to England following World War II as a domestic worker. She lived with a Jamaican man and had resorted to prostitution in Manchester's Moss Side in order to earn money to help to support her family. On the night of Tuesday, 16 May 1978 she left home for the Manchester Royal Infirmary to get painkillers to ease her chronic stomach pains. She died in a well-lit part of the hospital grounds, Sutcliffe hitting her three times on the head with a hammer and then slashing her across the stomach. Her corpse was discovered by a gardener the next morning, lying on a rubbish pile in the corner of the car park.

Three months later the police again visited Sutcliffe, this time because his car-registration number had cropped up during checks carried out in Leeds and Bradford. They subsequently returned to question him about the tyres on his car. (They were looking for treads that matched the tyre tracks found at the scene of Irene Richardson's murder 21 months earlier.) As always, Sutcliffe was helpful and unruffled, giving them absolutely no reason to suspect him. Indeed, they didn't even think it worth asking Sutcliffe what his blood group was – the Yorkshire Ripper's was rare – or for his shoe size, which was unusually small for a man.

Suddenly the Yorkshire Ripper's killing spree stopped: for 11 months there were no more murders. The police speculated that he had committed suicide, taking his identity to the grave with him. It was all eerily similar to the disappearance of Jack the Ripper 90 years earlier.

Sutcliffe was not dead, however, nor could he suppress his desire to murder for much longer. On the night of Wednesday, 4 April 1979 he drove to Halifax, getting out of his car at around midnight and accosting the 19-year-old Josephine Whitaker as she walked across Savile Park playing fields. They spoke briefly, and as they moved away from the street lights he smashed in the back of the head with a hammer and dragged her body into the shadows. Her body was found the next morning.

In common with Jayne McDonald, Josephine Whitaker was not a prostitute. She lived at home with her family and worked as a clerk at the headquarters of the Halifax building society. After her murder no woman felt safe on the streets of Yorkshire after dark.

Two weeks before Josephine Whitaker died a letter arrived at Bradford's police station; it was postmarked Sunderland and dated 23 March 1979. The letter said that the next victim would not be killed in Bradford's Chapeltown district because it was 'too bloody hot there' as a result of the efforts of the 'curserred coppers'. This odd misspelling so closely aped Jack the Ripper's notes that it should have rung warning bells, but the police believed it to be genuine. Handwriting experts confirmed that it had been written by the same person who had sent two previous letters purporting to come from the Yorkshire Ripper. This one furthermore mentioned that Vera Millward had stayed in hospital, information that the police (wrongly) believed could only have been gleaned from Vera herself. On this basis they concluded that the writer of the three letters was indeed the Yorkshire Ripper.

Traces of engineering oil had been found on one of the letters and similar traces were now discovered on Josephine Whitaker's body. Next the police called a press conference asking members of the public to come forward with any information that they might have about anybody who could have been in Sunderland on the days on which the letters were posted. Although the response was overwhelming it ultimately produced merely more useless information that had to be checked, analysed and filed.

Then, on the morning of 18 June 1979, two months after Josephine Whitaker's death, a buff-coloured envelope, addressed in the same handwriting as the previous letters that the Yorkshire Ripper had allegedly sent, arrived at the police station. The envelope contained an audio cassette on to which had been recorded a 257-word message delivered in a broad Geordie accent. A huge publicity campaign was mounted and the public was invited to dial up and listen to the 'Geordie Ripper tape' in the hope that someone might recognise the voice. Within a few days more than 50,000 people had called in. Language experts had confirmed that the accent was genuinely Wearside and had pinned it down to Castletown, a small, tightly knit suburb of Sunderland. Eleven detectives were consequently installed in a Sunderland hotel and a hundred officers combed the town. Although only 4,000 people lived in Castletown the police could still not find their man – a cruel hoaxer who had a cast-iron alibi. The identity of the Geordie Ripper remains a mystery to this day.

In July 1979 Detective Constable Laptew again visited Sutcliffe, whose car had by now been spotted in the red-light district of Bradford on 36 separate occasions. Laptew became increasingly suspicious of Sutcliffe, but because the police force's attention was focused on the Geordie Ripper tape at that time his report was not followed up and Sutcliffe therefore remained free to return to Bradford to dispatch his eleventh victim.

On Saturday, 1 September 1979 Sutcliffe was cruising the streets around Little Horton, a residential area of Bradford, when, at about 1am, he saw Barbara Leach, a student, moving away from a group of friends outside the Manville Arms. He attacked her when she was just 200 yards (183 metres) from the pub, dragging her into a back yard before stabbing her eight times. He then stuffed her body into a dustbin and slung an old carpet over it; it was discovered the following afternoon.

Two high-ranking officers from Scotland Yard were sent to Yorkshire, but made no progress. Although a police task force from Manchester reviewed the £5-note inquiry and narrowed the field down to 270 suspects it, too, could get no further.

Like everyone else in Yorkshire Sutcliffe spoke to his family and friends about the Ripper. He made a point of picking up Sonia from work in order to protect her and was later reported to have told a workmate 'Whoever is doing all these murders has a lot to answer for'. On one occasion his colleagues at the depot even made a bet that Sutcliffe himself was the Yorkshire Ripper, at which he laughed, but said nothing.

The Yorkshire Ripper now took another break from killing, which lasted for nearly a year. Then, on Thursday, 18 August 1980, he struck for the twelfth time. His victim was Marguerite Walls, a 47-year-old civil servant who had been working late at the Department of Education and Science in Leeds that evening, leaving at 10pm to walk home. Her body was discovered two days later, under a mound of grass clippings in the garden of a magistrate's house. She had been bludgeoned and strangled, but because her body had not been mutilated the police did not at first realise that she was another of the Ripper's victims.

Three months later, after he had just finished eating a chicken dinner, Sutcliffe saw Jacqueline Hill, a language student at the University of Leeds, getting off the bus outside a Kentucky Fried Chicken fast-food restaurant. His fingers were still greasy from his supper when he viciously struck her down before dragging her body to some waste ground behind the shops and attacking it savagely. Death had befallen Jacqueline so suddenly that one of her eyes had remained open, and Sutcliffe now stabbed it repeatedly with a rusty Phillips screwdriver that he had sharpened into a fine point.

The Home Office appointed a special squad with which to try solve the case, but only six weeks after Jacqueline Hill's murder it reached the same conclusion as had the West Yorkshire police force – it had no idea of how to crack the case. What it needed was a bit of luck.

On 2 January 1981 Sergeant Robert Ring and Police Constable Robert Hydes started their evening shift by cruising along Melbourne Avenue, in Sheffield's red-light district. On seeing Olivia Reivers climbing into a Rover V8 3500 they decided to investigate. The driver – a bearded man – identified himself as Peter Williams. After saying that he did not want any trouble he scrambled out of the car and asked if he could relieve himself. When the policemen agreed he went over to the bushes that lined the street and dropped a ball-peen hammer and sharp knife from a special pocket in his car coat while pretending to urinate. The policemen did not notice him doing this while Olivia Reivers was remonstrating loudly with them, complaining that they were ruining her livelihood.

By the time that the man strolled back to his car, however, the police had discovered that the car's number plates were false. He was accordingly taken to the police station, where he admitted that his name was really Peter William Sutcliffe. During his interview Sutcliffe said that his main concern was that the police would tell his wife that he had been picked up with a prostitute. Otherwise he was calm and forthcoming and readily confessed that he had stolen the number plates from a scrapyard in Dewsbury. He was even allowed to go to the lavatory alone, where he hid a second knife in the cistern.

There was no concrete reason to suspect Sutcliffe of being the Yorkshire Ripper, but the police working on the case had so little to go on that when any man was caught with a prostitute his details had to be forwarded to the West Yorkshire police before he could be released. Sutcliffe was thus locked up for the night before being taken, unprotesting, to a Dewsbury police station the next morning. In Dewsbury Sutcliffe proved himself to be a chatty and eager interviewee. Indeed, he was so full of himself that he made two fatal mistakes: in passing, he mentioned that he had been interviewed by the Yorkshire Ripper Squad about the £5 note and that he had also visited Bradford's red-light district.

The Dewsbury police next called the Yorkshire Ripper Squad in Leeds, where Detective Sergeant Des O'Boyle discovered that Sutcliffe's name had come up several times during the course of the investigation. Having driven to Dewsbury, when O'Boyle called his boss, Detective Inspector John Boyle, in Leeds that evening, he told him that Sutcliffe's blood group was B – the rare blood group that the police knew the Ripper shared. Sutcliffe was accordingly locked into his cell for a second night.

Meanwhile, Sergeant Ring had heard one of his colleagues casually mentioning that the man whom he had arrested was being interviewed by detectives from the Yorkshire Ripper Squad. After rushing back to Melbourne Avenue he found the ball-peen hammer and knife that Sutcliffe had hidden in the bushes. Sonia Sutcliffe was furthermore questioned and their house was searched. Early in the afternoon of the next day O'Boyle told Sutcliffe that they had found a hammer and knife in Sheffield, whereupon Sutcliffe, who had been talkative up to this point, fell silent. 'I think you're in trouble, serious trouble', said O'Boyle. Sutcliffe finally spoke: 'I think you are leading up to the Yorkshire Ripper', he said. O'Boyle nodded. 'Well,' said Sutcliffe, 'that's me.'

Sutcliffe's confession took almost 17 hours to complete. He said that he had begun killing after a Bradford prostitute had cheated him out of £10 in 1969. (He mentioned nothing about hearing a voice from God at that stage.)

Sixteen weeks later Sutcliffe stood trial at the Old Bailey. The Crown Prosecution Service's barrister, the defence counsel and the attorney general, Sir Michael Havers, had all agreed that Sutcliffe was mentally ill, and that he was suffering from paranoid schizophrenia. The presiding judge would have none of this, however, and told both counsels that the jury would listen to the evidence and then decide whether Sutcliffe was a murderer or a madman.

Sutcliffe pleaded guilty to manslaughter. During his testimony he remained calm and self-assured, even managing a laugh when he recalled that when he was questioned about the size 7 Wellington boot-print stamped on Emily Jackson's thigh and Tina Atkinson's sheet the policeman who had been interviewing him had not noticed that he was wearing the boots in question. He also claimed that he had been acting on instructions from God to 'clean the streets' of prostitutes.

The jury found Sutcliffe guilty of 13 murders and he was sentenced to life imprisonment, with the recommendation that he should serve at least 30 years.

19 ❖ Jack the Stripper

The file on Jack the Ripper has never been closed. Neither has the file on Jack the Stripper – even though Scotland Yard is sure that it knows who killed six women in 1964 and early 1965 and left their naked bodies lying along the bank of the river Thames.

The police found the first body under a pontoon at Hammersmith on 2 February 1964. The victim had been strangled and the remnants of her underwear had been shoved down her throat; she was small, at 5 foot 2 inches (1.60 metres) tall, and was naked, apart from her stockings.

The body was identified as being that of Hannah Tailford, who was 30 years old and lived with her boyfriend in the West Norwood district of London. She had a three-year-old daughter and an eighteen-month-old son and was pregnant again. She was employed as a waitress and a cleaner and supplemented her meagre wages by working as a prostitute on the streets of Bayswater (her record showed four convictions for soliciting). She had disappeared from her flat ten days before her body was found, although a couple had seen her on Charing Cross Road only two days before that. She had appeared depressed and suicidal and they had tried to cheer her up, they said.

Forensic experts concluded that she had been dead for just 24 hours when her corpse was found and believed that she may have been drowned in a bath or pond before she was dumped in the river. Tide tables showed that she must have been dropped in the Thames at Duke's Meadow, in Chiswick, a popular spot with prostitutes and their clients. The police discovered that Hannah had been a star turn at sex parties and that she had often attended kinky orgies in Mayfair and Kensington. A foreign diplomat known for his perverted tastes had been one of her clients, but he had been out of the country at the time of her disappearance.

This gave the police little to go on. Although they believed that Hannah had been attacked and sexually assaulted (her knickers having been shoved into her mouth to stop her from screaming as she was killed) they could not even prove that she had been murdered. The inquest into her death recorded an open verdict.

On 8 April 1964 the naked body of the 26-year-old Irene Lockwood was found among the tangled weeds and branches on the river bank at Duke's Meadow. Irene was a pretty, young redhead who, like Hannah, had also worked on the streets of Bayswater and Notting Hill and had attended kinky parties, too (she had furthermore performed in blue movies). Both girls had solicited cab drives late at night and both had been pregnant when they died.

It was impossible to determine how either Hannah or Linda had died, although marks on the back of Irene's head indicated that she could have been attacked from behind. Like Hannah, the police believed that Linda had been killed elsewhere and then brought to Duke's Meadow. The police also suspected that both girls had been mixed up in a blackmail racket. They had found an address book and photographic equipment in Hannah's flat, while Irene's flatmate, Vicki Pender (who had been found battered to death a year earlier), had once been beaten up after trying to blackmail a client who had been photographed with her without his knowledge. The most striking similarity between the two killings, however, was that the victims were found naked; there was no sign of their clothes, which were never discovered.

On 24 April 1964 another naked female corpse was found, this time in an alleyway off Swyncombe Avenue in nearby Brentford, Middlesex. The victim, the 22-year-old Helen Barthelemy, had been strangled, probably from behind. Strangely enough, three of her front teeth had been extracted after her death. It was also established that she had been stripped of her clothes post mortem; fresh tyre marks in the alley furthermore indicated that she had been killed elsewhere and then dumped there.

Helen was also a prostitute. Educated in a convent, she had later become a stripper in Blackpool. She had served a prison sentence in Liverpool for luring a man into a trap, after which he had been robbed. She had then come to London, where she had gone on the game. She was known to cater for any sort of perversion, but would often entertain local black men for free because they were more sympathetic to her than her kinky clientele. One Jamaican man admitted having been with her on the night of her disappearance, but because he had a strong alibi he was quickly ruled out as a suspect.

The newspapers soon picked up on the story of the three similar killings, and because the victims' nudity was the most sensational aspect the tabloids dubbed their murderer 'Jack the Stripper'.

On reviewing its records Scotland Yard identified another case that matched Jack the Stripper's *modus operandi*. On 8 November 1963, three months before Hannah's murder, the body of the 22-year-old Gwynneth Rees had been found buried in a shallow grave in an ash tip near Chiswick Bridge. She was naked, except for one stocking, and had been sexually assaulted. The body had lain there since May or June of 1963 and it was thought that she may have been sunbathing when she was attacked. The police concluded that she had been another victim of Jack the Stripper.

Kenneth Archibald, a 24-year-old caretaker, then walked into Notting Hill's police station and confessed to the murder of Irene Lockwood. (He was already a suspect because his cart had been discovered in Irene's flat.) He said that he had met her in a pub on the night of the murder, after which they had quarrelled over money on some open land near Barnes Bridge. He had lost his temper, he said, and after placing his hands around her throat to stop her from screaming he had accidentally strangled her. When she was dead he had taken off her clothing and had rolled her into the river. Then he had taken her clothes home and had burned them.

Archibald said that he knew nothing about the murders of Hannah Tailford, Helen Barthelemy or Gwynneth Rees, however. Although he was charged with the murder of Irene Lockwood, when he appeared in the Old Bailey he retracted his confession, and as there was no other evidence against him the jury acquitted him.

The forensic scientists paid special attention to Helen Barthelemy's body, which had not been buried, like that of Gwynneth Rees, and had not come into contact with water. It was, however, filthy, as if it had been stored somewhere dirty before being dumped. A minute examination of the corpse's skin showed that it was covered from head to toe in tiny flecks of paint and it was therefore concluded that Helen's naked body had been kept near a spray-painting shop.

It was clear that the man who had killed Helen Barthelemy and the others sought the company of prostitutes in the Bayswater area. The police next organised an amnesty for women working on the streets in that area and appealed to any who had ever worried about odd or eccentric clients – especially those who had made them strip naked – to come forward. The women's response was overwhelming. Policewomen posing as prostitutes were also sent out on to the streets.

On 14 July 1964 another body was found. At around 5.30am a man who was driving to work down Acton Lane had to brake hard in order to miss a van that was speeding out of a cul-de-sac. He subsequently called the police and at the end of the cul-de-sac, outside a garage, they found the naked body of Mary Flemming.

The murdered girl had again been a prostitute who had worked in the Bayswater area. As with Helen Barthelemy, her clothes had been removed after her death and there were tiny flecks of paint all over her body. It furthermore appeared that before being dumped her body had been kept for approximately three days after her killing. Mary had been warned of the dangers of continuing to work the streets which Jack the Stripper was prowling and had taken to carrying a knife in her handbag. It had done her no good, however, for she had been attacked from behind, like the Stripper's other victims. No trace of her handbag, knife or clothes were ever found.

By this time Scotland Yard had interviewed 8,000 people and taken 4,000 statements, but it was still no nearer to finding the culprit. Plainclothes policemen now blanketed the area in which the murdered girls had worked, but despite their presence the body of the 21-year-old Margaret McGowan was found lying on some rough ground in Kensington on 25 November 1964. Margaret had been a prostitute and an associate of the society pimp Dr Stephen Ward (who stood trial during the Profumo scandal). Her naked body had lain on the open ground for at least a week when it was found, but before that the forensic scientists believed that it had been stored somewhere else. She had been strangled and her skin was also covered in tiny flecks of paint. The hallmarks of Jack the Stripper were unmistakable..

On the evening on which she had gone missing Margaret and a friend had been in the Warwick Castle, a pub on the Portobello Road, where they had talked about the murders. Margaret had then met a client and she and her friend had gone their separate ways. Her friend gave a good enough description of Margaret's client for the police to issue an Identikit picture of the man, but no one answering the description was ever identified. The police also noticed that Margaret's jewellery was missing, but a check on all the local pawn shops drew a blank.

Although Christmas and New Year passed uneventfully, on 16 February 1965 the naked body of the 28-year-old Bridie O'Hara was found lying in the bracken behind a depot in Acton. In common with the Stripper's previous victims she was short – 5 feet 2 inches (1.60 metres) tall – and worked as a prostitute. Along with her engagement and wedding rings her clothes were nowhere to be found (and never were). The corpse was furthermore covered with minute flecks of paint. This time, however, there was a new clue: one of her hands was mummified, which meant that it had been kept near a source of heat, which had dried out the flesh.

Scotland Yard now threw all of its resources into the case and ordered every business premises within an area of 24 square miles (62 square kilometres) to be searched for samples of paint that matched the flecks on the victims' bodies. The police also worked out that all of the Stripper's victims had been picked up between 11pm and 1am, their bodies being disposed of between 5 and 6am. They concluded that the murderer was therefore a night worker, probably a night watchman who guarded premises near a spray-painting shop. In addition, they speculated that he was a man of about 40 who had a highly charged libido and curious sexual tastes.

The police now dismissed a theory that had been put forward earlier, which held that the culprit was on a crusade against prostitution. They instead believed that because he could not satisfy his bizarre sexual requirements at home he turned to the prostitutes who would do anything for money. The detectives felt sure that the man went into a frenzy during orgasm, which resulted in the women's deaths. He could not help himself, they guessed, and had thus learned to accept that murder was the price that he had to pay for his sexual satisfaction.

This was not much to go on, but the police nevertheless held regular press conferences at which they stated that a list of suspects had been drawn up which they were working their way through. The killer would soon be behind bars, they promised. In fact, although the police had no such list and were not nearly as confident as they pretended, they felt that this strategy was the best way in which to keep putting pressure on the culprit.

The murders coincided with a ten-week cycle, and the police were determined to prevent the next one. They therefore threw a cordon around a 20-square-mile (52-square-kilometre) area of central London and recorded every vehicle that entered or left it at night. Anyone who was found to have moved in or out of the zone on more than three occasions was traced, the police then visiting their home under the pretext of investigating a traffic accident (in order to avoid embarrassing those who had been where they were not supposed to have been). The suspect was then interviewed out of his family's earshot.

Weeks of searching at last paid off when a perfect match was made between the paint flecks on the victims' bodies and paint found under a covered transformer at the rear of a spray-painting shop in the Heron Factory Estate in Acton. (The transformer itself also generated enough heat to mummify any flesh that was left near it.) Every car entering or leaving the estate was then logged and all 7,000 people living in the vicinity were interviewed. At specially convened press conferences the police announced that the number of their suspects was being whittled down to three, then two, and finally one. Once again, these statements were not true, but it is likely that the strategy behind the press conferences worked.

In March 1965 a quiet, family man who lived in south London killed himself, leaving a suicide note that said that he could not 'stand the strain any longer'. At the time the police took little notice of the man's death. By June 1965, however, they had concluded that Jack the Stripper had not struck again – the ten-week cycle had been broken – and because they wanted to know why he had stopped killing they began investigating the suicides that had occurred since the murder of Bridie O'Hara in January 1965. They discovered that this particular suicide victim had worked at a security firm at night. Despite an intensive search of his house and extensive interviews with members of his family no evidence linking him directly to the murders was ever found. Nevertheless, the killings seemed to have stopped and from the circumstantial evidence alone the police were convinced that the man had been Jack the Stripper.

By July 1965 the murder inquiry had been scaled down, to be wound up in the following year. In 1970 Scotland Yard announced that the south London suicide had been Jack the Stripper. It never named him, however, and, indeed, the file on the Jack-the-Stripper case remains officially open.

20 ❖ The Co-ed Killer

One young man's irrepressible sexual appetite – he killed young women and mutilated their bodies for his sexual pleasure – terrorised a small town in the US state of Michigan for more than two years. After he was caught he showed no remorse and was convicted of only one murder, and then only by the flimsiest forensic evidence.

At about 9pm on a warm Sunday in June 1967 Mary Pleszar, an attractive, brunette student, was walking down a street in the small, university town of Ypsilanti when a car pulled over beside her and a young man leaned out to speak to her. An onlooker assumed that he was offering her a lift which she appeared to refuse, whereupon the car drove off. After turning at the next corner, moments later it sped past the girl again and drove into a private driveway. By this time Mary had reached her block of flats and was safe – or so she thought.

On the following day Mary's flatmate phoned her parents to say that Mary had not come home. Concerned, they called the police, who proved unhelpful: Mary was 19 and students often stayed out all night at parties or with boyfriends, they said, to which her parents protested that their daughter was not that sort of girl. On the day after that the police issued a missing-person's report on Mary. Although a witness who responded to it said that he had seen the young man who had offered Mary a lift he was unable to give a detailed description of the youth or of the car that he was driving.

Four weeks later two boys came across a fly-covered mass of rotting meat – which they took to be a deer's carcass – near a secluded lover's lane 2 miles (3 kilometres) north of Ypsilanti. A pathologist subsequently identified it as being human flesh, and more specifically the corpse of a young woman who had been stabbed in the chest more than 30 times. An extensive search of the area failed to uncover the victim's clothes, but the searchers did find one sandal close to the corpse, which Mary's parents identified as belonging to their daughter. Fresh tyre tracks were also found beside the body.

At the funeral home where Mary's body was lying prior to burial the young man was seen again. Having asked the receptionist if he could take a photograph of the body as a memento for his parents the receptionist had replied that that was impossible; it was only when he was going out of the door that she noticed that he was not carrying a camera.

Almost exactly a year later Joan Schell, a 20-year-old art student, left her flat (which was just three streets away from where Mary had once lived) to spend the night with a girlfriend in nearby Ann Arbor. Her flatmate accompanied her to the bus stop, where they waited for three-quarters of an hour. Then a red car pulled up and a young man, who was wearing an East Michigan University sweatshirt, asked if they wanted a lift. Joan was suspicious at first, but because were two other men in the back of the car she thought that she would be safe enough. As she climbed

John Norman Collins arriving for his trial, 1969.

into the car she told her flatmate that she would phone her when she arrived in Ann Arbor. She never called.

Five days later Joan's body was discovered rotting in a storm drain. Her blue mini-skirt and white slip had been pulled up, round her neck, and she had been raped and then stabbed to death. Although she had been dead for almost a week the pathologist noted that her body had been in the storm drain for less than a day.

Extensive inquiries revealed that Joan had been seen walking with a young man on the evening on which she went missing. The witnesses could not be certain, but thought that the youth was John Norman Collins, a fine football and baseball player, an honours student and a devout Catholic – in short, a regular, all-American boy. He had a troubled background, however: his father had abandoned his family soon after his son was born and his mother's second marriage had lasted for only a year; her third husband, who adopted John and his older brother and sister, was an alcoholic who beat his wife. Unbeknown to the police, Collins was suspected of stealing $40 from his fraternity house, as well as of other petty thefts. Although he lived directly opposite Joan, when the police interviewed him he claimed that he did not know her.

Ten months later a thirteen-year-old schoolboy saw a suspicious-looking shopping bag in a cemetery. After telling his mother about it she accompanied him to the spot where he had found it, there discovering a girl's body hidden under a yellow raincoat; her skirt had been pulled up and her tights rolled down. The corpse was that of the 23-year-old Jane Mixer, a law student who had been reported missing a few hours earlier. The man whom the press was now calling the 'Co-ed Killer' had struck again.

Four days after that the body of the sixteen-year-old Marilyn Skelton was found lying in a patch of undergrowth. She had been brutally beaten and a tree branch had been jammed into her vagina. The urges that were driving this sexually obsessed serial killer were plainly becoming more urgent, and the police feared that he would soon kill again. Sure enough, three weeks later the corpse of the thirteen-year-old Dawn Basom was discovered lying amongst some weeds. The youngest victim yet, she was wearing only a white blouse and a bra, which had been pushed up around her neck; the rest of her clothes had been strewn over a wide area. She had been strangled with a length of electric flex and her breasts had been repeatedly slashed.

On 9 June 1969 three teenage boys found the body of a girl in her twenties near a disused farmhouse. She had been shot in the head and repeatedly stabbed; her clothes were scattered around her. Pathologists established that she had been dead for less than a day. Although the use of a gun was new, the police were convinced that this killing was the work of the Co-ed Killer. The town was now in a state of panic; a $42,000 reward was offered for information leading to the killer's capture and the police were heavily criticised for not apprehending him. In their defence they argued that they had little to go on.

On 23 July 1969 the 18-year-old Karen Sue Beineman, another student, went missing. She had last been seen in a wig shop buying a $20 hairpiece. There were two foolish things that she had done in her life, she told the shop assistant – one was buying a wig and the other was accepting a lift on a motorbike from the stranger who was waiting for her outside. The assistant agreed that the latter was stupid and took a look out of the window at the young man on the motorbike. She had to admit, however, that he looked decent enough.

Four days later a doctor walking near his suburban home stumbled across Karen Sue's naked body, which was lying in a gully. She had been raped and her knickers had been stuffed into her vagina; somewhat strangely, there were hair clippings inside them. The police had already begun to suspect that the murderer returned to the spot where he had dumped each corpse on several occasions, even moving it if he had the chance. Before the news of her death was made public the police therefore replaced Karen Sue's mutilated body with a tailor's dummy and staked out the area. It rained heavily that night, which diminished the visibility, but shortly after midnight an officer nevertheless spotted a man running out of the gully. Although the policeman tried to summon help his radio had been soaked by the rain and failed to work. The man got clean away.

It was then that a young campus policeman put two and two together. The description of the young man on the motorbike that had been circulated reminded him of a member of his fraternity house who had dropped out of college after having been suspected of stealing. The young man's name was John Norman Collins, and he had already been interviewed by the police. The policeman then showed a photograph of Collins to both the shop assistant from the wig shop and the owner of the shop next door; both identified it as being a picture of the man on the motorbike. After that the policeman went to interview Collins himself, expecting a confession from him; none was forthcoming, however, and Collins even refused to take a lie-detector test. On the following night Collins was seen by his flatmate emerging from his room and carrying a box that was covered with a blanket. The flatmate caught a glimpse of its contents: a handbag, as well as some women's clothing and shoes.

Police Corporal David Leik had been on holiday with his family and had therefore missed the latest developments in the Co-ed-killer case. After they had returned home his wife had taken some washing to the laundry room in the basement and had noticed that the floor was covered in black spray paint. Only one person had been in the house while they were away: Leik's nephew, John Norman Collins, who had been letting himself in to feed their dog. But why would he paint the basement floor? After receiving an urgent phone call telling him to report to work Leik went to the police station where he was told, to his surprise and disbelief, that Collins was a prime suspect in the Co-ed-killer case.

That evening Leik scraped some of the black paint from the basement floor with a knife; underneath the paint were brown stains, which Leik thought could be blood. Within two hours lab technicians had identified the brown stains as being varnish that Leik had spilled when he had painted some window shutters. A more extensive examination of the basement floor, however, revealed what later proved to be nine tiny bloodstains. Even more significantly, forensic experts discovered some hair clippings lying on the floor next to the washing machine which were subsequently proved to match the clippings that had been found in the knickers that had been stuffed into Karen Sue Beineman's vagina.

Collins was arrested that afternoon. Although he was shaken – and even tearful – he refused to make a confession. A search of his room revealed nothing, his box of gruesome mementos already having been disposed of.

The police knew that Collins ran four motorbikes and funded his activities by means of petty theft. On closer examination, however, it was found that his background was even more disturbed than had first been thought. His sister had become pregnant at the age of 18 and had married the child's father. Although the marriage did not last, when Collins discovered her dating another man he lost control of his temper, beating the man unconscious and hitting his sister repeatedly while screaming that she was a tramp. He furthermore seemed unable to express his sexual feelings in any normal way, and when his girlfriend moved close to him while dancing he chastised her for inciting lustful feelings in him. Later, when his defence attorney was trying to ascertain how well Collins would stand up to cross-examination, he called Collins' mother (who had a new boyfriend, but had not remarried) a 'kept woman', whereupon Collins' usually calm demeanour dissolved into uncontrollable rage.

The police case against Collins was still flimsy, so they began to try to track down Andrew Manuel, Collins' former room-mate, who had committed a number of burglaries with him. Using false names, he and Collins had also once hired a caravan, which they had not returned after their trip – it had been left in Manuel's uncle's back yard in Salinas, California. At around that time the 17-year-old Roxie Ann Philips had vanished from Salinas after telling a friend that she had a date with a man called John, from Michigan, who was staying with a friend in a caravan. Two weeks after her disappearance her body was discovered in a ravine; she had been strangled and her corpse also bore all of the other trademarks of the Co-ed Killer.

Manuel was found in Phoenix, Arizona, and was charged with burglary and stealing the caravan. He knew nothing about the murders, he said, although he did admit to leaving Ypsilanti after he had heard that the police suspected Collins of being the Co-ed Killer. Manuel was sentenced to five years' probation.

Collins went to trial charged only with the murder of Karen Sue Beineman. The prosecution's case centred on the identification of Collins by the wig-shop sales assistant and the hair clippings that were found in Karen Sue's knickers. For his part, the defence counsel questioned the wig-shop assistant's eyesight and contended that the comparison of 61 hairs from the knickers and 59 from the basement floor was insufficient evidence with which to convict a man of murder.

After long deliberation the jury returned a unanimous verdict of guilty and Collins was sentenced to a recommended period of imprisonment of from 20 years to life.

21 ❖ Women are doing it for themselves

Aileen Wuornos never made any secret of the fact that she hated men. When she hung out, drinking and popping pills, in the Last Resort, a Hell's Angels' bar in Port Orange, Florida, she would curse all men and boast that she would get even with this rotten, masculine world. For their part, the Hell's Angels put up with her, regarding her as just another outcast – like them – and calling her 'Spiderwoman', on account of the black-leather outfits that she wore.

Wuornos certainly came from a tough background. Her first recollections were of her mother screaming while her alcoholic father administered another brutal beating; when she was five he abandoned his family. Her mother died when she was 14, and by the time that she was 19 she was all alone in the world, her father having died in prison after having been convicted for sex offences and her only brother having died of cancer. Wuornos then took to prostitution and armed robbery. Although she occasionally worked as a barmaid or cleaner, with her love of alcohol and drugs she could never hold down a job for long. More often than not she spent her time hitchhiking around the highways of Florida, sleeping on the beach or at the roadside.

The Last Resort was more of a home to her than anywhere else. She sometimes slept on the porch or in the so-called 'Japanese hanging gardens', from whose trees the Hell's Angels would hang the Japanese motorcycles that they despised. She was known to one and all as a foul-mouthed, ill-tempered drunk.

When Wuornos was 27 she fell in love with the 22-year-old Tyria Moore. It was a deeply romantic affair and Wuornos believed that Tyria would put an end to her loneliness, never abandoning her as all the men in her life had. She petted and pampered Tyria, stealing in order to lavish her with luxuries.

In September 1990 Wuornos stole a car for Tyria, but when the two women took it for a spin down a dirt road the car went out of control and they subsequently abandoned it. The pair had been spotted, however, and had been reported to the police. Their descriptions were entered into the Marion County police computer, which then linked the two women to six murders that had occurred in the area. The victims had all been men whose bodies had been dumped miles from their cars. Each had been shot exactly nine times and a condom wrapper was found on the back seat of each of their cars.

Shortly after the incident with the stolen car Tyria left Wuornos and fled. In January 1991 the police traced her to Pennsylvania, where they arrested her for car theft. Tyria then broke down and blamed everything on Wuornos, who, she said, had enticed Tyria into a life of crime, also murdering and robbing in order to buy expensive gifts for her.

Wuornos was sleeping on the porch of the Last Resort when she was apprehended. At first she thought that she was being arrested for a five-year-old firearms' charge, but when the police dropped the names of the murder victims into the conversation she freely admitted having killed them.

She explained that she had usually been hitchhiking when her victim stopped his car to offer her a lift, although she had sometimes pretended that her car had broken down and that she needed help. Either way, once she had got into the car she had offered to have sex with the man and had then asked him to drive to a deserted spot. After having had sex she had then exacted her vengeance on all mankind, killing her victim and robbing him of his money, as well as his jewellery.

Even the hardened Hell's Angels were shocked that they had been harbouring a man-slayer in their midst. 'It's scary, man', said Cannonball, the barman at the Last Resort. 'Every one of those guys could have been one of them [Hell's Angels], and we would never have known where it was coming from . . . Mind you, I sorta think she would not have gone for a biker . . . we were her only folks . . . She was a lost soul, like most of us.'

22 ❖ The Night Stalker

On the night of 28 June 1984 the mutilated body of the seventy-nine-year-old Jennie Vincow was found lying spread-eagled on the bed of her one-bedroom flat in the Eagle Rock district of Los Angeles. She had been raped and her throat had been slashed so savagely that she had almost been decapitated; there was blood on the walls of the bedroom and bathroom and her flat had been ransacked. In violent LA, however, it was regarded as just another murder.

Nine months later the killer struck again. Maria Hernandez had just parked her car in her garage in the Rosemeade suburb of Los Angeles and was walking towards her flat when she heard footsteps behind her. On turning around she was confronted by a man holding a gun. Although he aimed the gun at her and pulled the trigger, the bullet miraculously ricocheted off her car keys and dealt her only a glancing blow. Even so, the impact was enough to knock her to the ground, whereupon the gunman stepped over her, giving her a vicious kicking as he did so, and made his way into her flat. Maria then heard a gunshot from inside the flat and staggered to her feet, only to come face to face with the gunman as he ran from the building. 'Please don't shoot me again', she begged, and after freezing momentarily the gunman took to his heels. Inside the flat Maria found her boyfriend, the 34-year-old, Hawaiian-born traffic-manager Dayle Okazaki, lying dead on the kitchen floor. He had been shot through the head.

There was only one clue to the murder: Maria told the police that the gunman was wearing a baseball cap which had the AC/DC logo embroidered on the front of it. AC/DC, an Australian heavy-metal rock band, had recently released an album called Highway to Hell, on which a track called 'Night Prowler' appeared. 'Night Prowler' was the nom d'assassin , or assassin's name, that Richard Ramirez, the killer responsible for the deaths of Jennie Vincow and Dayle Okazaki, preferred, and he therefore became annoyed when the newspapers insisted on calling him the 'Night Stalker'. Despite having killed Okazaki, his lust for blood was still not satisfied that night, and less than an hour later, when he was on his way home, Ramirez pulled the 30-year-old Tsai Lian Yu, a Taiwanese law student, from her car and shot her repeatedly. She died before the ambulance arrived.

Ten days later Ramirez entered the home of Vincent and Maxine Zazzara, which was half a mile from the San Gabriel motorway. Maxine was a successful lawyer, while Vincent had just fulfilled his lifetime's ambition to open his own pizzeria. Both of them were shot at point-blank range, and Maxine's naked body was mutilated after her death, Ramirez stabbing her repeatedly (the wounds making a pattern resembling a large, ragged 'T') and also gouging out her eyes. The bodies were found by their son, Peter, when he called in at the house on the following day.

On 14 May 1985 Ramirez broke into the home of William and Lillie Doi, shooting the 66-year-old William in the head as he lay sleeping. His wife, the 63-year-old Lillie, who was lying in bed next to William, was beaten repeatedly around the head until she told the intruder where their valuables were hidden. After that Ramirez handcuffed her and ransacked the house before returning to rape her.

A fortnight later Carol Kyle was awoken in her Burbank flat by a torch shining into her eyes, a man then pointing a gun at her and dragging her out of bed. Carol's terrified 12-year-old son was handcuffed and locked into a cupboard in the next room before his mother was raped. Despite her ordeal Carol was compassionate towards Ramirez, saying 'You must have had a very unhappy life to have done this to me'. Ramirez, however, shrugged off her compassion, replying 'I don't know why I'm letting you live. 'I've killed people before.' He then ransacked the flat looking for valuables. Satisfied with the jewellery that he had found, he finally went away, sparing both Carol and her son's lives.

At around the same time two elderly women, the 83-year-old Mabel Bell and her 80-year-old sister, Florence Long, an invalid, were attacked in their home in the LA suburb of Monrovia. On 1 June 1985 Carlos Venezuela, a gardener who did chores for the sisters, found Florence lying on her bed in a coma; there was a huge wound over her ear and a blood-stained hammer had been left on the dressing table. The barely conscious Mabel was found lying in a pool of her own blood on her bedroom floor. Both women had been beaten with the hammer, as well as having been cut and tortured – there were even signs that Ramirez had tried to rape the older sister, Mabel. The police concluded that the sisters had been attacked two days earlier.

As on previous occasions the culprit had ransacked the house; this time, however, some clues to the attacker's identity were discovered. Along with the hammer, a half-eaten banana was found on the dining table. He had also left what was soon to become his trademark: an inverted pentagram (the encircled, five-pointed star that is used in witchcraft). One was scrawled in lipstick on Mabel's thigh, while another was drawn on Florence's bedroom wall. Tragically, Mabel died six weeks after the attack, but Florence eventually regained consciousness and survived.

Now the Night Stalker's onslaught began in earnest. On the night of 27 June 1985 Ramirez slashed the throat of the 32-year-old Patty Elaine Higgins in her home in Arcadia. The same fate befell Mary Louise Cannon five days afterwards. Three days later, again in Arcadia, Ramirez savagely beat the 16-year-old Whitney Bennett with a crowbar; she survived. On 7 July Ramirez once again turned his attention to Monterey Park (where he had attacked Tsai Lian Yu and the Dois), the 61-year-old Joyce Lucille Nelson being found beaten to death in her home, while the 63 year-old Sophie Dickmann had been raped and robbed in her flat.

On 20 July Ramirez murdered the 66-year-old Maxson Kneiding and his 64-year-old wife, Lela, in their Glendale home before going on to kill

The 'Night Stalker'
Richard Ramirez.

the 32-year-old Chainarong Khovananth at his house in Sun Valley. After shooting Chainarong as he lay asleep in his bed Ramirez raped and beat up his 29-year-old wife, Somkid. He furthermore forced Somkid to perform oral sex on him and stole $30,000 in cash and jewellery, before raping her eight-year-old son also making her swear in Satan's name that she would not cry out.

Although the police had long ago concluded that they had a serial killer on their hands, their primary problem was that he followed no set *modus operandi*. He killed people with guns, hammers and knives; he raped both children and women – young and old – orally, anally and vaginally; sometimes he mutilated the bodies of his victims after death, but sometimes he didn't.

Some patterns in the Night Stalker's attacks were nevertheless emerging. The killer stalked quiet suburbs away from the city's main centres of crime, where home-owners were less security-conscious, for instance. He also tended to pick houses that were painted in beige or pastel yellow and that were usually close to a motorway. He made his entry through an open window or an unlocked door. Although burglary was clearly one of his motives, he also seemed to enjoy rape and sheer brutality. Pentagrams and other satanic symbols were furthermore commonly left by the killer.

On the night of 5 August 1985 Virginia Petersen, a postal worker, was woken by the sound of an intruder. Sitting up in bed, she cried out 'Who are you? What do you want?', whereupon the burglar laughed and shot her in the face. The bullet entered her cheek, just below her eye, and exited through the back of her head (miraculously, she survived). Her husband, Christopher, who was lying beside her, was woken by the shot and leapt to his wife's defence, which earned him a bullet in the temple. Christopher, who worked as a lorry driver, was, however, a tough guy whom it would have taken more than one small-calibre bullet to subdue. Diving out of bed, he chased his attacker. The intruder, who was not prepared for this, panicked and ran.

Like his wife, Christopher Petersen survived the ordeal, although he suffered from partial memory loss thereafter and had to live with a bullet lodged in his brain. For the first time, however, the Night Stalker had been put to flight, although this did not end his violent rampage. Three days later he shot a 35-year-old Asian man and beat up and raped his 28-year-old wife. In common with Somkid Khovananth she was forced to swear by Satan that she would not cry out, but this time he did not molest the couple's two young children, apart from tying up their three-year-old son, Amez.

By this time the public state of panic had reached fever pitch in Los Angeles. In the affluent suburbs locksmiths and burglar-alarm outfits were doing a roaring trade, while gun shops quickly sold out of their stock and local residents set up neighbourhood-watch committees. It was now that Ramirez took a holiday and travelled north to San Francisco, where, on the night of 17 August 1985, he shot both the 66-year-old Asian accountant Peter Pan and his 64-year-old wife, Barbara, through the heads in their home in the suburb of Lake Merced. Before leaving the scene of the crime Ramirez drew an inverted pentagram in lipstick on the bedroom wall, underneath it writing 'Jack the Knife'. At first the police thought that the Pans' murders were copycat killings, until they discovered that the bullets that had killed the couple matched the small-calibre rounds that had been used in the Los Angeles murders.

A week later Ramirez travelled to the small town of Mission Viego, south of Los Angeles, where he shot William Carns, a 29-year-old computer engineer, three times in the head before raping his fiancée, Inez Erickson (also 29), twice and ordering her to say 'I love Satan'. 'You know who I am, don't you?' Ramirez taunted. 'I'm the one they're writing about in the newspapers and on TV.' (William Carns survived the shooting, but suffered permanent brain damage. The couple never married.)

Inez had managed to observe Ramirez's rusty, old, orange Toyota leaving the house. James Romero III, a sharp-eyed youth, had also noticed the orange Toyota as it cruised the area and had noted down its licence-plate number. The car would prove to be the vital clue that put an end to the reign of the Night Stalker. After the police had circulated a description of it it was found in a car park in LA's Rampart suburb two days later.

Forensic scientists used a radical new technique when examining the car: they put a dab of Superglue on a saucer and sealed the doors and windows before placing the saucer in the car, the theory being that the fumes from the Superglue would react with the moisture contained in any fingerprints in the car and would then turn them white. The interior of the car was also scanned using a laser beam, which would be able to pick up any fingerprints on the car, including those that the culprit had tried to wipe off. The scan yielded one fingerprint, which a computer matched to a fingerprint belonging the twenty-five-year-old Ramirez, who had been arrested on three previous occasions in El Paso for marijuana possession.

Richard Ramirez,
arriving at the court
for his trial.

Soon afterwards Ramirez's photograph was on the front page of every newspaper in California.

Ramirez was quite unaware of these developments when he stepped off a Greyhound bus at Los Angeles' main bus station. He had been in Phoenix, Arizona, where he had obtained some cocaine, and was now on a high: he had killed 13 people so far and felt good about it – surely, he reasoned, he must be Satan's favourite son.

On going into a shop to buy a Pepsi he saw his face splashed across the Spanish language paper *La Opinion* that was lying on the counter by the till. He was also recognised by the cashier, as well as by other customers in the shop, causing him to make a run for it. Out on the street someone cried 'It's the Night Stalker' and Ramirez soon heard the wail of police sirens behind him. He knocked on a door, and when Bonnie Navarro opened it he shouted 'Help me' in Spanish. She slammed the door in his face, however. Ramirez tried to pull a woman from her car in the next street, but some bystanders rushed to her rescue. He then jumped over a fence into the garden where Luis Munoz was cooking a barbecue and was hit with Munoz's tongs. In the next garden he was prevented from stealing a red, 1966 Mustang by the 56-year-old Faustin Pinon, who had been working on the car's transmission and now grabbed him in a headlock. Ramirez broke free, but José Burgoin, a 55-year-old construction worker who had heard Pinon's shouts from across the street, picked up a steel rod and hit Ramirez with it. Although Ramirez stumbled away Burgoin soon caught up with him and clubbed him to the ground.

Deputy Sheriff Andres Ramirez pulled up in his patrol car in the nick of time, as far as Ramirez was concerned. 'Save me!' yelled the Night Stalker, commenting as his namesake handcuffed him 'Thank God you came. I am the one you want. Save me before they kill me'. Only the arrival of further police patrol cars stopped the angry mob from taking the law into their own hands, and even outside the police station a crowd soon gathered calling for him to be lynched.

Ramirez showed no contrition for his crimes, explaining to the police

I love to kill people. I love watching them die. I would shoot them in the head and they would wiggle and squirm all over the place, and then just stop. Or I would cut them with a knife and watch their faces turn real white. I love all that blood. I told one lady one time to give me all her money. She said no. So I cut her and pulled her eyes out.

In court he made satanic signs and even appeared with the inverted pentagram scratched into his palm. He told the judge 'You maggots make me sick. Hypocrites one and all. You don't understand me. You are not expected to. You are not capable of it. I am beyond your experience. I am beyond good and evil'.

Ramirez was found guilty of 63 crimes, including 13 murders. He was sentenced to 12 death penalties and over 100 years' imprisonment. When he was on death row many women wrote to him, sending provocative pictures, pledging undying love and even proposing marriage. When Ramirez accepted the proposal of Christine Lee, a divorcée, over that of the nude model Kelly Marquez it made headlines. Christine, a mother of two, bombarded Ramirez with pin-up-style pictures of herself and visited him over 150 times. She was undaunted by the fact that her husband-to-be was a serial killer: 'We really love each other and that's all that matters', she said. 'From the moment I saw him in prison I knew he was special. I couldn't believe he was the evil monster people were calling him. He's always been sweet and kind to me.'

23 ❖ Leonard Lake and Charles Ng

When a young Chinese man took a vice from a shop without paying for it the sales assistant ran to find a policeman. The officer followed the man to his car, who dumped the vice in the boot before running off when he spotted the policeman. Although the police officer gave chase the youth was too fast for him, and when he returned to the car he found a bald, bearded man standing next to it. The man explained that it had all been a mistake: he had now paid for the vice, he explained, and showed the officer the receipt. The policeman was suspicious, however, and examined the car, finding a holdall in the boot containing a .22 pistol, as well as a silencer. (Although it is legal to carry a handgun in the USA adding a silencer is against the law and usually indicates that the gun is likely to be used for some illegal purpose.)

The bearded man's Californian driving licence said that he was called Robin Scott Stapley. He hardly knew the youth who had run away, he told the policeman, but had been about to hire him for a job. Despite his explanation the officer took him to the police station for questioning. Once there the man asked for – and received – paper, a pencil and a glass of water. He then scribbled a note to his wife on the paper, which read 'Cricket, I love you. Please forgive me. I forgive you. Please tell Mama, Fern and Patty I'm sorry'. After that he swallowed a cyanide capsule, washing it down with the water. Within seconds he was dead.

The police subsequently discovered that the dead man was not Robin Scott Stapley, who had gone missing five months earlier. A few weeks after his disappearance, however, his camper van, which was being driven by a young Chinese man, had collided with a lorry. Although the young man had begged the lorry driver not to report the accident the latter was driving a company vehicle and therefore had no option but to do so.

It later transpired that the car that the bearded man had driven was registered to a Paul Cosner. When questioned, Cosner's girlfriend said that he had told her that he was selling it to a weird-looking man who had said that he would pay cash for it. Cosner had never returned after he had driven off to deliver the car.

When forensic scientists examined the car they found two bullet holes in the front seat and two spent rounds lodged in the upholstery; there were also bloodstains – human bloodstains – in the car. In the glove compartment they discovered some papers belonging to a Charles Gunnar, of Wilseyville, Calavers County, which was 150 miles (241 kilometres) north of San Francisco.

A call to Wilseyville's sheriff revealed that the Calavers County police already had their eye on Gunnar, as well as his young friend, a Chinese man named Charles Ng. They were suspected of handling stolen goods – videos, television sets, furniture and other household items – and had been selling furniture belonging to Brenda O'Connor and Lonnie Bond. Gunnar had explained to the police that the couple had moved to Los Angeles with their baby and had given Gunnar the furniture in settlement of a debt. There had furthermore been another mysterious disappearance in the area: a young couple had vanished from a camp site at the nearby Schaad Lake, leaving behind their tent, as well as a coffee pot sitting on the stove.

Following a computer check the dead man's fingerprints revealed that his real name was Leonard Lake. Lake had been charged with grand larceny and burglary in Mendocino County and had then jumped bail. It also seemed that he was linked with a number of other disappearances, including that of his younger brother, Donald, who had gone missing two years before, after setting off to visit Lake at a survivalist camp in Humboldt County. Charles Gunnar, the man whose identity Lake was using, had disappeared earlier that year after having acted as best man at Lake's wedding.

The trail inexorably led to the small ranch on Blue Mountain Road where Gunnar – that is, Lake – and Ng lived, and a team of policemen from San Francisco consequently visited it. Set within three acres of wooded grounds, the ranch was an ordinary-looking, two-bedroomed bungalow. Inside, however, it was far from ordinary, for the master bedroom was fitted out like a medieval torture chamber: there were hooks in the ceiling and walls, as well as boxes full of chains and shackles that could be used to immobilise someone who was lying on the bed. There was also a wardrobe full of flimsy nightgowns and sexy underwear, along with expensive video gear. The serial numbers confirmed that the video equipment belonged to Harvey and Deborah Dubbs; following the disappearance of the couple and their 16-month-old baby it had last been seen being carried from their flat by a Chinese removal man.

Lake had been a dedicated survivalist who had built a nuclear-fallout shelter in the garden. Inside the shelter the police found a storeroom containing food, water, candles and guns. Set into the floor was a sinister-looking trapdoor which led to another chamber. This subterranean room was also hung with hooks and chains, and the walls were covered with photographs of frightened-looking girls posing in their underwear. It was clear that all of the pictures had been taken in that very room. Next to this chamber was a tiny cell with a one-way mirror in its wall, which meant that anyone being held inside the room could be subjected to twenty-four-hour surveillance.

The bomb-shelter basement also contained filing cabinets, in which the police found more pictures, as well as a huge collection of video tapes. The first video cassette that they viewed was marked 'Kathy/Brenda'. It began by showing a terrified girl, who was handcuffed to a chair, being menaced by Charles Ng. Then Lake entered the frame and removed the girl's handcuffs, instead shackling her feet, after that ordering the girl to strip. She undressed reluctantly – she could clearly hardly bring herself to remove her knickers, but was forced to do so. 'You'll wash for us,' announced Lake, 'clean for us, fuck for us.' Later she was shown naked, being strapped to the bed and being told by Lake that her boyfriend was dead.

'Brenda' – who was later identified as Brenda O'Connor – also appeared in the video. Shown handcuffed to a chair, she entered into a chilling dialogue with Lake while Ng slowly cut her clothes off her. First she asked where the baby was, to which Lake replied that it had been placed with a family in Fresno. 'Why do you guys do this?' she then asked. 'We don't like you. Do you want me to put it in writing?' was the response. 'Don't cut my bra off', she pleaded, to which Lake replied 'Nothing is yours now'. 'Give my baby back to me. I'll do anything you want' Brenda begged, only to be told 'You're going to do anything we want anyway'.

Other videos showed women being shackled, raped, tortured and murdered. They featured all of the missing women of whom the police already knew and others that they recognised from missing-person's reports, along with over 25 more whom they never identified. It was plain that Leonard Lake and Charles Ng had been making 'snuff' movies for two years, for each of the tapes, which were clearly marked 'M Ladies' ('Murdered Ladies'), ended with the death of its reluctant female star.

The police also discovered a bloodstained chainsaw which had been used to cut up the bodies of Lake and Ng's victims; the body parts had then been incinerated and the bones scattered across the hillside at the back of the house. Other bodies were found intact, while in a narrow trench that ran across the garden the police discovered a number of corpses that were too decomposed to identify. Among the latter were the bodies of a man, woman and child, which could have belonged to Bond, O'Connor and their baby, the Dubbs family or, indeed, to any other man, woman and child who had had the misfortune to fall into Lake's gruesome trap. Two weeks of digging produced a total of nine entire bodies and 40 lbs (18 kilogrammes) of human bones. Identifying the corpses themselves was well-nigh impossible, but driver's licences and other papers confirmed that Robert Stapley, Paul Cosner and the couple from the camping site were all among the victims.

The police found Lake's diary in the files in the basement which indicated that his grisly career of murder had begun long before he moved into the ranch on Blue Mountain Road. Born in San Francisco in 1946, Leonard Lake had been rejected by both parents, being brought up with military discipline by his grandparents. Leonard's brother, Donald, was a sadist who tortured animals and tried to rape his sisters. Leonard protected his sisters, but at a price: they had to perform certain sexual favours for him. He also took nude pictures of his sisters and cousins, later also making pornographic films featuring his wife, 'Cricket' Balazs.

Although he was not the front-line hero that he subsequently claimed to have been, the Vietnam War changed him. Despite disguising his feelings by teaching, becoming a volunteer fire-fighter and doing charity work, he became deeply pessimistic. This pessimism eventually led him to survivalism, as well as to a life financed by petty theft and burglary.

Then Lake's marriage broke up, although his wife still acted as a fence for the credit cards and other items that he stole. After that the idea slowly began to grow in his mind that women were the cause of all his problems. He eventually found the release that he sought by killing his troublesome brother, Donald, whereupon he embarked upon a murder spree. (The police discovered a crude map of California that he had marked with crosses labelled 'buried treasure'. The crosses were believed to represent the graves of his early victims, but the map was too inaccurate for the police to investigate this theory.)

While staying in the isolated village of Miranda, in northern California, Lake came up with the idea for 'Operation Miranda': he planned to stockpile weapons, food, water and kidnapped women in preparation for the nuclear holocaust that he believed was nigh. 'The perfect woman is totally controlled,' he wrote, 'a woman who does exactly what she is told to and nothing else. There is no sexual problem with a submissive woman. There are no frustrations – only pleasure and contentment.' He then put Operation Miranda into practice with the help of Charles Ng.

Ng, the son of a wealthy Hong Kong family, was born in 1961. He was educated at a private school in North Yorkshire before being expelled for theft, therefore completing his studies in San Francisco. At the age of 18 he was involved in a hit-and-run accident and joined the US Marines in order to escape going to jail. Having been posted to Hawaii, his lifelong kleptomania then reasserted itself and he was arrested for the theft of ammunition and weapons worth over $11,000. After escaping from jail in Hawaii Ng returned to San Francisco where he met Lake, whom he looked up to. Together they embarked upon a full-time life of crime, later being arrested in Mendocino County for burglary. Ng was imprisoned (also serving time for his earlier theft in Hawaii) and spent some of his sentence at Fort Leavenworth. When he was paroled he joined Lake at the ranch and helped him to transform his paranoid fantasies into brutal reality.

Lake's journal describes how his sex slaves were obtained. Having invited unwitting couples and families to the ranch for dinner the men and children would be murdered straightaway. The women would then be stripped, shackled, sexually abused, humiliated and forced to perform menial chores around the house. Kept in a Spartan cell, they would also be used as the unwilling subjects of sexually sadistic videos. When a woman showed any sign of rebellion against her submissive role – or when her tormentor grew tired of her – Lake and Ng would kill her and film her death.

Psychological studies of Lake showed that he was in the final phase of the serial-murder syndrome when he was arrested: sated with blood, he felt that he had reached the end of a cul de-sac from which there was no way back. Having caused untold misery to others he was now bringing misery upon himself – the only way out was suicide.

Ng escaped to Canada, where he shot a security guard after having been caught shoplifting. He served a four-and-a-half-year sentence for armed robbery before being extradited to California to face charges of mass murder.

24 ✦ Son of Sam

At 1am on 29 July 1976 the 19-year-old Jody Valente and her friend, the 18-year-old Donna Lauria, were sitting in Jody's car outside Donna's home in the Bronx area of New York. It was a hot summer night and they were discussing their boyfriends. Finally Donna said goodnight and opened the car door to get out. As the door opened a young man who was standing a few feet away reached into the brown-paper bag that he was holding, pulled out a gun and dropped into crouching position. 'What does this guy want?' asked the alarmed Donna. The words had just left her mouth when a bullet struck her in the side of the neck, a second bullet smashing the window in the door and a third shattering her elbow as she raised her hands to protect her face. Fatally wounded, she tumbled out of the car on to the pavement, whereupon her killer shot Jody in the thigh, causing her to fall forward on to the car's horn. As the horn blared the killer made off.

Donna's father, Mike Lauria, who was about to take the dog for a walk, was halfway down the stairs of the family house when he heard the shots. Running outside, he found Jody conscious, though hysterical, and Donna lying collapsed on the ground. In the ambulance he entreated his daughter not to die, but it was too late: when Donna reached the hospital she was pronounced DOA – dead on arrival. Although Jody was treated for hysteria she nevertheless managed to give the police a good description of their assailant: he was a young, white male, about 30 years old, clean shaven, with dark, curly hair. He was not a rejected boyfriend (as the police at first speculated), Jody said – in fact, she had never seen him before. The only other clue to his identity was a yellow car that had been parked near Jody's, but it had gone by the time that the police arrived, and in any case New York is full of yellow cars.

(The car in question actually belonged to David Berkowitz. In the days leading up to the murder he had been looking for a job, but had spent the nights, he later said, 'Looking for a victim, waiting for a signal'. Demonic voices inside his head had told him to kill, he explained. 'I never thought I could kill her', he said of Donna Lauria. 'I just fired the gun, you know, at the car, at the windshield. I never knew she was shot.')

The northern Bronx, where the Laurias lived, is a predominantly Italian area, and the police therefore immediately suspected Mafia involvement in Donna's murder. However, the Mafia are usually scrupulous when it comes to contract killings: women and children are out of bounds. Besides, ballistics tests showed that the murder weapon was a Charter Arms, five-round, .44 Bulldog revolver, which had a powerful recoil and was grossly inaccurate at distances of more than a few yards – hardly a hit man's weapon.

On the other side of the East river from the Bronx lies the Queens area, a comfortable, middle-class district. Twelve weeks after the murder of Donna Lauria the eighteen-year-old Rosemary Keenan, a student at Queens College, went to a bar in the Flushing area of Queens where she met the twenty-year-old record salesman Carl Denaro, who was enjoying his last days of freedom before joining the United States Air Force. After having left the bar together in her red Volkswagen, Rosemary and Carl had parked and were talking when a man crept up on them. He may have thought that Carl, who was sitting in the passenger seat, was a woman on account of his long, brown hair. He pulled out the .44 Bulldog handgun that was tucked into his belt and fired through the passenger window five times. His shooting was wildly inaccurate, however, and only one bullet found its mark: as Carl threw himself forward to protect himself from the flying glass the bullet clipped the back of his head, knocking away part of his skull, but not damaging his brain. Although Carl was lucky, in that he recovered completely after a two-month stay in hospital, the metal plate that the surgeons had had to insert into his head ended his air-force career before it had even begun.

On the evening of 27 November 1976 two schoolgirls – the 16-year-old Donna DeMasi and her 18-year-old friend, Joanne Lomino – were sitting talking on the front porch of Joanne's home on 262nd Street in Queens. At the end of their conversation Joanne stood up and reached into her handbag for her front-door keys. It was then that the two girls noticed a man walking down the other side of the road. He was acting rather suspiciously: when he saw them he suddenly changed direction. After crossing the street at the corner he came over to them as if he was about to ask for directions, but instead he pulled a gun from his waistband and began firing at them. The two girls ran towards the front door, Joanne frantically searching for her keys. The first bullet hit her in the back; the second lodged in Donna's neck. They stumbled into the bushes as the gunman fired his remaining three shots, all of which missed. He then ran off down 262nd Street and was spotted by a neighbour still holding his gun.

The two wounded girls were rushed to Long Island Jewish Hospital, where Donna was found not to be badly injured (she made a full recovery after three weeks). But Joanne was not so lucky: the bullet had smashed her spinal cord, paralysing her from the waist down, and she would spend the rest of her life in a wheelchair. The neighbour who had spotted the gunman making his escape gave the police a description of him. One key feature that he mentioned was the young man's dark, curly hair, which was strange because the girls themselves said that he had had long, fair hair. Despite the discrepancy, the description nevertheless linked the shootings of Donna DeMasi and Joanne Lomino to the man who had killed Donna Lauria and wounded Jody Valente.

On 29 January 1977 the 30-year-old John Diel and his 26-year old girl-friend, Christine Freund, went to see the film *Rocky* in Queens. Afterwards they had dinner at the Wine Gallery, in Austin Street, where they discussed their forthcoming engagement. Soon after midnight the couple walked along several streets to where their Pontiac Firebird was parked. It was cold outside, and once inside the car their breath fogged up the windows. Although they were eager to get home they stopped for a moment to kiss, John then turning the key in the ignition. Before he could pull away, how-ever, he heard the blast of gunfire, whereupon the passenger window shat-tered and Christine slumped forward, bleeding. She died a few hours later in St John's Hospital of bullet wounds to her right temple and neck. She had never even seen her killer, but he had seen her – and so had the demon within him: Berkowitz later claimed that he had heard a voice command-ing him to 'Get her, get her and kill her'. After firing three shots and real-ising that he had hit her he felt calm again. 'The voices stopped', he said. 'I satisfied the demon's lust.'

After the murder of Christine Freund Berkowitz surrendered himself completely to his impulse to kill. After all, he reasoned, he was being rewarded by all of the publicity that he was generating: 'I had finally con-vinced myself that I was good to do it, and that the public wanted me to kill', Berkowitz later explained.

However, the New York Police Department (NYPD) was on his trail. Its ballistics lab had ascertained that the bullet that had killed Christine Freund had come from a .44 Bulldog handgun, which tied it to the murder

of Donna Lauria and the shootings of Jody Valente, Carl Denaro, Donna
DeMasi and Joanne Lomino. Yet apart from the mention of his dark, curly
hair by Jody Valente and the neighbour in the DeMasi-Lomino case the
descriptions of the gunman varied so widely that no one in the NYPD had
concluded that the shootings were the work of a single individual.

Six weeks later, on 8 March 1977, Virginia Voskerichian, a 19-year-old
Armenian student, left Columbia University in Manhattan and set off for
her home in Forest Hills, Queens. At around 7.30pm she was nearing her
home on Exeter Street when a young man approached her on the pavement. She politely stepped aside, whereupon he pulled out a gun, shoved
it into her face and fired. Although Virginia raised her books in a vain
attempt to protect herself, the bullet tore through them, entering her body
through her upper lip, smashing several teeth and lodging in her brain. She
collapsed in the bushes at the side of the street and died instantly. A witness saw a young man running away and later estimated that he was aged
about 18 and was 5 feet 8 inches (1.75 metres) tall. No dark, curly hair was
noted, however, because the murderer was wearing a Balaclava.

The killer was almost caught that very day. Minutes after Virginia's
murder the police put out a 'Code .44' alert and two police officers were
assigned to the southern end of the Bronx with orders to stop any car that
contained a lone white man. Berkowitz had driven up to the checkpoint
with his loaded .44 Bulldog lying in full view on the passenger seat of his
Ford Galaxie and was third in line when the police called off the search. He
could not believe his luck as he watched the officers walk away.

It was quickly proved that the bullet that had killed Virginia
Voskerichian was of a .44 calibre and that the riflings on it matched the
marks on the bullet that had killed Christine Freund six weeks before and
just a few miles away. Two days later it was established that the same gun
was responsible for the shooting of seven people.

On the afternoon of 10 March 1977 a press conference was held at One
Police Plaza, the 13-storey, red-stone building that is New York's equiva-
lent of London's New Scotland Yard. As Police Commissioner Mike Codd
stood with some trepidation before New York's hard-bitten crime reporters
and started to read his carefully prepared statement he had an inkling that
he was about to unleash a wave of hysteria that would engulf the city. He
began by saying that the murder of Donna Lauria nine months before was
linked to the killing of Virginia Voskerichian a mere two days earlier. In
both cases, he stated, the killer had used a .44 Bulldog revolver and the

same gun had also been used in three other incidents. Worse still, in terms of securing his arrest, the killer apparently chose his victims completely at random. As the reporters pushed for further information Codd revealed that the police were looking for a Caucasian male, about 6 feet (1.83 metres) tall, of medium build, 25 to 30 years old, with dark hair. The .44 killer made the headlines the next day.

The policeman in charge of the investigation was Deputy Inspector Timothy J Dowd. Working under Dowd was Chief of Detectives John Keenan, who had a special reason for wanting to capture the .44 killer: his daughter was the young woman who had been in the car with Carl Denaro when he was shot in the head. 'I know he was aiming for her', Keenan subsequently said. 'So let's just say I put a little more than I had to into this case.'

The police realised that their chances of catching a lone, seemingly motiveless, murderer on the streets of New York were remote, so they asked for the help of every New Yorker. As a result tip-offs jammed the police switchboards and Dowd and his detectives had to follow up 250 to 300 leads a day. Berkowitz took pity on the police, however, and wrote them a letter, although dropping it into a letter box and letting the postal service deliver it was too mundane an option for him.

On the night of 16 April 1977 another young couple went to a cinema in New York. After the 18-year-old Valentina Suriani and her boyfriend, the 20-year-old Alexander Esau, had seen the film they went on to a party. At around 3am they were sitting in a borrowed Mercury Montego that was parked outside Valentina's block of flats in the northern Bronx, only three streets away from where Donna Lauria had been killed. Valentina was sitting on Alexander's lap, her legs stretched across the passenger seat, enjoying a prolonged series of goodnight kisses when a hail of bullets suddenly shattered the passenger window. Two hit Valentina's head, killing her instantly. Another two struck Alexander on the top of the head as he dived across the seat towards the passenger door; he died two hours later.

When the police arrived they found a white envelope lying in the middle of the road next to the car. It was addressed to Captain Joe Borelli, Dowd's second-in-command. The letter was written in capitals, was full of spelling mistakes and appeared to be the work of a madman. The writer claimed that he had been ordered to kill by his father, who was a vampire. His father's name, the writer said, was Sam (hence the killer's subsequent macabre sobriquet 'Son of Sam'). In the letter he professed to love the people of Queens, but nevertheless stated his intention of killing more of them – particularly the women (he spelt the word as if it rhymed with 'demon'). The writer signed off with a farewell message:

I SAY GOODBYE AND GOODNIGHT. POLICE: LET ME HAUNT YOU WITH THESE WORDS; I'LL BE BACK! I'LL BE BACK! TO BE INTERPRETED AS – BANG BANG, BANG, BANG, BANG, BANG – UGH!! YOURS IN MURDER, MR MONSTER.

By the time that the letter reached the police labs eight policemen had handled it and only tiny traces of the writer's fingerprints remained. He furthermore appeared to have held the letter by the tips of his fingers and there was therefore not enough of a print on the paper with which to identify the sender. Although the police consequently kept the existence of the letter a secret they showed a copy of it to the celebrated New York columnist Jimmy Breslin, who dropped hints about it in his column in the New York Daily News.

On 1 June 1977 Breslin himself received a letter from the .44 killer. It had been posted two days earlier, in Englewood, New Jersey, just across the George Washington Bridge from Manhattan. The New York Daily News, which was then the biggest-selling newspaper in the USA, held back publication of the full letter for six days as speculation about it, and therefore also the newspaper's circulation, mounted. On 3 June the New York Daily News ran the front-page headline: 'THE .44 CALIBER KILLER – NEW NOTE: CAN'T STOP KILLING'. On the next day the headline read: '.44 KILLER: I AM NOT ASLEEP'. In the Sunday edition it said: 'BRESLIN TO .44 KILLER: GIVE UP! IT'S THE ONLY WAY OUT'. This edition had sold out within an hour of going on sale, so the presses kept rolling and by the end of the day the paper had sold 1,116,000 copies – a record that was beaten only on the day on which Berkowitz was arrested.

The paper's editors assumed that public interest in the story had peaked on Sunday and therefore reproduced the letter in full in the Monday edition. Like the first letter that had been received by Borelli it was written entirely in capital letters and showed the same uncertain grasp of basic spelling. The letter was something of an anti-climax to the newspaper's readers as it was as rambling and incoherent as the letter that the .44 killer had sent to the police.

The writer signed off with the words:

NOT KNOWING WHAT THE FUTURE HOLDS I SHALL SAY FAREWELL AND I WILL SEE YOU AT THE NEXT JOB, OR SHOULD I SAY YOU WILL SEE MY HANDIWORK AT THE NEXT JOB? REMEMBER MS LAURIA.

THANK YOU. IN THEIR BLOOD AND FROM THE GUTTER, 'SAM'S
CREATION' .44.

Then there was a long postscript:

HERE ARE SOME NAMES TO HELP YOU ALONG. FORWARD THEM TO
THE INSPECTOR FOR USE BY THE NCIC: 'THE DUKE OF DEATH'. 'THE
WICKED KING WICKER', 'THE TWENTY TWO DISCIPLES OF HELL',
JOHN 'WHEATIES' – RAPIST AND SUFFOCATER OF YOUNG GIRLS.
    PS: J B PLEASE INFORM ALL THE DETECTIVES WORKING THE
SLAYINGS TO REMAIN.

At the police's request this last page was withheld from publication
because the police said that they did not want the existence of the NCIC –
the National Crime Information Center – to become public knowledge. Yet
the .44 killer certainly knew about it. Perhaps the real reason for their
request lay in the satanic undertones of the list of pseudonyms that the
killer gave: the 'Wicked King Wicker' presumably refers to 'Wicca' (witchcraft), while the 'Twenty Two Disciples of Hell' certainly sounds like a
satanic organisation. The name 'Wheaties' was enclosed within inverted
commas as if it were the nickname of the John who was supposedly the
'rapist and suffocater of young girls'. When they ran some checks, however, the police could find no trace of him. In fact, none of the names given
were much help either to the Omega team that was working on the case or
the NCIC. Nor were they any use to Breslin, who now began calling the .44
killer the 'Son of Sam'.

    The 17-year-old Judy Placido went to the same Bronx school as
Valentina Suriani, whose funeral she had attended. On 25 June 1977, three
weeks after the publication of the letter that the .44 killer had written to
Breslin, Judy celebrated her high-school graduation at Elephas, a discotheque in Queens. There she met a handsome young man called Salvatore Lupo, who worked at a petrol station; they hit it off immediately and
soon went outside for some privacy. While sitting in a car Salvatore slipped
his arm around Judy's shoulders as they discussed the Son of Sam killings.
It was at that precise moment that their lurid speculations turned into murderous reality. A .44 bullet smashed through the passenger window, passing through Salvatore's wrist and into Judy's neck; a second bullet hit her
in the head, but miraculously failed to penetrate her skull, while a third
entered her right shoulder. The terrified Salvatore threw open the car door
and ran into the discotheque to get help, but it was too late: the shooting

was over and the attacker had fled. Although she had been hit three times Judy was quite unaware of having been shot and was shocked to see that her face was covered with blood when she glanced into the rear-view mirror. She, too, then jumped out of the car and headed for the discotheque, but only managed to cover a few yards before collapsing. Salvatore nursed a shattered wrist and cuts from the flying glass; in hospital it was ascertained that Judy had been fortunate to escape without serious injury.

The city was now in a state of panic and takings at discotheques and restaurants – particularly in Queens – plummeted. Newspapers' circulation soared: not only did they contain the gory details of the latest shooting, but they also speculated about the next killing. In the Son of Sam's letter to Breslin he had written 'TELL ME JIM, WHAT WILL YOU HAVE FOR JULY TWENTY-NINTH?' It was noted that 29 July was the date on which he had carried out his first murder. Was he planning to celebrate the killing of Donna Lauria with another?

New York's mayor, Abraham Beame, who was running for re-election, could not afford to wait to find out and quickly announced that even more officers were being seconded to the investigation. Overnight it became the largest single operation in the history of the New York Police Department: 200 men, recruited from every borough of the city, were seconded to the case and the investigation cost more than $90,000 a day to run. Volunteers, like Donna Lauria's father, Mike, furthermore manned special Son of Sam patrols, as well as a hot line, which was receiving at 5,000 calls a day by then. For their part, a team of psychiatrists tried to compile a profile of the killer, but the best that they could come up with was that he was 'neurotic, schizophrenic and paranoid'. This description was duly released by the police, but did not help anyone to identify the gunman.

Fortunately 29 July passed without incident and two days later, with a sense of relief, two sisters from Brooklyn, the fifteen-year-old Ricki Moskowitz and the twenty-year-old Stacy, decided to go out. While in a Brooklyn restaurant they were approached by a handsome young man who introduced himself as Bobby Violante. The next day Bobby and Stacy went to see the film *New York, New York*. Afterwards they went out to dinner before heading off for a quiet place where they could be alone. They drove to a secluded spot on Shore Parkway, near Coney Island, southern Brooklyn, which was used as an urban type of lovers' lane. They felt safe enough there: so far there had been no Son-of-Sam killings in Brooklyn; the nearest shooting had taken place 22 miles (35 kilometres) away, in Queens. What they did not know, however, was that a week beforehand a man claiming to be the Son of Sam had phoned the Coney Island police station to say that he would strike in that area next. Extra patrol cars had therefore been assigned to Brooklyn and Coney Island and Shore Parkway was patrolled regularly.

Bobby and Stacy pulled up under a street lamp, the only available parking spot on Shore Parkway. There was a full moon that night and because it was not dark enough for what they had in mind the pair went for a stroll in a nearby park. They walked over a bridge and spent a few minutes playing on the swings. Near the public lavatories they noticed a jeans-wearing man – whom they described as a 'hippie type' – leaning against a wall, but he was no longer there when they returned to the car. They were kissing in the front seat when Stacy suggested that they move on. Bobby, however, insisted on one more kiss. This was a mistake, for while they were embracing Bobby was hit in the face by two bullets, which blinded him and caused his eardrums to explode. Although he could neither see nor hear he felt Stacy jerk violently in his arms before falling forward. Fearing that she was dead, Bobby threw himself against the car's horn, fumbled at the door, called for help and then collapsed on to the pavement.

Tommy Zaino, who was sitting in the car in front, had seen the shooting in his rear-view mirror. He had watched as a man approached the car from behind before pulling out a gun; from a crouching position he had then fired four shots through the open passenger window. When Tommy's girlfriend, Debbie Crescendo, had heard the shooting she had asked 'What's that?' Tommy believed that he knew: 'Get down', he said. 'I think it's the Son of Sam.' Tommy had seen the gunman run towards the park and had then looked at his watch: it was exactly 2.35am. (A patrol car was just five streets away at the time.)

Stacy Moskowitz was still conscious when the ambulance arrived. Although one bullet had grazed her scalp the other had lodged in the back of her brain and she died 38 hours later. Bobby Violante survived, but his sight could not be restored.

Tommy Zaino gave a good description of the killer: he was stocky, with stringy, fair hair. This matched the description given by Donna DeMasi and Joanne Lomino, but did not fit the man with the dark, curly hair who had been described by Jody Valente and the neighbour in the DeMasi-Lomino case. The police therefore wondered whether he had been wearing a wig.

There were other witnesses, too. A beautician and her boyfriend had been sitting by the entrance to the park when they had heard the shots. They had then seen a man wearing a denim jacket and what they took to be a nylon wig jump into a light-coloured car and drive off, as if he had just robbed a bank. A young girl who had been riding a bicycle identified the car as being a yellow Volkswagen, while a nurse who had looked out of her window when she had heard the shooting also said that she had seen a yellow VW. It had almost collided with another car at an intersection and the second driver had been so incensed that he had chased the VW, only to lose it a few streets later. The VW's driver, the other motorist said, had had stringy, brown hair.

An even more vital witness took a little longer to come forward, however. She was Cacilia Davis, a 49-year-old widow who had been out with a male friend on the night in question. They had returned to her flat, which was two streets from the park, at around 2am and had then sat in her friend's car and talked for a few minutes, keeping an eye open for other cars as they did so because they had been forced to double-park. Cacilia had noticed a police car a little way ahead, along with two patrolmen, who were writing out parking tickets. Some way behind them was a yellow Ford Galaxie that had been parked by a fire hydrant; a few minutes beforehand a patrolman had issued it with a parking ticket. Next Cacilia had seen a young man with dark hair walk up to the Galaxie and irritably pull the parking ticket from the windscreen. After that she had invited her friend in for coffee, but he had declined, saying that it was late – it was 2.20am by then. At that moment the police car had pulled away, as had the Galaxie shortly thereafter, but because he could not get past her friend's car the Galaxie's driver had impatiently honked his horn. Cacilia had hurriedly got out of the car and her friend had driven off, whereupon the Galaxie had followed and quickly passed him before speeding off after the police car.

Minutes later Cacilia had taken her dog for a walk in the park and had noticed Tommy Zaino and Bobby Violante's cars, as well as a VW van. On her way home she had seen a man with dark hair and a blue-denim jacket striding across the road from the cars. As he glared at her she had observed that he was walking with his right arm held stiffly, as if something was concealed up his sleeve. He also looked rather like the driver of the Ford Galaxie whom she had seen earlier, she thought.

Cacilia did not come forward with this information immediately, however, for she realised that she was in danger if the man whom she had seen was indeed the Son of Sam: he could easily identify her and knew where she lived. It was not until two days after the shootings that she told a couple of close friends what she had seen. Thinking that she might be able to provide a vital clue as to the killer's identity they urged her to call the police, eventually doing so on her behalf. Although Detective Joseph Strano visited her and took her statement it caused hardly a ripple of interest among his colleagues, who considered Tommy Zaino to be the best witness to the shooting. Tommy had seen a man with fair, not dark, hair; moreover, the driver of the Ford Galaxie had left the scene of the crime before the shooting began.

By this time, however, Cacilia – who felt that she had risked her life to come forward – was no longer going to be ignored and threatened to go anonymously to the newspapers with her story. In order to humour her Strano interviewed her again, this time bringing a police artist to make a sketch of the man whom she had seen. He also took her on an expedition to the shops to see if she could pick out a similar denim jacket to the one which the man had been wearing. Yet nothing further was done to investigate her story.

The primary problem with Cacilia's evidence was that the local police said that they had not issued any parking tickets in the area on the night on which the shootings had taken place. The police cars that had been patrolling the area had been seconded from other boroughs, however, and it was thus ten days before four further parking tickets materialised. Three of the four cars that had been penalised were quickly eliminated. The fourth, a yellow Ford Galaxie with the number plates 561-XLB, was found to belong to a David Berkowitz, of 35 Pine Street, Yonkers – a suburban area just north of the Bronx. When Detective James Justus called the Yonkers police headquarters to investigate further, a switchboard operator named Wheat Carr answered. On explaining that he was working on the Son-of-Sam case and that he was running a check on David Berkowitz the woman shouted 'Oh, no'.

It turned out that not only did Wheat Carr know David Berkowitz, but that she had suspected that he was the Son of Sam for some time. It had begun the previous year, when her father, Sam Carr, had started to receive anonymous letters complaining about his dog. In October 1976 a petrol bomb had been thrown through the window of the Carrs' house at 316 Warburton Avenue, Yonkers. A neighbour had also been receiving anonymous letters and abusive phone calls, and on Christmas Eve a number of shots had been fired through their window; their Alsatian had also been killed. Then, on 27 April 1977, someone had entered the Carrs' back yard and had shot their black Labrador, Harvey.

On 10 June 1977 Sam Carr had received a phone call from Jack Cassaras, who lived in New Rochelle, on Long Island Sound, who wanted to know why Sam had sent him a get-well card. The card had mentioned that Jack had fallen off a roof, but Jack had claimed that he had not – and, indeed, had never – been on one. Sam, who could offer no explanation for the mystery, had invited Jack over to his house to discuss the matter. On Jack's arrival, about 20 minutes later, Sam had examined the card, which had a picture of an Alsatian on it. He had then told Jack about the bizarre things that had been happening.

Jack had driven home feeling even more puzzled, but his son had then told him that he thought that he had the answer to the enigma. In the previous year the Cassarases had rented a room above their garage to a certain David Berkowitz, who had complained about their Alsatian before suddenly leaving a few weeks later without asking for the $200 deposit on his room. Jack's son suspected that Berkowitz might have something to do with the card. When Mrs Cassaras had looked him up in the telephone directory she found that he had moved to 35 Pine Street, Yonkers. She had then called Sam Carr to ask him whether Pine Street was near his house; it was just around the corner from him, Sam had replied. Convinced that Berkowitz was responsible for the harassment that his family had suffered, Sam had therefore gone to the police, but they had explained that they could take the matter no further without more concrete evidence.

Craig Glassman – a police officer who lived in the flat beneath Berkowitz – had also been receiving abusive letters, and when rubbish was piled against his front door and set alight on 6 August 1977 (a week after the Moskowitz murder) he reported it. He also showed detectives two anonymous letters that he had received, which accused Glassman of being a spy who had been planted in the building by Sam Carr. Glassman and the Carrs were members of a black-magic sect that was to get him, the author alleged. The detective who examined the letters recognised the handwriting to be that of a man whom he was investigating – David Berkowitz.

Berkowitz was not the only suspect in the Son-of-Sam case, however – indeed, New York has a rich supply of potential serial killers. Besides, Berkowitz did not fit the description given by Tommy Zaino, nor did he drive a yellow VW. It was not until 10 August 1977 that detectives John Longo and Ed Zigo went to Yonkers to check out Berkowitz. On their arrival Zigo spotted Berkowitz's Ford Galaxie parked outside the block of flats in Pine Street. On closer investigation they saw that there was a bag on the back seat from which a rifle butt protruded. Although possession of a rifle does not require a licence in New York, Zigo nevertheless forced open the car. Inside he found another, more formidable, weapon: a Commando Mark III semi-automatic. He also discovered a letter in the glove compartment addressed to Deputy Inspector Timothy Dowd – the head of the Son-of-Sam investigation – which said that the next shooting would be in Long Island. Detective Zigo phoned the police station and told Sergeant James Shea 'I think we've got him'.

Police who had been rapidly ordered to Pine Street from all over the city staked out the car until Berkowitz – a stocky man, with a round, cherubic face and dark hair – turned up six hours later. When he got into the driver's seat he found himself looking down the barrel of a police revolver. 'Freeze!' yelled Detective William Gardella. 'Police!' Berkowitz simply smiled. Detective John Falotico then opened the passenger door, held his .38 to Berkowitz's head and told him to get out. When Berkowitz placed his hands on the roof of the car Falotico asked 'Who are you?' 'I am Sam', replied Berkowitz.

At One Police Plaza Berkowitz confessed to the shootings, as well as to sending the anonymous letters, furthermore admitting that his crime spree had begun on Christmas Eve in 1975. At about 7pm on that day he had driven to Co-op City in the Bronx, where his adoptive father lived. On seeing a young, Hispanic woman leaving a shop he had followed her before pulling out a knife and stabbing her in the back. Not realising what had happened, she had turned, screamed and grabbed his wrist, whereupon he had run away. On his way home, however, he had stalked the 15-year-old Michelle Forman and had stabbed her in the back and head. When she fell screaming to the pavement Berkowitz had again fled. Michelle had somehow managed to stagger to the block of flats where she lived and her parents had then rushed her to hospital, where it was discovered that she had a collapsed lung. Her other injuries were superficial, however, and she only spent a week in hospital. Berkowitz's first victim had not even reported the attack and was never identified. These early attacks had convinced Berkowitz that he needed a gun, and a friend called Billy Dan Parka had accordingly bought him a .44 Bulldog revolver in Houston, Texas, for $130.

Under interrogation, Berkowitz explained that he had been ordered to commit the murders by Sam Carr, via Carr's demonic dog, Harvey. Other demonic voices had accompanied him when he was stalking his victims, he claimed. Berkowitz was so forthcoming that his confession took only half an hour to complete.

Further inquiries revealed that Richard David Berkowitz had been an illegitimate child who had been given up for adoption as a baby. His natural mother, Betty Broder, was Jewish. At the age of 19 she had married the Italian-American Tony Falco, who had left her for another woman six years later. Betty had begun an affair with Joseph Kleinman, a married real-estate agent, in 1947 and had become pregnant by him, but when she told him that she was going to have a child he replied that she had better get rid of it if she wanted to continue seeing him. Their child was born on 1 June 1953 and was immediately adopted by a Jewish couple, Pearl and Nathan Berkowitz, who were unable to have children of their own. They called their new son David. When Pearl succumbed to cancer in 1967 the 14-year-old David was deeply upset by this new loss.

Two years later Nathan decided to move to Co-op City, in the Bronx. It had been a middle-class suburb, but gangs of youths soon began terrorising the neighbourhood. David's school marks plunged and he seemed to lose his sense of direction. A shy boy, he found himself becoming the victim of bullying, although others regarded him as being spoilt and something of a bully himself. He was big for his age, strong and an excellent baseball player, but preferred to play with children who were younger than himself. His biggest problem, however, was with girls (one friend recalled Berkowitz asking him if he wanted to join the 'girl-haters' club'). He only dated one girl in Co-op City: Iris Gerhardt. Although Iris liked his warm and obliging nature the relationship was never consummated, and while Berkowitz remained chaste it seemed to him that almost everyone else was having sex: 'After a while, at Co-op City there wasn't one girl who was a virgin', he said resentfully. In prison, Berkowitz later wrote 'I must slay women for revenge purposes to get back at them for all the suffering they caused me'.

When his friends started smoking marijuana Berkowitz was too inhibited to join in. Things became worse in 1971, when his father remarried, whereupon Berkowitz, who resented his stepmother and stepsister, joined the army (his spell in uniform did not last long, however). By the time that he returned home in 1974 Berkowitz had rejected Judaism and had become a Baptist. Nathan Berkowitz furthermore remembered watching his son standing in front of a mirror while beating his head with his fists. Things became so uncomfortable in the Berkowitz household that David moved out, renting a drab, one-room flat at 2151 Barnes Avenue in the Bronx. By this time Nathan was convinced that his son needed psychiatric help, but because he and his new family were moving to Florida nothing was done. With his adoptive father gone another door to sanity closed on Berkowitz.

Having known since the age of seven that he was adopted, because he was feeling isolated he now tried to trace his natural family. It took a year. Through the Bureau of Records he discovered that his real name was Richard Falco and that he had been born in Brooklyn. With the help of an old telephone directory he managed to locate his mother and an elder sister. A few days after dropping a card into his mother's letterbox she called him and they had an emotional reunion. He also met his 37-year-old sister and became a regular visitor to the house in which she lived with her husband and children. Berkowitz had found his family and was happy at last – or so it seemed.

During the first half of 1976 his visits to his mother and sister became increasingly rare. He complained of headaches. In February he rented the room above the Cassarases' garage in New Rochelle, but two months later suddenly moved to Pine Street, Yonkers. In July he killed Donna Lauria, marking the start of his year-long killing spree.

Now, however, the police had Berkowitz under lock and key. Judged sane enough to stand trial, Berkowitz pleaded guilty to all of the charges against him and was sentenced to 365 years in prison. Sergeant Joseph Coffey, who had conducted Berkowitz's initial interrogation, commented 'I feel sorry for him. The man is a fucking vegetable'.

Not everyone was satisfied with Berkowitz's conviction; the young, Yonkers-born investigative journalist Maury Terry was one who noted a number of inconsistencies in Berkowitz's story. For example, Berkowitz claimed that he had acted alone, but because descriptions of the killer varied wildly he could have had an accomplice. Terry also noted that some of the Son-of-Sam killings had been performed with ruthless efficiency, while others had been inept and bungled. He eventually concluded that Berkowitz had committed only three of the killings – those of Donna Lauria, Valentina Suriani and Alexander Esau.

Terry believed that Berkowitz was a member of a satanic organisation – the Twenty Two Disciples of Hell mentioned in the letter sent to Jimmy

Breslin from the Son of Sam – and that further members of the cult were actually responsible for the other murders (the killer in the Balaclava, Terry speculated, was a woman). However, when he managed to track down some of the cult's members – including Sam Carr's sons, John 'Wheaties' and Michael – in order to investigate his theory further he learned that they had all died mysteriously.

In February 1979 Berkowitz issued a statement from Attica Correctional Facility, where he was being held, saying that he was indeed involved with a satanic group. Then, on 10 July 1979, he was slashed with a razor by another inmate. The cut ran from the left-hand side of his throat to the back of his neck; it needed 56 stitches and nearly killed him. Berkowitz claimed that the attack was a warning from the cult that he should keep his mouth shut.

25 ◆ The Zodiac Killer

A brutal assassin who styled himself the 'Zodiac Killer' stalked the Bay area around San Francisco for over ten years. Like Jack the Ripper, he taunted the police with letters and clues. Also in common with the Ripper, he, too, was never caught and may even have moved on, to kill again.

His reign of terror began on a chilly, moonlit night at Christmas in 1968. A teenage couple had drawn up in their car in an open space next to a pump house on the Lake Herman road in the Vallejo hills overlooking San Francisco. This was the local lovers' lane and David Faraday and Bettilou Jensen were indifferent to the cold. Indeed, they were so wrapped up in each other that they did not notice another car pulling up about 10 feet (3 metres) away. Their amorous reverie was then rudely interrupted by gunfire, however. One bullet smashed through the back window, showering them with glass, while another thudded into the car's bodywork. Bettilou threw open the passenger door and leapt out. David, who was trying to follow her, had his hand on the door handle when the gunman leant in through the driver's window and shot him in the head, causing his body to slump across the front seat. Bettilou's attempt at flight was futile; as she ran screaming into the night the gunman ran after her; she had covered just 30 feet (9 metres) when he fired five shots at her. After she had collapsed

Artists impression of the 'Zodiac Killer'.

and died the gunman walked calmly back to his car and drove away.

A few minutes later another car drove down the quiet road. Its driver, a woman, saw Bettilou's body sprawled on the ground, but did not stop, instead speeding on, towards the next town, Benica, to get help. On the way she saw the flashing blue light of a police car approaching her and frantically switched her headlights on and off to try to attract the driver's attention. The car stopped and she told the patrolmen what she had seen. They then followed her back to the pump house, arriving there about three minutes later. Although Bettilou was dead David was still alive, but because he was unconscious he could not give them any information about what had happened. He died shortly after his arrival at the hospital to which they had rushed him.

There was little for the police to go on: the victims had not been sexually assaulted and nothing was missing (the money in David's wallet was still there). Detective Sergeant Les Lundblatt, of the Vallejo-county police force, investigated the possibility that they had been murdered by a jealous rival, but there were found to be no jilted lovers and no other amorous entanglements. The two teenagers were ordinary students whose lives were an open book. Six months later Bettilou Jensen and David Faraday's files had become just two of a huge number relating to unsolved murders in the state of California.

On 4 July 1969 their killer struck again. At around midnight at Blue Rock Park – another romantic spot, just 2 miles (3 kilometres) from where Bettilou and David were murdered – Mike Mageau was sitting in his car with his girlfriend, the 22-year-old waitress Darlene Ferrin. They were not entirely alone because other courting couples had also parked their cars there. Like Bettilou and David before them, Mike and Darlene were too engrossed in each other to notice when a white car pulled up beside them. It stayed there for only a few minutes before driving away, but then it returned and parked on the other side of the road. A powerful spotlight was suddenly shone on Mike's car, whereupon a figure approached them. Thinking that it was a policeman, Mike reached for his driver's licence. As he did so, however, he heard the sound of gunfire and saw Darlene slump in her seat; seconds later a bullet tore into Mike's neck. The gunman then walked unhurriedly back to the white car, paused to fire another four or five shots at them and then sped off, leaving the smell of cordite and burning rubber in his wake.

A few minutes later a man called the Vallejo-county police station and reported a murder on Columbus Parkway, telling the switchboard operator 'You will find the kids in a brown car. They are shot with a 9mm Luger. I also killed those kids last year. Goodbye'. When the police arrived Darlene was dead, and although Mike was still alive the bullet had passed through his tongue and he was unable to speak.

There was another lead for the police to follow up, however. Four months earlier Darlene's babysitter had noticed a white car parked outside Darlene's flat. Thinking that it looked suspicious, she asked Darlene about it. It was plain that the young waitress knew the driver: 'He's checking up on me again', she told the babysitter. 'He doesn't want anyone to know what I saw him do. I saw him murder someone.' The babysitter had had a good look at the man in the white car and told the police that he was middle-aged, with brown, wavy hair and a round face. When Mike could talk again he confirmed that the gunman had had brown hair and a round face. After that, however, the clues to the killer's identity petered out.

Then, on 1 August 1969 – almost two months after the shootings of Darlene and Mike, three local newspapers received handwritten letters. They all began: 'DEAR EDITOR, THIS IS THE MURDERER OF THE 2 TEENAGERS LAST CHRISTMAS AT LAKE HERMAN & THE GIRL ON THE 4TH OF JULY . . .' (Like

David Berkowitz's letters, they were written in capital letters and contained basic errors in spelling and syntax.) The author gave details of the ammunition that he had used, leaving no one in any doubt that he was indeed the gunman. Each letter also contained a third of a sheet of paper covered with a strange code, which the writer demanded that the papers print on their front pages; if they did not, he warned, he would go on 'killing lone people in the night'. The letters were signed with another cipher – a circle with a cross inside it which looked ominously like a gun sight.

All three of the newspapers complied with the writer's demands and the coded message was also sent to Mare Island Naval Yard, where cryptographers tried to crack it. Although it appeared to be a simple substitution code the US Navy's experts could not break it. Dale Harden, a teacher at Alisal High School in Salinas, however, could. Having had the idea of looking for a group of ciphers that might spell the word 'kill', he managed to locate them and after ten hours' intense work he and his wife had decoded the whole of the message, which read: 'I like killing people because it is so much more fun than killing wild game in the forrest [sic] because man is the most dangerous of all to kill . . .' The killer then went on to boast that he had already murdered five people in the San Francisco Bay area and added that after he had been reborn in paradise his victims would become his slaves.

After the murderer's cryptic message was made public a tidal wave of information was offered by ordinary citizens: over 1,000 calls were received by the police, but none of them led anywhere. So the killer helpfully volunteered another clue, this time revealing a name, or rather a nickname, that he knew would attract the attention of the headline-writers. Writing again to the newspapers, he began his letters 'DEAR EDITOR, THIS IS ZODIAC SPEAKING . . .' He again gave details of the slaying of Darlene Ferrin that only the killer could have known. Yet although the killer's strategy increased his publicity profile the police were still no nearer to catching him.

On 27 September 1969 the 20-year-old Bryan Hartnell and the 22-year-old Cecelia Shepard – both students at the nearby Seventh-day Adventists' Pacific Union College – went for a picnic on the shores of Lake Berryessa, some 13 miles (21 kilometres) north of Vallejo. At around 4.30pm they had finished eating and were lying on a blanket, kissing, when they noticed a stocky man, with brown hair, walking towards them across the clearing.

Having disappeared momentarily into a copse, when he re-emerged he was wearing a mask and carrying a gun. As he came closer Bryan saw that the mask had a symbol on it: a white cross within a circle.

The man was not particularly threatening in his manner and his voice was soft. 'I want your money and your car keys', he said. Bryan explained that he only had 76 cents, but said that the masked man was welcome to that. The gunman then began to chat, telling them that he was an escaped convict and that he was going to have to tie them up with the clothesline that he had brought with him. Having forced Cecelia to tie up Bryan, he then trussed her up himself.

The gunman talked some more before calmly announcing 'I am going to have to stab you people', whereupon Bryan begged to be stabbed first, saying 'I couldn't bear to see her stabbed'. Having quietly agreed to this, the gunman sank to his knees and stabbed Bryan repeatedly in the back with a hunting knife. Although he was feeling dizzy and sick, Bryan was still conscious when the masked man turned his attention to Cecelia. Having initially appeared calm, after the first stab he went berserk, plunging the hunting knife into her body again and again while she frantically twisted and turned beneath him in a futile attempt to escape the blows. When she was finally lying still the man regained his composure. He got up, walked to their car, pulled a felt-tip pen from his pocket and then drew something on the door before strolling away.

A fisherman who had heard their screams ran towards them, to find both Bryan and Cecelia still alive. Napa Valley police officers were already on their way, having been alerted by an anonymous phone call in which a man's gruff voice had said 'I want to report a double murder', then going on to give the precise location at which the bodies could be found before leaving the phone hanging from its cord.

When the police arrived Cecelia was in a coma; she died two days later, in hospital, without having regained consciousness. Bryan recovered slowly and was able to give a full description of their attacker, but the police had already guessed who he was, for the sign that the killer had drawn on the door of their car was a circle with a cross within it. The police also located the phone booth from which the killer had reported the murder: it was less than six streets away from the headquarters of the Napa Valley Police Department. They furthermore managed to lift three good-quality fingerprints from it, although their owner's details were unfortunately not found among the police's records.

On 11 October 1969, just two weeks later, a fourteen-year-old girl was looking out of a window of her home in San Francisco when she witnessed a crime in progress. A taxi was parked on the corner of Washington and Cherry streets and she could see a stocky man, who was sitting in the front passenger seat, going through the pockets of the driver, who appeared to be dead. She called to her brothers to come and watch what was happening and together they observed the man getting out of the taxi, leaving the cab driver lying slumped across the seat, and wiping the door handle with a piece of cloth before walking off in a northerly direction. Although the children promptly called the police they did not give their evidence very clearly and the telephone operator who took the call (which was logged at 10pm) made a note that the suspect was an 'NMA' – Negro male adult – even though he was, in fact, white. Indeed, after the police had put out a general alert a patrolman actually stopped a stocky man near the scene of the crime and asked whether he had seen anything unusual; the man replied in the negative and because he was furthermore white the patrolman waved him on his way.

A stocky man was later seen running into the nearby Presidio – a military compound that contains housing and a park – whereupon the floodlights were switched on and the area was searched by patrolmen with dogs, but with no success. When they inspected the taxi the police found the driver, the 29-year-old Paul Stine, lying dead from a gunshot wound to the head. The motive for his killing, they thought, was robbery.

Three days later the San Francisco Chronicle received a letter from Zodiac. 'THIS IS THE ZODIAC SPEAKING', it said. 'I AM THE MURDERER OF THE TAXI DRIVER OVER BY WASHINGTON ST AND MAPLE ST [sic] LAST NIGHT, TO PROVE IT HERE IS A BLOOD STAINED PIECE OF HIS SHIRT.' (The piece of cloth enclosed with the letter was indeed found to match the shirt of the murdered taxi-driver. The bullet that had killed Stine was also identified as a .22 that had been fired from the same gun that had been used to kill Bettilou Jensen and David Faraday.) The letter went on to say: 'I AM THE SAME MAN WHO DID IN THE PEOPLE IN THE NORTH BAY AREA'. 'THE S. F. POLICE COULD HAVE CAUGHT ME LAST NIGHT', it taunted, before concluding: 'SCHOOL CHILDREN MAKE NICE TARGETS. I THINK I SHALL WIPE OUT A SCHOOL BUS SOME MORNING. JUST SHOOT OUT THE TIRES AND THEN PICK OFF ALL THE KIDDIES AS THEY COME BOUNCING OUT.' The letter was signed with the now familiar circle containing a cross.

The description of the man supplied by the children, as well as by the policeman who had stopped the stocky, white male as he was leaving the scene of the crime, matched those given by Darlene Ferrin's babysitter, Mike Mageau and Bryan Hartnell. A new composite image of the Zodiac Killer was now drawn up and issued to the public by San Francisco's chief of police, Thomas J Cahill. It depicted a white male, 35 to 45 years old, with short, brown hair, which possibly had a red tint; he was described as being around 5 feet 8 inches (1.75 metres) tall, heavily built and a wearer of glasses. This 'wanted' poster was plastered around San Francisco.

The Zodiac Killer's appetite for publicity seems to have been insatiable. At 2am on 22 October 1969, 11 days after the murder of Paul Stine, a man with a gruff voice called the police department in Oakland, just across the bay from San Francisco. After introducing himself as Zodiac he said 'I want to get in touch with F Lee Bailey. If you can't come up with Bailey I'll settle for Mel Belli. I want one or other of them to appear on the Channel 7 talk show. I'll make contact by telephone'.

The men for whom he had asked were the USA's two leading criminal lawyers, and although F Lee Bailey was not available at such short notice Melvin Belli agreed to appear on Jim Dunbar's talk show at 6.30 on the following morning. The show's ratings soared as people throughout the Bay area tuned in. At around 7.20am a man called in and told Belli that he was Zodiac, although he preferred to be called Sam. Then he said 'I'm sick. I have headaches'. The mystery caller was eventually traced to Napa State Hospital and proved to be a psychiatric patient.

The actual Zodiac continued his correspondence, however, writing to Inspector David Toschi, of San Francisco's homicide squad, and threatening to commit more murders. In another letter he claimed to have killed seven people – two more than the Zodiac Killer's official body count up till then. He later said that he had murdered 10, taunting the San Francisco Police Department (SFPD) with the score line 'ZODIAC 10, SFPD 0'. He furthermore gave cryptic clues as to his real name and shared his fantasy of blowing up school children with a bomb with the recipients of his letters.

The following Christmas Melvin Belli received a card saying 'DEAR MELVIN, THIS IS THE ZODIAC SPEAKING. I WISH YOU A HAPPY CHRISTMAS. THE ONE THING I ASK OF YOU IS THIS, PLEASE HELP ME . . . I AM AFRAID I WILL LOSE CONTROL AND TAKE MY NINTH AND POSSIBLY TENTH VICTIM'. Another piece of Paul Stine's bloodstained shirt was enclosed. Forensic handwriting experts feared that Zodiac's mental state was deteriorating.

On 24 July 1970 the Zodiac Killer wrote a letter that included the words: 'THE WOEMAN [sic] AND HER BABY THAT I GAVE A RATHER INTEREST-ING RIDE FOR A COUPLE OF HOWERS [sic] ONE EVENING A FEW MONTHS BACK THAT ENDED IN MY BURNING HER CAR WHERE I FOUND THEM'. The afore-mentioned woman was Kathleen Johns. On the evening of 17 March 1970 she was driving in the Vallejo area, with her baby in the car with her, when a white Chevrolet drew up alongside her. The driver indicated that there was something wrong with her rear wheel, so she pulled over and the other driver also stopped; according to Kathleen he was a 'clean-shaven and neatly dressed man'. He told her that her wheel had been wobbling and offered to tighten the wheel nuts for her, which she gratefully agreed to. When she drove off, however, the wheel that he had said that he had fixed came off altogether, whereupon the driver of the Chevrolet offered her a lift to a nearby service station. She again accepted his offer of help, but when they reached the service station he drove straight past it, reply-ing to her query as to why he had done so in a chillingly calm voice. 'You know I am going to kill you', he said.

Kathleen managed to keep her head, however, and when her abductor slowed down on the curve of a motorway ramp she jumped from the car while holding her baby in her arms, ran off and hid in an irrigation ditch. The driver then stopped the Chevrolet and started to search for her, using a torch that he had taken out of the boot of the car. Fortunately for Kath-leen, he was approaching the ditch in which she was cowering with her child when he was caught in the beam of a lorry's headlights. An hour later, having watched him drive off, Kathleen made her way to a police sta-tion to report what had happened to her. On seeing Zodiac's 'wanted' poster pinned to the wall of the police station she identified him as the man who had threatened to kill her. When the police drove her back to her car they found that it was now a burnt-out shell – it seemed that the Zodiac Killer had returned to set it alight.

Despite the new leads that Kathleen Johns had provided the police were still no nearer to catching the Zodiac Killer, although the Vallejo-county police believed that he was now the driver of a new, green Ford. The reason behind their suspicion was that the driver of such a car had once stopped and ostentatiously watched a highway patrolman who was parked on the other side of the motorway. After the patrolman had decided to ask him what he was doing and had driven through an underpass to reach him he had found the green Ford gone: it was now parked on the other side of the motorway, exactly where the squad car had been moments before. Zodiac subsequently played this cat-and-mouse game every day for two weeks.

Detective Sergeant Lundblatt was becoming increasingly convinced that the Zodiac Killer was a man named Andy Walker. Walker had known Darlene Ferrin and Darlene's sister had also identified him as the man who had waited outside Darlene's flat in the white car. He bore a marked resemblance, too, to the description of the man who was seen near Lake Berrylessa when Cecelia Shepard was stabbed to death. Walker was also known to suffer from bad headaches and to get on badly with the women with whom he worked. He had furthermore studied codes while in the army.

However, neither did his fingerprints match the one that had been left in Paul Stine's taxi nor did his handwriting equate to that on Zodiac's notes. The police then discovered that Walker was ambidextrous, which meant that his handwriting would change depending on which hand he used to write with. They also formulated the theory that the murder of Paul Stine had been so meticulously planned that the Zodiac Killer may have used the severed finger of an unknown victim with which to plant fingerprints in the taxi and thereby throw the police off his scent.

The police decided that they had to obtain Walker's palm prints in order to see if they matched those that had been found on the telephone that had been left dangling after the Paul Stine killing. An undercover policeman therefore asked Walker to help him to carry a goldfish bowl, but although Walker obliged the palm prints that he left were smudged. Walker soon realised that he was being targeted by the police, however, and approached a judge, who issued a court order which forced them to stop harassing Walker.

Letters from Zodiac threatening more murders were received; some were authenticated, but rendered few new clues. The only thing that the police could be sure of was that Zodiac was a fan of the comic operettas of Gilbert and Sullivan. He had taunted them with a parody of 'The Lord High Executioner', listing those people whom he intended to kill and using the refrain 'Titwillo, titwillo, titwillo', and there were furthermore no letters or killings during the entire run of San Francisco's Presentation Theater's The Mikado .

The police also deduced that Zodiac had a curious connection with water. Not only did all of the names of his crime scenes have some association with water, but in one of his letters he had claimed that the body count would have been higher if he had not been 'swamped by the rain we had a while back'. The police therefore reasoned that he lived in a low-lying area that was susceptible to flooding or that he perhaps had a basement in which he kept equipment for making his long-threatened bomb.

Next a K-Mart shop in Santa Rosa, California, was evacuated following a bomb threat made by a man who identified himself as the Zodiac Killer. Two months later Zodiac wrote another letter to the *San Francisco Chronicle* claiming to have killed 12 people and enclosing a map with an 'X' marking the peak of a mountain in Contra Costa Country, across the bay from San Francisco, from which an observer, he said, would be able to see the entire panorama of the area in which the murders had taken place. When detectives examined the location more closely, however, the spot marked was found to be within the compound of a naval relay station, to which only service personnel with security clearance were granted access.

The letters, which continued to come, now demanded that everyone in the San Francisco area wear lapel badges bearing the Zodiac Killer's symbol. When they did not comply he threatened Paul Avery, the *San Francisco Chronicle*'s crime writer who had been investigating the Zodiac story, whereupon journalists (including Avery), began wearing badges saying 'I am not Paul Avery'. Avery, who was a licensed private eye and a former war correspondent in Vietnam, also started carrying a .38 and practised shooting regularly at the police firing range.

An anonymous correspondent then tied the Zodiac slayings to the unsolved murder of Cheri Jo Bates, an 18-year-old college student who had been stabbed to death after leaving the college library in Riverside, California, on Hallowe'en in 1966. Although the police could not rule out a connection they could not prove a concrete link either. When Avery investigated it, however, he discovered that the police had received what they considered to be a crank letter about the murder five months after the killing. It was signed with the letter 'Z'. In a series of typewritten letters the author furthermore gave details of the murder that only the killer could have known. He also threatened more killings and wrote of a 'game' that he was playing. Handwritten letters were received, too, whose writing matched that of Zodiac's. Armed with this evidence, Avery managed to persuade the police to re-open the Bates case in the light of the Zodiac murders.

During 1971 there were a number of murders which could have been committed by Zodiac. Indeed, letters purporting to have come from him confessed to them, but he could easily have been claiming the credit for other people's handiwork.

At around 9pm on 7 April 1972 the 33-year-old Isobel Watson, who worked as a legal secretary in San Francisco, got off a bus in Tamalpais Valley. She had just begun walking home, up Pine Hill, when a white Chevrolet swerved across the road and nearly hit her. After the car had come to a halt the driver apologised and offered to give her a lift home; when Isobel declined he got out of the car, pulled out a knife and stabbed her in the back. Her screams alerted her neighbours, who came running out of their homes, whereupon the man jumped back into his car and sped off. After Isobel had recovered she gave a description of her attacker: he was a white man in his early forties, around 5 feet 9 inches (1.78 metres) tall, and had been wearing black-rimmed reading glasses. The police believed that there was a better than 50-50 chance that he was the Zodiac Killer.

As time went by, many of the detectives working on the Zodiac case were reassigned, and eventually only Inspector David Toschi was left. Agents from the Federal Bureau of Investigation (FBI) looked at the files, but even they could take the case no further. Zodiac's correspondence now ceased for nearly four years, but although psychologists believed that he was the type to commit suicide Toschi was not convinced that he was dead. He reasoned that Zodiac got his kicks from the publicity that his murders generated rather than from the killings themselves and that he would therefore have left a note or some other clue that he was Zodiac if he had killed himself. Then, on 25 April 1978, Toschi received confirmation that Zodiac was still alive when the *San Francisco Chronicle* received a letter from him. It mentioned Toschi by name and said that the writer wanted the people of San Francisco to know that he was back.

Robert Graysmith, the author of the book *Zodiac*, deduced that the eponymous murderer was a film buff. In one of his cryptograms, for example, he had mentioned the 'most dangerous game', which is the title of a film, in another calling himself the 'Red Phantom', which is also the name of a film. He furthermore frequently mentioned going to the cinema to see The *Exorcist* or *Badlands*, the latter a fictionalised account of the murderous spree of the Nebraskan killer Charles Starkweather.

The police used the information supplied by Graysmith, as well as the Zodiac Killer's obvious love of publicity, to try to trap him. When a film about the Zodiac killings was shown in San Francisco a suggestions box was installed in the lobby of the cinema, into which the audience was invited to drop notes containing any information or theories that they may have had regarding the murders. Inside the huge box was hidden a detective, who read every note by torchlight as it fell through the slot; he had been ordered to raise the alarm if any looked as though they could have come from the Zodiac Killer, but none did.

The Oakland police thought that they had captured the Zodiac Killer at one point. The suspect was a veteran of the Vietnam War who had seen the Zodiac film three times and had been apprehended while masturbating in the cinema's lavatory after a particularly violent scene. They were soon proved wrong, however, for his handwriting did not match Zodiac's. Amid a welter of recrimination Toschi was transferred from homicide following (baseless) accusations that he had forged the Zodiac letters for self-promotion. The police in the Bay area now began to believe that the Zodiac Killer was either dead or serving time for another crime in a prison outside the state. On the other hand, maybe he reckoned that his time was running out, having nearly been caught following the killing of Paul Stine.

Robert Graysmith was not convinced by these theories, however. He had managed to link the Zodiac killings with the unsolved murders of 14 young girls, usually students or hitchhikers, in the Santa Rosa area during the early 1970s. Although most of them had been found naked, with their clothes missing, they had generally not been sexually molested. Each had been killed in a different way, as if the murderer had been experimenting to ascertain which method was best. Graysmith now reckoned that Zodiac's body count could be as high as 40.

Graysmith believed that Zodiac's symbol - a cross within a circle – was not intended to represent a stylised gunsight, but rather the projectionist's guide that is shown on screen during the lead-in to a film. He traced a promising-sounding suspect through a cinema in San Francisco on whose ceiling the constellations were painted: the man, Graysmith was told, had filmed some murders and kept the gruesome footage in a booby-trapped can. Another suspect of Graysmith's was a former boyfriend of Darlene Ferrin, who had also been a resident of Riverside at the time when Cheri Jo Bates was murdered. He lived with his mother, whom he loathed, and dissected small mammals as a hobby. During the crucial 1975 to 1978 period, when the Zodiac Killer had been quiet, he had been in a psychiatric institution after having been charged with molesting children at the school where he was employed. Graysmith could not pin the Zodiac murders on either of his suspects, however. He published the story of his investigation in 1985.

In 1990 a series of murders was perpetrated in New York by someone who claimed to be Zodiac. Although descriptions of the New York killer did not match those given by the witnesses to the Zodiac murders in California, a man can change a lot over 20 years. Who can tell where he may strike next?

26 ✦ The Hillside Strangler

Between October 1977 and January 1979 the Los Angeles area was plagued by a series of killings. Although these were attributed to the 'Hillside Strangler they turned out to be the work not of one man, but of two murderous cousins.

It had started as a discussion over a beer, when Kenneth Bianchi had asked his cousin, Angelo Buono Jr, what it would be like to kill someone. This was no drunken banter and they consequently decided to find out exactly how it would feel.

The 25-year-old Bianchi had been raised by foster parents in Rochester, New York State. In 1977 he had moved to Los Angeles, where he stayed with his cousin, Buono, who was 17 years his senior. The intellectually subnormal, yet streetwise, Buono used to bring prostitutes back to his house in Glendale, where he ran an upholstery business. Within months of Bianchi's arrival in California the aforementioned question of murder came up and they accordingly resolved to kill one of the prostitutes whose services Buono used. It would be the beginning of a murder spree that would claim the lives of 12 young women.

Their first victim was the 21-year-old Hollywood prostitute Elissa Kastin, whose naked body was found on a hillside on Chevy Chase Drive on 6 October 1977. The police believed that she had been murdered elsewhere and that her body had later been dumped there. Indeed, like those that were to follow her, she had been lured to Buono's home, where she had been savagely raped and killed.

By the end of November 1977 five more young women had fallen victim to the putative Hillside Strangler, and a pattern to the killings was beginning to emerge. The bodies of all of the women, who were mainly part-time prostitutes, had been discovered on hillsides around Los Angeles. Their wrists and ankles bore the marks of ropes and they had been stripped naked, raped and sometimes also sodomised. Their corpses had subsequently been carefully cleaned by the killers so that no clues to their own identities remained. From analysing samples of the sperm that had been left inside the women, however, the police knew that two men had been involved, but they kept this information from members of the press, who, presuming that the perpetrator was a single man, had come up with the nickname the 'Hillside Strangler'.

The murderers were clearly enjoying their notoriety, for all of the naked bodies – often arranged in lascivious poses – had been dumped by roadsides, where they were certain to be discovered. Because the corpses had also been left near police stations it was speculated that the killer was taunting the police. In fact, Bianchi had applied for a job with the Los Angeles Police Department (LAPD), and although he had been turned down police officers had taken him on patrol during the course of the investigation.

The killers chose their victims by cruising around Los Angeles in Buono's car. When they saw a likely target they would stop and get out. Flashing fake badges, they would claim to be undercover policemen and order the woman to get into what they said was an unmarked police car. The woman would then be driven to Buono's home, where she would be tied up, tortured and abused by both men before being strangled.

Their second victim was the 19-year-old Yolanda Washington, whose corpse was discovered lying beside the Forest Lawn cemetery on the night of 18 October 1977. Her spread-eagled, naked body had been meticulously cleansed and the only clues to her death that remained were the marks of the ropes that had restrained her during her final hours of torment. Two weeks later the 15-year-old Judith Miller was found dead on a hillside above a Glendale road. Her neck, wrists and ankles all bore rope marks and she had been violently raped before being strangled.

On the night of 20 November 1977 Bianchi and Buono murdered three girls, one of whom – Dolores Cepeda – was only 12 years old. Dolores' body was found lying alongside that of the 14-year-old Sonja Johnson in Elysian Park. On the same night the corpse of the 20-year-old Kristina Weckler was discovered on a hillside in Highland Park. Three days later the casually discarded body of the 28-year-old Jane King was found lying on an exit ramp of the Golden State motorway.

Things went quiet for a bit after that, until, on 17 February 1978, the naked body of Cindy Hudspeth was discovered in the boot of a car. Cindy had been registered with a modelling agency which kept a record of its clients' assignments, leading the LAPD to hope that a breakthrough was at last in sight. Although police officers interviewed a security guard named Ken Bianchi, nothing came of it. The killings, however, mysteriously ceased.

Buono's home was filthy and because Bianchi could no longer stand living there he left his cousin's house and moved to Bellingham, in Washington state, where he took a job as a security guard and again applied to join the local police force. For the rest of 1978 there were no more killings and the special murder squad that had been formed in Los Angeles to track down the Hillside Strangler was therefore disbanded.

However, in January 1979 the bodies of two young women were found in the back of a locked car in Bellingham. Diane Wilder and Karen Mandic had been hired by a young man from a security firm to 'house-watch' a luxury residence in Bellingham while the alarm system was being repaired, or so he had said. Their corpses were subsequently discovered near the house and on investigating further detectives learned that there had been nothing wrong with the alarm system. On checking with the Coastal Security Company (for which Bianchi worked) Bianchi's name came up and it was established that he was the security guard who had hired the women to look after the house. The police then found a note of the address of the house, as well as its front-door key, in Bianchi's lorry. A number of blood- and semen-stained articles of clothing were furthermore discovered in his house, along with Karen Mandic's telephone number. Meanwhile, forensic experts were examining both car and bodies in an attempt to link him to the killings.

Bianchi now claimed to be suffering from multiple-personality disorder and said that one of his personalities – Steve – was a sex killer. Six Washington-state psychiatrists duly certified him insane, which, according to the law in Washington, saved him from receiving the death penalty (hanging) for the two murders. Bianchi then plea-bargained a deal with the state prosecutors: if he was allowed to serve out his life sentence in California (where he thought the jails to be more comfortable) he would turn state's evidence again Buono in the Hillside-strangler case.

The Los Angeles prosecutors, however, considered Bianchi's evidence to be worthless – after all, he had been declared insane by six psychiatrists in Washington state. Thereafter the Hillside-strangler case became one of the longest and most expensive trials in US criminal history. Halfway through it Bianchi even tried to sabotage it by protesting that he was innocent.

More than 400 witnesses were heard before the two men were finally convicted, of whom one of the most important was the 27-year-old daughter of the actor Peter Lorre. Catherine Lorre identified Bianchi and Buono as the two men who had stopped her in Hollywood claiming to be police officers. Along with her identity card, she had showed them a photograph of herself with her famous father. This had saved her life, for the murderers had decided that killing the daughter of a celebrity would have caused the police to redouble their efforts to catch them.

The trial dragged on from 16 November 1981 to 14 November 1983, and at the end it Judge Ronald George told the pair 'I am sure, Mr Buono and Mr Bianchi, that you will only get your thrills by reliving over and over the tortures and murders of your victims, being incapable as I believe you to be, of ever feeling any remorse'. Bianchi – who was considered to have broken the terms of his plea bargain – was transferred to Washington state to serve his sentence of life imprisonment in Walla Walla Prison, while Buono, who was also sentenced to life, was sent to Folsom Prison in California.

27 ✦ The Wests

Number 25 Cromwell Street, Gloucester: an ordinary house in an ordinary terrace. The man of the house, Fred West, was cheerful and hard-working. His wife, Rosemary, was a busy, lively mother. They were generally liked by their neighbours. Although there was some gossip about the number of men who visited the house late at night, and some said that they disciplined their children too harshly, it was nothing that they felt that they should tell the police or social services about. The Wests, however, had some minor legal problems: during the 1970s the upper floors of the house had been divided into cheap bedsits and Fred, a builder by trade, had added a single-storey extension to the rear of the property without obtaining planning permission for it.

The story of what was actually going on behind the façade of this apparently ordinary house began to unravel during the summer of 1992. Police Constable Steve Burnside was patrolling his Gloucester beat when a group of young people came up to him and told him that children were being abused at a house in Cromwell Street, which was owned by a man named 'Quest'. Although the young informants were unsure of the facts, it was enough to warrant further police attention and as a result social services eventually took the five of Wests' children who were under sixteen into care. Fred and Rosemary were charged with a number of sexual offences, including rape and buggery, but the case against them was dropped when two prosecution witnesses refused to testify. Fred and Rosemary hugged each other in the dock and then returned to their old ways as if nothing had happened.

Detective Constable Hazel Savage, however, who had investigated the initial allegations, remained convinced something terrible was going in Cromwell Street. During quiet chats with the West children she had won their trust; they seemed particularly concerned about the disappearance of Fred and Rosemary's 16-year-old daughter, Heather, who had last been seen on 29 May 1987. Her parents had not even reported her as being missing, and when questioned had said that she had left home of her own accord, 'with a lesbian in a blue Mini'. But the children said that Fred would often joke about Heather being 'under the patio', and Savage believed that these 'jokes' were made a little too often to be simply the product of poor taste. On 23 February 1994 she therefore obtained a search warrant enabling her to gain access to the property at Cromwell Road and the following day the police started to dig up the garden.

A mechanical digger was brought in to remove the topsoil. Then, in the pouring rain, an 'archaeological-type dig' began, under the aegis of the Home Office pathologist Professor Bernard Knight. Supervised by Detective Superintendent John Bennett, a team of 30 officers, working in relays, began sifting shovelfuls of sodden earth through a sieve in the search for clues. At night the work continued under the glare of arc lights. On the second day a trowel hit something hard and the loose soil was scraped away to reveal a human skull. It was thought to be Heather's, and on 25 February 1994 Fred and Rosemary West were arrested. 'I didn't kill her', shouted Fred, as the couple was driven away in a police car.

Rosemary West - the serial killer poses at a birthday party.

After the police had interviewed her Rosemary was released without charge. By the time that her husband appeared in Gloucester magistrates' court a few days later to be formally charged with murder two more bodies had been found. Both were badly decomposed, having lain in the garden for 16 years.

One of the bodies was identified as being that of Shirley Ann Robinson, a lodger at 25 Cromwell Street who had last been seen in 1977. At the time of her death she had been 18 years old and heavily pregnant. According to Liz Brewer, another lodger, Fred West was the father of her child and Rosemary West had also been pregnant with another man's child at the time. 'The Wests had told Shirley they had an open marriage', said Liz. 'Fred didn't seem to mind his wife expecting by another man.' When Shirley had disappeared the Wests had informed Liz that Shirley could not cope with the growing tension between Fred and Rosemary and had gone to visit relatives in Germany. 'I was told she probably wasn't coming back', she said.

Over the next five days the bodies of two more women were unearthed in the cellar of the house. The situation was becoming so gruesome that the police officers involved in the excavation were given stress counselling; 40 more policemen were also seconded to the investigation. The police now

Fred West who, along with his wife Rosemary, buried many of their victims around the garden or in the house.

thought that there were five more bodies in the house and two further corpses buried in a field near Fred West's former home in Much Marcle. At 25 Cromwell Street the floorboards were lifted, fittings were ripped out and 200 tons of soil were excavated from the garden. In addition, the police opened up the chimney breast and broke up the bathroom floor using pneumatic drills. They furthermore discovered that the basement had been dug out to a depth of 5 feet (1.5 metres), which had undermined the foundations of the house.

Next a sixth body – again that of a young woman – was found buried under the cellar and it was then that the police brought in a ground-penetrating radar system. Developed during the Falklands Conflict to locate plastic landmines, it was the first time that this technology had been used in a murder investigation. The device cost £2,000 a day to rent. A seventh body was located under concrete in the cellar; the eighth was buried 4 feet (1.2 metres) beneath the bath on the ground floor (Fred's brother-in-law, Graham Letts, had helped him to lay the concrete floor there in 1987). The ninth, that of the 15-year-old Carol Ann Cooper, was discovered behind a false wall in the bathroom. Carol had last been seen on 10 November 1973; she had been in care at a children's home in Worcester at the time, but had been let out for the weekend to visit her grandmother.

The police also sealed off the nearby 25 Midland Road, the Wests' former home. Other bodies were thought to have been buried in a cornfield, known as Fingerpost Field, on the road between Much Marcle and Dymock. They decided that up to 30 properties at which Fred West had lived or worked would also have to be searched.

By 11 March 1994 Fred West had been charged with eight murders. Throughout the investigation he had been questioned by relays of detectives, who had found him to be co-operative 'some of the time'. From their interviews with him they had been able to piece together the bare bones of his life story.

Frederick Walter Stephen West was born on 29 September 1942 in Much Marcle. He lived with his parents and siblings at Moor Court Cottages and developed his powerful physique while working as a farm labourer. His mother's favourite son, Daisy was believed to have seduced him when he was 12. His father, Walter – also a farm labourer – enjoyed incestuous relationships, too, and regarded his daughters as sexual playthings; Fred would follow in his father's footsteps.

At the age of 19 Fred was arrested after having impregnated a 13-year-old girl. When questioned by the police he was unabashed and openly admitted to molesting young girls, asking 'Doesn't everyone do it?' Although West escaped a charge of statutory rape when his victim refused to give evidence in court, his mother threw him out of the house and he went to live nearby, with his Aunt Violet. He then started work as a lorry driver, soon afterwards meeting the woman who would become his first wife: a blonde, 18-year-old waitress named Catherine 'Rena' Costello.

Rena was already five months pregnant by another man when she married Fred on 17 November 1962. Fred gave the baby, Charmaine, his surname, and he and Rena then had a child of their own, Anne-Marie. They moved briefly to Lanarkshire and then to a caravan park in Bishop's Cleeve, near Cheltenham. The marriage was already in trouble because West wanted to play sadistic sex games, which Rena hatred. When she subsequently disappeared West told friends that she had taken up with an engineer and had returned to Lanarkshire. She was never seen again. Meanwhile, West had started seeing the 15-year-old Rosemary Letts.

Rosemary Pauline Letts was born on 29 November 1953 in Barnstaple. Her father, William Letts, was a steward in the Royal Navy who battered and bullied his wife and treated their seven children with appalling severity (he was later diagnosed as being schizophrenic). As the third-youngest of his children, Rosemary escaped the worst of his father's attentions, however. When the family moved to Bishop's Cleeve her mother walked out, taking Rosemary and her two younger brothers with her. Later in the same year Rosemary met the 27-year old Fred West at a bus stop and they soon began going steady. Fred had probably already committed one murder – maybe two – by this time, while the 15-year-old Rosemary was making a little pocket money from prostitution.

Rosemary's parents disapproved of the relationship and put Rosemary into care, but when Rosemary attained her independence at the age of 16 she moved in with West and his two daughters at the local caravan site. In 1970 they had a daughter of their own, Heather. Thereafter the Wests moved to a two-storey, pebble-dash house in Midland Road, Gloucester, along with Fred's daughter, Anne-Marie. Charmaine had been put into care in 1969, but was later returned to Fred, going missing shortly afterwards. The Wests apparently abused her viciously, on the grounds that she was 'not one of theirs', and at Rosemary's trial witnesses told of seeing Charmaine standing on a chair, her hands tied behind her back, while Rosemary beat her with a wooden spoon.

The police believed that Fred had killed Charmaine at around this time and that when Rena had come looking for her daughter he had killed her, too. Neither was reported missing and when Rosemary was asked where Charmaine was she replied 'She's gone off with her mother'. West certainly did not expect any problems to be caused by his first wife when he married Rosemary on 29 January 1972 at Gloucester Registry Office, for on the marriage certificate he entered his marital status as 'bachelor'. Three days later the Wests moved into 25 Cromwell Street. Here they would create their own fantasy world, a world in which Rosemary not only gave free reign to Fred's desire for sadistic sex, but actively indulged in it herself. The house in Cromwell Street was also home to a family of nine children, at least two of which were fathered by another man (West was furthermore said to have fathered as many as 24 children by different women). Because his wages were not enough to support such a large family the Wests supplemented their income by taking in lodgers and by Rosemary's prostitution under the working name of 'Mandy Mouse'.

Neighbours remembered Fred West as being a devoted father who loved taking his children to the seaside and worked hard for a number of local employers. Using his do-it-yourself skills he turned 25 Cromwell

Street into a temple to Formica. The downstairs front room was turned into a bedroom for Rosemary; set into the floor was a trap door which led down to the cellar, which West converted into two rooms in which four of the children slept. There was another bedroom, with a lace-canopied bed, on the first floor, as well as a sitting room containing a fully stocked bar, television and video (this storey was out of bounds to the children). On the top floor was one more bedroom, which was kept locked. It contained a four-poster bed that was fitted with spotlights and a concealed microphone; whips, chains, manacles and bondage gear were also to hand. It was here that they shot home-made, hard-core pornographic films starring the Wests and the punters who paid for Rosemary's services as a prostitute.

The couple lived for sex and were both constantly on the lookout for young women whom they could use as sexual playthings. Rosemary played a key role in this, Fred later explaining that it was a lot easier to pick up girls when he had Rosemary in the car with him because their victims felt more secure with a woman being present. After the young women had been lured to Cromwell Street their faces were bound with sticky, brown parcel tape and plastic breathing tubes were stuffed into their nostrils. Then their limbs were tightly bound and they were repeatedly raped and tortured. After they had died their bodies were mutilated – some say cannibalised – and their remains were then tossed unceremoniously into pits that had been dug in the cellar or back garden. (No one thought it odd that Fred did a lot of do-it-yourself work around the house – after all, he was a builder.)

By 8 April 1994 the police had identified every one of the nine bodies that had been found at 25 Cromwell Street. They were all those of young women aged between 15 and 21. Four had last been seen waiting for buses.

Lynda Gough, a seamstress who worked at the Co-op in Gloucester, had disappeared in April 1973 – just two weeks before her twentieth birthday – when she had left her parents' home to move into a flat in Gloucester. Her distraught parents had made enormous efforts to find her. The Swiss-born Thérèse Siegenthaler, a 21-year-old sociology student at Woolwich College in south London, had left her Lewisham home for the Holyhead ferry on 15 April 1974 to hitchhike to Ireland. She had boasted that because she was a judo expert she could take care of herself. The third body found in the garden was that of the 17-year-old Alison Chambers, who had been placed with a firm of solicitors in Gloucester under the Youth Training Scheme. Alison had run away from her home in south Wales and had written to her mother saying that she was staying with a 'big family'.

The police team then moved to Letterbox Field, on Stonehouse Farm at Kempley. After a trench 135 feet (41 metres) long had been dug and 160 tons of soil removed the remains of West's first wife, Rena, were found. She had gone missing at the age of 24 and her remains were identified on 14 April 1994, which would have been her fiftieth birthday. A quarter of a mile away, at Fingerpost Field, in Stonehouse Coppice, police found the remains of Anna McFall, a nanny who had been employed by Rena who had vanished during the early 1970s at the age of 22. The remains of Charmaine West, who had disappeared in 1971 at the age of eight, were found under the kitchen floor at 25 Midland Road.

Up until this time it had been assumed that Fred West alone was responsible for the murders. On 21 April 1994, however, Rosemary West was jointly charged with a 67-year-old man with raping an 11-year-old girl and assaulting a 7-year-old boy, causing actual bodily harm. Although man was released on bail Rosemary continued to be held. Two days later she was charged with having sexual intercourse with the same girl without her consent. After that she was charged with the murders of Lynda Gough, Carol Ann Cooper, Lucy Partington, Thérèse Siegenthaler, Shirley Hubbard, Juanita Mott, Shirley Robinson, Alison Chambers, and finally, on 26 May 1994, of her own daughter, Heather. Fred West had already been accused of all nine murders, as well as of the murders of two people whose remains had been found at Midland Road and Letterbox Field, but who had not yet been identified. His younger brother, John Charles Edward West, was accused of raping two underaged girls, along with Rosemary.

The most extraordinary thing about the West case was that they had got away with it for so long: for more than two decades the Wests' secret careers as sadistic sexual torturers and murderers of young women had flourished unchecked. West had killed his first victim – Anna McFall, from Sandhurst, Gloucestershire –before he had even met Rose. West had made Anna pregnant while she was working as a nanny for him and Rena in 1967 and had murdered her because she wanted him to leave Rena. The next two to die were Rena and little Charmaine. The police believed that West had killed his wife when she came looking for her daughter in 1971 and that Charmaine was strangled a few hours later.

Victim number four was the nineteen-year-old Lynda Gough. A local girl, she had become friendly with some of the Wests' lodgers at the Cromwell Street house and had moved in herself in March 1973. She had found herself becoming unwillingly involved in the Wests' twisted sex games and was dead within a matter of weeks. Her body had been buried under the bathroom floor; tape had been wound thickly around her head and her dismembered limbs had been piled on top of one another.

The fifth victim was the 15-year-old Carol Ann Cooper, who lived in a children's home in Worcester and was last seen boarding a bus on the way to her grandmother's on the night of 10 November 1973. Although West admitted killing her he said that Rosemary had not been involved. Number six was the twenty-one-year-old Lucy Partington. A devout religious student, she was studying medieval English at Exeter University when the Wests spotted her waiting at a bus stop in Cheltenham as they drove back from a Christmas visit to Rosemary's parents in Bishop's Cleeve on the night of 27 December 1973. At 25 Cromwell Street she endured a week-long ordeal of rape and torture. West did such a sloppy job dismembering her body that he cut his hand and had to go to hospital.

The next of the Wests' known victims was the Swiss-born Thérèse Siegenthaler. The 21-year-old had been hitchhiking to Ireland for a holiday when West had picked her up in his lorry near Chepstow. She was then taken to Cromwell Street, where she was imprisoned, tortured and raped. When the police unearthed her remains at Cromwell Street some of her body parts were found to be missing. Number eight was the fifteen-year-old Shirley Hubbard, a schoolgirl from Droitwich who had disappeared on 14 November 1974 while she was travelling by bus from Worcester to her parents' home. She, too, had been forced to wear one of West's 'mummy'-style masks before being repeatedly raped.

The 18-year-old Juanita Mott was picked up as she hitchhiked into Gloucester from her home in Newent on 11 April 1975. Lured to their home by the Wests, she was then trussed up with 17 feet (5 metres) of grey, plastic clothesline and her own stockings. After the Wests had finished with her Fred killed her with a blow from a hammer before decapitating her body and burying it in the cellar. Their tenth victim was Shirley Robinson. A bisexual, the eighteen-year-old had shared three-in-a-bed sex sessions with the Wests during early 1978 before becoming pregnant with West's child and falling in love with him (Rosemary had also been pregnant in 1978 with the child of a West Indian man). Rosemary had become jealous of Shirley and had put pressure on her husband to get rid of her. He had complied: Shirley's body was found next to that of her unborn child in the garden of 25 Cromwell Street.

A few months after Shirley had disappeared the Wests had latched on to the 16-year-old Alison Chambers, who was living in a children's home in Gloucester at the time and was exactly the kind of vulnerable girl that they liked. One of her friends was a lodger at 25 Cromwell Street and she visited the house regularly. The Wests had asked her to become their nanny and shortly after she had moved in they had involved her in their sadistic sex play. The police found her body underneath the Wests' lawn.

Their last-known victim was Heather West. Born in 1970, Heather was thought to have been the product of an incestuous relationship between Bill Letts and his daughter, Rosemary. Fred had made her life a living hell: when she had refused to let him molest her he had beaten her viciously. When she vanished, on 17 June 1987, the Wests told friends that she had run away from home.

The Wests were reunited in the dock of Gloucester's magistrates' court on 30 June 1994. West brushed his wife's neck with his hand and bent down to speak a few words to her, but Rosemary ignored him and refused even to glance at him. As they rose to leave the court after the brief hearing West tried to touch his wife again, only to receive the same response. They appeared together again for one last time in December 1994, when Rosemary West again pointedly ignored her husband.

On New Year's Day, 1995, Fred West was found hanged in his cell in Winson Green Prison. He had made a rope by plaiting strips of sheet together. Standing on a chair, he had then tied his home-made rope to a ventilator shaft, put the noose around his neck and kicked away the chair. (Things had not gone to plan, however, for the fall had not broken his neck and he was slowly strangled to death instead.) His suicide left Rosemary to face ten murder charges alone, along with two counts of rape and two of indecent assault. Her trial, which was presided over by Mr Justice Mantell, opened at Winchester Crown Court on Tuesday, 3 October 1995.

An early witness was Caroline Owens, who had been picked up by the Wests while she was hitchhiking in 1972. They had bound, beaten and raped her, she said, further alleging that Fred West had threatened that he would murder her. A witness described as 'Miss A' also said that she had been abused by the Wests at 25 Cromwell Street. And Anne-Marie, Fred's daughter, described how she had been raped by Fred and Rosemary at the age of eight; West had told her that she 'should be grateful' and that all fathers did this to their daughters. She had become pregnant by her father at the age of 15, but he had arranged an abortion.

In her defence Rosemary West claimed that she was innocent. She said that her husband had manipulated her into participating in the assault on Caroline Owens, but stated that she did not know 'Miss A'. She furthermore denied all knowledge of the murders, as well as of the alleged assault on her stepdaughter, Anne-Marie. The defence played four of Fred West's taped interviews with the police, in which he had admitted to committing the murders and had said that Rosemary had played no part in them. The prosecution then called Janet Leach as a rebuttal witness. She had sat in on the police interviews with West and testified that when she and West were alone together after the interviews he had given a different version of his story, explaining that he had lied to the police in order to protect Rosemary, who had committed some of the murders. West had also told her that there were at least 20 more bodies that had not been discovered by the police.

The jury found Rosemary West guilty of all ten counts of murder. In passing sentence Mr Justice Mantell said 'Rosemary Pauline West, on each of the ten counts of murder of which you have been unanimously convicted by the jury the sentence is one of life imprisonment. If attention is paid to what I think you will never be released. Take her down'. He also ordered that the outstanding rape charges against her should be left on file.

On 19 March 1996 Rosemary West lost her appeal against her conviction. Meanwhile, the police continued their investigations into the deaths of nine other girls who had visited Cromwell Street and were never seen again.

28 ◆ The Backpacker Killer

After meeting in Australia in 1992, two British backpackers, Caroline Clarke and Joanne Walters, teamed up together to hitchhike around the south of the country, leaving a hostel in Sydney in April and then heading south. In September a jogger found their remains in a shallow grave at a place called Executioner's Drop in the Belanglo Forest. In the October of the following year, 1993, two more corpses were discovered in the same area. They belonged to James Gibson and Deborah Everist, both of whom were 19 and from Melbourne, who had disappeared in 1989.

It was soon begun to be feared that a serial killer was at work and an intensive search of the region was therefore set in motion. On 1 November 1993 the body of the 23-year-old Simone Schmidl, from Germany, was unearthed nearby; she had last been seen in January 1991. On the following day the skeletons of the 21-year-old Gabor Neugebauer and his 20-year-old girlfriend, Anja Habschied – two more German backpackers, who had disappeared two years previously – were found. Both victims had died from multiple stab wounds and Anja had also been beheaded.

Over 300 police officers were then ordered to comb a vast area of remote woodland and scrub for clues and other graves. It was the biggest murder hunt in Australia's history. One clue was identified: cartridges from a .22 Ruger were found near the grave of the 22-year-old Caroline Clarke which matched some spent cartridges that had been discovered at an isolated farmhouse.

After searching their records the New South Wales police thought that they had identified the serial killer's eighth victim. In 1991 the body of a 29-year-old Australian mother, Diane Pennacchio, had been found in a wood; last seen leaving a bar near Canberra, she had been stabbed to death sometime thereafter. Although her body had been found more than 100 miles (161 kilometres) from the others, she had been buried in the same, distinctive way. All eight had been found lying face downwards, with their hands behind their backs, alongside a fallen tree trunk; a small wigwam of sticks and ferns had been constructed over each body.

By the beginning of 1994 the 'Backpacker Killer' was making the headlines world-wide. Then a 24-year-old British woman came forward and told the police that she had been hitchhiking in the Belanglo Forest in January 1990 when she had been picked up by a lorry driver. When he had started acting strangely she had leapt out of the vehicle and had run into the woods. As she fled the driver had fired a gun at her, but had missed. Another British backpacker, the 25-year-old Paul Onion, also told the police that he had been hitchhiking in the same area in 1990 when he had accepted a lift from a man who had later pulled a gun out of the glove compartment. As Paul was fleeing the man had shot at him, thankfully missing his intended victim. Paul was able to identify the driver's car, as well as picking out his photo from the New South Wales police's collection of mug shots.

Following a dawn raid on 22 May 1994 a 49-year-old lorry driver and gun fanatic named Ivan Milat was arrested. Parts of a rare, .22-calibre, Ruger rifle were found hidden in his bungalow and ballistics tests later linked it to cartridge cases that had been picked up at the scenes of two of the killings. It was also identified as the weapon that had been used to kill Caroline Clarke, Milat's fingerprints furthermore being found on the gun.

Ivàn Robert Marko Milat was consequently charged with the deaths of seven backpackers. Although he pleaded not guilty the jury did not believe him and Milat was accordingly sentenced to life imprisonment.

29 ❖ The Gay Slayer

Colin Ireland, London's 'Gay Slayer', wanted to achieve notoriety as a serial killer. He revelled in the fact that the details of his hideous murders were reported week by week by a fascinated press and furthermore telephoned police detectives to taunt them: 'I've got the book', he would say (meaning the FBI Handbook). 'I know how many you have to do.' After he had murdered his fifth victim – which officially classed him as a serial killer – he phoned up and boasted 'I've done another one'.

There is no doubt that Ireland was deranged character. The illegitimate son of a newsagent's assistant in Dartford, Kent, he never knew his father. His mother remarried when he was 12 and he did not get on with his step-father, who beat the boy for the slightest reason. Always something of a loner, he then became 'difficult' and was sent to a school for maladjusted children. After having been expelled for arson he began a life of petty crime, which took him firstly to borstal and eventually to prison. At the same time he became obsessed with both uniforms and the newly fashionable cult of survivalism, moreover making it plain to his friends that he hated 'queers'.

In 1990, at the age of 35, the 6 feet (183 metre) tall Ireland, who now weighed 15 stones (95 kilogrammes), married the landlady of a pub in Newton Abbot. He dumped her on their honeymoon, however, before returning to the pub, plundering it and then making off in her car. By the end of 1992 he had two failed marriages behind him and was working at a night shelter for the homeless in Southend. Shortly before Christmas he had a violent row with a gay man at the shelter and upon being sacked set about taking his revenge on all homosexuals. He began frequenting the Coleherne, a pub in the Earl's Court district of London that was popular with homosexual men who were into sado-masochism (S & M). Ireland later told detectives: 'I had gone there with the idea that if someone approached me something would happen. It would be some sort of trigger – a stepping over the line in a way'.

On 8 March 1993 Peter Walker, a 45-year-old theatre director, stepped over that line when he accidentally spilled some water on Ireland's jacket and begged Ireland to punish him for it by beating him. They then took a taxi to Walker's flat in Battersea for a sado-masochistic sex session, Ireland having come equipped with a cord, knife and pair of gloves. Walker eagerly submitted to being tied to the bed. 'Once I had tied him up I knew my intentions were different from his', Ireland said later. 'I'm not sure if I really set out to kill him, but it went from there . . . In the end I killed him with a plastic bag. I put it over his head.' Two days later he called the Samaritans, as well as a newspaper, asking them to visit the flat to take care of Walker's dogs.

On 28 May 1993 Ireland returned to the Coleherne and fell into conversation with Christopher Dunn, a 37-year-old librarian. Like Peter Walker, Dunn was a masochist who was into bondage – perfect for Ireland's purposes. The two men went back to Dunn's flat in Wealdstone, where Ireland handcuffed the willing Dunn to his bed. Dunn's pleasure

**Colin Ireland -
London's 'Gay Slayer'.**

Colin Ireland who was described as having an aggressive character. He was deeply disturbed since childhood.

quickly turned to dismay, however, as he watched Ireland rifle through his wallet and pull out the money that it contained, along with his cash-point card. When Dunn refused to tell Ireland his PIN (personal identification number) Ireland burnt Dunn's testicles with a cigarette lighter until he complied, then strangling him with a length of cord.

Ireland's third victim was Perry Bradley III, a 35-year-old sales director from Sulphur Springs, Texas, whose father was a congressman. The bisexual Bradley was another *habitué* of the Coleherne, where, on 4 June 1993, he met Ireland, shortly thereafter taking him to his smart, Kensington flat. Although Bradley was not really into S & M Ireland eventually persuaded him to let Ireland tie him up, going through his wallet once Bradley was trussed up and helpless. 'At one point I was thinking of letting him go', Ireland said in his statement to the police. 'Then I thought it's easier to kill him. I walked round and pulled the noose.' Ireland was becoming increasingly afraid of being caught and now feared that he would look conspicuous walking the streets alone while it was dark. He therefore settled down to listen to the radio until morning, wiping away his fingerprints after dawn and then leaving the flat.

Andrew Collier, the 33-year-old warden of a block of sheltered-accommodation flats in east London, was another Coleherne regular. After having been picked up by Ireland on 7 June 1993 Collier took him to his flat in Dalston. While the two men were having a drink they heard an altercation on the street and went to the window to see what was happening, Ireland leaning out of the window and accidentally leaving a fingerprint on the outside of the window frame. Afterwards Collier consented to Ireland tying him up and once he was helpless Ireland strangled him with a noose. Ireland was then inspecting the contents of Collier's wallet when he found some medical papers: 'I was going through his documentation and I became aware he had AIDS', Ireland said. 'He didn't warn me . . . I went fucking crazy. I burnt certain areas of his body. He loved his cat, that was his life – so I did the cat with a noose, draped it over the body.' The cat was actually arranged so that its mouth was around Collier's penis, its tail having been stuffed into his mouth. Ireland later told the police 'I wanted him to have no dignity in death. It was a way of saying to the police "What do you think of that?" It was like a signature to let them know I'd been there. I was reaching a point where I was just accelerating. It was just speeding up, getting far worse.'

After Collier's killing Ireland phoned the police and asked them whether they were still investigating the murder of Peter Walker. He taunted them, saying 'I will do another. I have always dreamed of doing the perfect murder'. Then Ireland laughed about killing Collier's cat – following the call that he had made about Peter Walker's dogs the press had been speculating that the killer was an animal lover.

On 13 June 1993 Ireland killed for the fifth, and last, time. His victim was the 42-year-old, Maltese-born chef, Emanuel Spiteri. 'I'd seen him a couple of times at the Coleherne', said Ireland. 'He was obviously the leather type.' Having accompanied Spiteri to his flat in south London, Ireland then tied him up and tortured him in an attempt to make him reveal the PIN for his cash-point card. Spiteri, however, resisted, screaming 'You will just have to kill me'. 'He was a very brave man, but I couldn't allow him to stick around', explained Ireland, continuing 'I killed him with a noose.'

It was at this point that Ireland telephoned the police and bragged that he had now taken five lives, which, he claimed, made him a real serial killer and hence 'famous'. What Ireland did not know, however, was that when he and Spiteri had passed through Charing Cross station on their way to Spiteri's home in Hither Green they had been filmed by the station's security cameras. A description of the man whom the police wanted to question was first issued to the public and then the British Transport Police's video of Spiteri with his killer was shown on television.

On 20 July 1993 Ireland walked into a solicitor's office in Southend and revealed that he was the man who had been filmed with Spiteri, whereupon the solicitor advised him to go to the police. Having done so, Ireland told police officers at New Scotland Yard that although he had indeed gone to Spiteri's flat with him he had left shortly afterwards; a third man had also been present, he claimed. The police quickly demolished Ireland's story, however: one of his fingerprints was found to match that left on the frame of Collier's window and the police also recognised Ireland's voice from his anonymous phone calls. Realising that the game was up Ireland confessed to all five murders en route to the magistrates' court.

At the Old Bailey Ireland pleaded guilty to five counts of murder. On sentencing him to serve five life sentences Mr Justice Sachs said

By any standards you are an exceptionally frightening and dangerous man. In cold blood and with great deliberation you killed five of your fellow human beings in grotesque and cruel circumstances. The fear, brutality and indignity to which you subjected your victims are almost unspeakable. To take one human life is outrageous. To take five is carnage. You expressed your desire to be regarded as a serial killer – that must be matched by your detention for life. In my view it is absolutely clear you should never be released.

30 ❖ The Monster of Florence

In 1968 Antonio Io Bianci was making love to Barbara Locci in the front seat of his car when they were both shot dead, Barbara's husband being subsequently arrested and convicted of the murders. It would be six years before Signor Locci could prove his innocence and establish that the double murder was the first atrocity committed by a serial killer who preyed on courting couples in Tuscany who later became known as the 'Monster of Florence'.

While Signor Locci was languishing in jail another courting couple was killed in a car. The police established that they had been shot with the same .22-calibre Beretta pistol that had been used in the Bianchi and Locci murders; the female victim had furthermore been mutilated. During the course of the next year two more people were killed in a similar manner. Although a German couple was murdered, too, neither of them was mutilated (they were homosexuals and their killing was probably a mistake).

Upon Signor Locci's release the Monster of Florence appeared to suspend his activities. He struck again in 1981, however, stabbing his female victim some 300 times. Four months later, in October 1981, another woman was murdered and mutilated. The Monster of Florence continued to wage his campaign of murder over the next four years. The slayings followed a rigid pattern: all of the men were shot through the driver's window before the women were killed, their bodies then being dragged from the car and mutilated with a knife (their left breasts were generally hacked off). Ballistics tests revealed that all of the 67 bullets that were fired in a total of 16 murders came from the same gun, all also being marked with the letter 'H'. The Monster of Florence's final attack, in 1985, differed slightly from the rest, however. He slaughtered his last victims – a French couple – in their tent, cutting off a section of the woman's genitalia (which he later posted to the police) during his grisly mutilation of her body.

The Florence police handled the case badly. Numerous false accusations were made and one man who had been named as the killer committed suicide by cutting his throat. Another five were jailed for the killings, three of whom were released when the Monster struck again while they were behind bars; because there was no evidence against a fourth a judge released him, while the fifth man remained the subject of controversy.

During the course of the Monster of Florence's bloody reign of terror the police received scores of anonymous notes identifying Pietro Pacciani as the killer. Pacciani was a peasant farmer who had been convicted of murder in 1951 and jailed for 13 years for killing a rival in love. (Pacciani had followed his 16-year-old fiancée upon seeing her going into the woods with another man; when he could no longer stand the sight of them making love he had stabbed the man 19 times before raping the terrified girl next to the mutilated corpse.) The police speculated that if he was indeed the Monster of Florence the embittered Pacciani had sought to avenge himself on other couples. Key to their thinking was the theory that it had been the sight of his fiancée's exposed left breast during her seduction that had triggered Pacciani's initial attack and that this was also why the Monster usually amputated the left breasts of his female victims. Pacciani had again come to the police's attention in 1987, subsequently being convicted of molesting his two daughters and accordingly being jailed.

His name was fed into a computer, along with those of more than 100,000 people who had had the opportunity of carrying out the Monster of Florence's crimes. The computer identified just one suspect, however: Pacciani. Convinced that Pacciani was the perpetrator of the murders, the police searched his farm in minute detail for evidence, but nothing was found. They were on the point of giving up when a bullet was unearthed which was later found to match those that had been used in the murders.

Although a weapon was never recovered Pacciani was charged with murder. His trial dragged on for six months before the jury finally convicted him, whereupon he was jailed for life in 1994. Subsequently, however, a judicial review reassessed the flimsy evidence against him and after its ruling that his conviction was unsafe Pacciani was released from prison in 1996. As far as anyone knows the Monster of Florence is still at large.

31 ✦ The Rostov Ripper

Following the collapse of the Soviet Union during the early 1990s the rest of the world – as well as its own people – discovered that Russia, along with the other former Soviet republics, could produce serial killers that were more than a match for any found in the West.

The first such notable case was that of Nikolai Dzhumagaliev, the killer cannibal who was known as 'Metal Fang' because of his white-metal, false teeth. Dzhumagaliev operated in Kazakhstan during 1980, picking up tall, attractive women in the capital, Alma-Ata, before taking them for a walk along the river bank, where he raped them and then hacked them to death with an axe. On the night following each murder he would invite friends to dinner and serve them roast meat, his reign of terror coming to an end when two of his guests found a woman's head and entrails in his fridge. Charged with seven murders, Dzhumagaliev was found to be insane and was sent to a psychiatric hospital in Tashkent. He escaped in 1989, however, and after trying to pick up women in Moscow fled to Uzbekistan, where he was eventually captured. Yet terrible as his crimes undoubtedly were, Metal Fang's reputation as a serial killer would soon be eclipsed by that of the 'Rostov Ripper'.

At first sight Andrei Romanovich Chikatilo, a former schoolteacher, was a mild-mannered grandfather. He was also an apparently happily married man – if slightly henpecked – although some thought his habit of sleeping in the bathroom a little odd. Those who were closer to him, however, knew that he was haunted by the memory of a cousin who had been killed and his body subjected to cannibalism during the 1934 Ukrainian famine. Even so, no one who knew Chikatilo would have believed that he had tortured, murdered, raped, mutilated and eaten as many as 53 victims, many of them children, between 1978 and 1990. (There may have been more: because Chikatilo's victims were loners and strays some disappearances may have gone unreported.) During the course of the 12-year murder investigation 500,000 people were questioned; Chikatilo himself was arrested and interrogated twice, but was released on both occasions.

It was Chikatilo's sexual problems that sparked his murder spree. His wife, Fayina, later admitted that her husband had not been able to make love to her properly. He had therefore turned to prostitutes and had bought a shack to which he would take them for sex. This strategy ultimately proved unsuccessful, too, however, and his inability to perform sexually seems to have enraged him.

His first victim was a pretty nine-year-old named Lena Zakotno. In December 1978 he lured her to his shack, where he tried to rape her; having failed to do so, he then murdered her. It was then that he discovered that he was only able to have sex with someone when they were dead. Afterwards he disposed of Lena's body in a river. Chikatilo was suspected of being involved in Lena's death after neighbours reported seeing a light burning in the shack during the night on which Lena had vanished. He was interviewed nine times about the murder before suspicion fell on another man who lived nearby. The man confessed, was found guilty and executed.

Chikatilo then embarked upon a career of prolific murder – 11 bodies were found in 1984 alone. With the sixth sense of the natural predator he would pick out the weak and vulnerable, hanging around bus stops and railway stations looking for prostitutes and runaways. He would also stalk potential victims on buses and trains or target them in the street. His favourite targets were homeless drifters who were unlikely to be missed, or else solitary children on their way to school.

A lone child could be tempted by a packet of chewing gum, while a drifter would jump at the offer of a meal or a chance to watch a video. After all, Chikatilo looked for all the world like a kindly grandfather.

'As soon as I saw a lonely person I would have to drag them off to the woods', he later told the police. 'I paid no attention to age or sex. We would walk for a couple of miles or so through the woods and then I would be possessed by a terrible shaking sensation.' He then murdered his victims before raping and mutilating their corpses. Sometimes he disembowelled them and cut out or bit off their organs; fearing their deathly gaze, he would usually pluck out their eyes, and would furthermore bite off their nipples in a sexual frenzy.

The police found themselves out of their depth: 'We just couldn't imagine what sort of person we were dealing with', said Lieutenant Colonel Viktor Burakov, who led the murder hunt. 'This was the height of sadism, the like of which we had never seen.' At the height of the murders the police mounted a regular surveillance of the woods around Rostov. Although Chikatilo himself was stopped in an isolated, wooded area in 1979, he persuaded the police that he was an innocent hiker and after noting down his name and address they let him go.

Chikatilo's wife and friends were baffled when he gave up his teaching job of ten years in 1981 for the position of a lowly supply clerk in a loco-motive-repair shop in Rostov. His new job gave him the opportunity to travel, however, and he extended his murderous activities to St Petersburg, the Ukraine and Uzbekistan. The manhunt, which was led by detectives seconded from Moscow, now stretched to Siberia.

In 1983 he was arrested close to the scene of one of the murders, the police finding a length of rope and a knife in his briefcase. A sample of his blood was taken, but because it proved to belong to a different group to that of the semen samples that had been recovered from the victims' bodies Chikatilo was released. (At that time the Soviet police did not know that in extremely rare cases secretions from various parts of the body can have different serological groupings; Chikatilo was one of those rare cases.)

During the summer of 1984 Chikatilo was forced to take a break from murder when he was arrested and jailed for three months for the theft of three rolls of linoleum. Over the month following his release Chikatilo relieved his pent-up frustration by slaughtering eight people.

Chikatilo's murderous campaign was only halted because the police had a stoke of luck. In November 1990 a policeman stopped Chikatilo in the street after spotting bloodstains on his face. When the body of his final victim, a young boy, was later discovered nearby witnesses reported having seen a middle-aged man hanging around the railway station while the boy bought a ticket. Having run a check on 25,000 possible suspects detectives put Chikatilo under heavy surveillance on reading the police report pertaining to his having been stopped while covered with blood. Six-hundred policemen were drafted in to cover the station and adjoining woods and some were watching on 20 November 1990 when Chikatilo approached a teenage boy at the railway station. He was immediately arrested.

Under interrogation Chikatilo readily confessed to murdering 11 boys and 42 women and girls during his reign of terror, although he claimed that 'there may be more'. Of his known victims the youngest was Igor Gudkov, a seven-year-old who had strayed from his home; the oldest was the 44-year-old prostitute Marta Ryabyenko. Upon realising that her husband was the Rostov Ripper Chikatilo's wife, as well as his two grown-children, went into hiding.

Chikatilo was 56 when he went on trial in Rostov on 14 April 1992. Throughout the proceedings he sat in chains within an iron cage that had been built around the dock. On the first day of the trial proceedings were delayed for half an hour while the hysterical crowd bayed for his blood, Chikatilo merely rolling his eyes and waving pornographic magazines to inflame the audience further as first-aiders administered sedatives to the families of his victims. The two-volume indictment listed thirty-five child victims and eighteen women. The facts of the case were not contested and the only matter upon which the court had to decide was whether or not Chikatilo was sane; experts from Moscow's Serbsky Institute, Russia's leading institute of psychiatry, testified that he was.

It took Judge Leonid Akabzhanov an hour and a half to read the verdict on 15 October 1992, during which he concluded that 52 of the 53 murders had been proven. He expressed fierce criticism of the police, however: 'If they had done their job in 1978 after the first killing 52 lives could have been saved', he said, continuing: 'Or if they had not released him after questioning in 1984 at least 20 people would not have died'. Of the accused he said: 'He ruthlessly and cold-bloodedly dismembered his victims, pulling them apart while they were still alive'. The judge then sentenced him to death, outraging Chikatilo: 'I fought in Afghanistan', he ranted. 'I was a partisan who defended the barricades; I fought for a free Russia.' The courtroom was in pandemonium when he was finally taken from the iron cage for the last time.

On 14 February 1994 Andrei Chikatilo, whom the press was now calling the 'world's most sadistic and perverted killer', was executed by means of a single bullet to the back of the head after President Boris Yeltsin had rejected his appeal for clemency.

32 ❖ The Terminator

The Ukrainian serial killer Anatoly Onoprienko was sentenced to death in 1999 after having been convicted of murdering fifty-two people, including ten children in villages across Ukraine, most of them during a three-month killing spree. The former sailor, who had become known as 'The Terminator', admitted the killings, saying that he had been driven by a higher force.

In its eagerness to join the European Union (EU) the Ukraine had in the meantime complied with EU requirements in suspending its death sentence, however, and in 1999 Onoprienko was therefore still being held in a tiny, 9- by 5-feet (2.7- by 1.5-metre) cell at the nineteenth-century prison in Zhitornir, 8 miles (13 kilometres) west of Kiev, while his fate was being decided. Because Onoprienko relished killing even the toughest guards on death row took no chances with him.

'The first time I killed I shot down a deer in the woods', he later reminisced. 'I was in my early twenties and I recall feeling very upset when I saw it dead. I couldn't explain why I had done it, and I felt sorry for it. I never had that feeling again.' Onoprienko's first human victims were a couple whom he had seen standing by their Lada car on a motorway. 'I just shot them', he said. 'It's not that it gave me pleasure, but I felt this urge. From then on it was almost like some game from outer space.'

After that he terrorised the Ukraine for months, slaughtering men, women and children alike, wiping out entire families in cold blood, battering children and raping one woman after having shot her in the face. 'To me killing people [was like] ripping up a duvet', he explained. 'Men, women, old people, children – they are all the same. I have never felt sorry for those I killed. No love, no hatred, just blind indifference. I don't see

Ukranian serial killer Anatoly Onoprienko who was sentenced to death in 1999 after killing 52 people.

them as individuals, but just as masses.' On one occasion he had killed a young girl who was praying, having just seen him kill both of her parents. 'Seconds before I smashed her head [in] I ordered her to show me where they kept their money', he said. 'She looked at me with an angry, defiant stare and said "No, I won't". That strength was incredible. But I still felt nothing.'

The Ukraine had been plunged into panic when Onoprienko's savagery reached its climax in early 1996, when he committed about forty murders in three months. The determined force that he used was almost unbelievable: he blew the doors off homes on the edges of villages, gunned down adults and beat children with metal cudgels, stealing money, jewellery, stereo equipment and other valuable items before burning down his victims' homes. 'To me it was like hunting. Hunting people down', he explained. 'I would be sitting, bored, with nothing to do. And then suddenly this idea would get into my head. I would do everything to get it out of my mind, but I couldn't. It was stronger than me. So I would get in the car or catch a train and go out to kill.'

Although he took pleasure in the 'professionalism' of his crimes, Onoprienko claimed that he had derived no pleasure from killing. 'Corpses are ugly', he confided. 'They stink and send out bad vibes. Once I killed five people and then sat in the car with their bodies for two hours not knowing what to do with them. The smell was unbearable.' Investigators feared that his final tally of victims was higher than 52 – with some justification, for there appeared to have been a long gap between murders when he roamed illegally around other European countries.

After weeks of tests and interviews a commission consisting of the Ukraine's top psychiatrists and psychologists concluded that Onoprienko was not mentally ill, rather that his main motivation for murder appeared to have been money: he killed to steal. The fact that he had grown up without parents and had been sent to an orphanage by his elder brother may have explained why he had slaughtered entire families, they speculated. Indeed, his most frenzied killing spree had occurred after he had moved in with a woman (who said that he had always been very loving) and her children. The couple had intended to marry, Onoprienko having proposed to his girlfriend with a ring that he had forcibly removed from the finger of one of his victims only a few hours earlier.

For his part, Onoprienko – who claimed that he was a good-natured person and a sensitive music-lover – maintained that he was possessed. 'I'm not a maniac', he said.

It's not that simple. I have been taken over by a higher force, something telepathic or cosmic, which drove me. For instance, I wanted to kill my brother's first wife, because I hated her. I really wanted to kill her, but I couldn't because I had not received the order. I waited for it all the time, but it did not come . . . I am like a rabbit in a laboratory, part of an experiment to prove that man is capable of murdering and learning to live with his crimes. To show that I can cope, that I can stand anything, [I] forget everything.

Onoprienko was finally caught after the Ukraine had staged its biggest manhunt, which involved 2,000 police officers and more than 3,000 troops. He was eventually arrested in April 1996 at his girlfriend's house, near the Polish border, as the result of an anonymous tip-off.

During his trial, which took place in his home town of Zhytomyr, Onoprienko stood locked within a metal cage in the courtroom. He described himself as 'the devil' and boasted about being the world's greatest serial killer. He expressed no remorse for his crimes, continuing to claim that a higher force had driven him to commit them. 'He is driven by extreme cruelty', disagreed Dmytro Lypsky, the presiding judge at his trial. 'He doesn't care about anything, only about himself. He is egocentric and has a very high opinion of himself.'

Five judges, including Lypsky, sat in judgement on Onoprienko during his four-month trial. It took three hours to read out their verdict, after which Lypsky told the court: 'In line with the Ukraine's criminal code Onoprienko is sentenced to death by shooting'. In March 1997, however, the Ukraine was admitted to the Council of Europe, and in compliance with EU rules the Ukraine's president, Leonid Kuchma, announced a moratorium on capital punishment. Yet Onoprienko's crimes had caused such revulsion in the Ukraine that commuting the serial killer's death sentence to 20 years in jail caused outrage. Even Onoprienko himself refused to ask for his sentence to be commuted, instead insisting that he should be executed and warning:

If I am ever let out I will start killing again. But this time it will be worse, ten times worse. The urge is there. Seize this chance because I am being groomed by Satan. After what I have learnt out there I have no competitors in my field. And if I am not killed I will escape from this jail and the first thing I'll do is find Kuchma and hang him from a tree by his testicles.